Understanding the
U.S. Supreme Court

Understanding the U.S. Supreme Court

Cases and Controversies

Kevin T. McGuire

University of North Carolina
at Chapel Hill

Boston   Burr Ridge, IL   Dubuque, IA   Madison, WI   New York
San Francisco   St. Louis   Bangkok   Bogotá   Caracas   Kuala Lumpur
Lisbon   London   Madrid   Mexico City   Milan   Montreal   New Delhi
Santiago   Seoul   Singapore   Sydney   Taipei   Toronto

McGraw-Hill Higher Education

A *Division* of *The* **McGraw-Hill** *Companies*

UNDERSTANDING THE U.S. SUPREME COURT: CASES AND CONTROVERSIES

Published by McGraw-Hill, a business unit of The McGraw-Hill Companies, Inc.,
1221 Avenue of the Americas, New York, NY 10020. Copyright © 2002 by The McGraw-Hill

Some ancillaries, including electronic and print components, may not be available to
customers outside the United States.

This book is printed on acid-free paper.

4 5 6 7 8 9 0 DOC/DOC 0 9 8 7 6 5 4

ISBN 0–07–233731–1

Editorial director: *Jane E. Karpacz*
Sponsoring editor: *Monica Eckman*
Editorial coordinator: *Shannon Morrow*
Marketing manager: *Janise A. Fry*
Senior project manager: *Gloria G. Schiesl*
Senior production supervisor: *Laura Fuller*
Coordinator of freelance design: *Michelle D. Whitaker*
Freelance cover designer: *Nathan Bahls*
Compositor: *GAC--Indianapolis*
Typeface: *10/12 Palatino*
Printer: *R. R. Donnelley & Sons Company/Crawfordsville, IN*

Cover image: View of the Great Hall from the west end, and toward the open Courtroom
doors at the east end, taken August 10, 1998; photographer Franz Jantzen; Reproduced from
the collection of THE SUPREME COURT OF THE UNITED STATES OFFICE OF THE
CURATOR

Library of Congress Cataloging-in-Publication Data

McGuire, Kevin T.
     Understanding the U.S. Supreme Court : cases and controversies / Kevin T. McGuire.
— 1st ed.
         p.   cm.
     Includes index.
     ISBN 0–07–233731–1
     1. United States. Supreme Court. I. Title.

KF8742 .M343   2002
347.73'26—dc21   2001032710
                                                                 CIP

www.mhhe.com

*For David, Jay, and Mike
and in Memory of Ralph*

Contents

Preface

Any doubts about the importance of the U.S. Supreme Court were erased in the late fall of 2000. In a remarkable turn of events, an agonizingly close presidential election gave rise to a legal conflict over the counting of votes in what turned out to be the critical state of Florida. George W. Bush had prevailed by only a handful of votes, and Al Gore, believing that more Floridians may have instead voted for him, initiated efforts to reconsider some ballots that might not have registered a vote. Bush challenged these actions, and with the presidency in the balance, the case quickly made its way to the high court. Reflecting a concern about the standards for recounting these disputed ballots, the Court issued an opinion that effectively brought an end to the election and determined its winner. In this very dramatic way, the decision in *Bush v. Gore* brought home the Court's role as the final arbiter of federal law.

Aside from its obvious importance, this case enabled observers to learn a great deal about the Court—how parties petition the Court, the content of the written briefs, the nature of oral arguments, the substance of the justices' written opinions. Examples such as this case can be quite illuminating, because they offer a very useful window into how the Supreme Court operates. Relying upon a series of these individual cases, this book introduces readers to some of the principal research on the Court. Each chapter uses different features of a case to draw out and highlight the findings of political scientists who systematically study the justices and their decisions.

This idea for this book was formulated at the University of North Carolina at Chapel Hill, an especially agreeable professional environment. As the project took shape, my fellow faculty were very generous, extending their time and expertise at every turn. James Stimson was especially accommodating, always indulging my need for advice and data. Thomas Oatley listened patiently to many of my ideas and saved me from numerous embarrassing errors. My frequent conversations with Virginia Gray, David Lowery, Stuart Macdonald, Michael MacKuen, and George Rabinowitz also provided a steady supply of suggestions for improvement.

Beyond my home institution, guidance came from a number of other insightful scholars. The following reviewers read portions of the manuscript and offered constructive critiques as it was still taking shape: David Allen, *Colorado State University*; Robert Behrman, *Marshall University*; Roy Flemming, *Texas A & M University*; Robert Gilmour, *University of Connecticut*; Timothy Hagle, *University of Iowa*; David Klein, *University of Virginia*; Tim Lenz, *Florida Atlantic University*; John Anthony Maltese, *University of Georgia*; Nancy Maveety, *Tulane University*; Richard Pacelle, *University of Missouri, St. Louis*; H.W. Perry, Jr., *University of Texas at Austin*; Mark Silverstein, *Boston University*; James Stoner, *Louisiana State University*.

Gregory Caldeira offered his characteristic discriminating judgment at several critical stages, and Frank Sorauf provided his comprehensive knowledge of the complexities of campaign finance. I also owe a special debt to a number of others for their extended discussions on this project—John Clark, Gregg Ivers, H.W. Perry, Jr., Jennifer Segal, and Charles Smith—each of whom has affected my thinking about the Supreme Court. Welcome recommendations and information also came from Roy Flemming, Jon Gould, Forrest Maltzman, Shannon Smithey, and Stephen Wasby. In developing many of my ideas, I was fortunate to have the help of three fellow distance runners, Sue Davis, Marie Hojnacki, and Lynn Mather. These scholars offered perspective and advice—as well as wonderful companionship—across the miles of a number of very rewarding runs.

Some of the work for this book required spending time with the papers of Justice Lewis F. Powell, Jr., archived at Washington and Lee University. My efforts there were made infinitely more easy by John Jacob, as gracious and helpful a host as one could imagine.

The good people at McGraw-Hill merit particular praise. Jane Karpacz offered her steadfast support from the outset. Hannah Glover helped to guide the book through its earliest stages. As the constant voice of cheerful enthusiasm, the effervescent Shannon Morrow was always available to offer her counsel, reassurance, and expertise. Kevin Campbell copyedited the manuscript with particular skill, smoothing over savage syntax and generally improving my prose. Most notable among the McGraw team was Monica Eckman, who demonstrated an ideal blend of patience, professionalism, and support, all set against a consistently sunny disposition. She is a splendid editor.

Finally, I am grateful to my wife Nancy who—on more occasions than I can count—gave me the time that I needed to work on this project. As she well knows, she shouldered far more than her share of responsibility for the care of our two rambunctious young daughters, while somehow maintaining both her poise and sense of humor.

K. T. M.

January 2001
Chapel Hill, North Carolina

CHAPTER 1

An Overview of the Supreme Court

It was an improbable start for the nation's highest court. In February 1790, the U.S. Supreme Court began its work in an upstairs room of a New York City building known as the Royal Exchange. Below the Court was a thriving open-air butchers' market, but in the courtroom itself there was considerably less activity: During its first session, the Court had no cases to decide. Of the six justices who were appointed, only four were initially present; the remaining two resigned without ever sitting on the Court. For those who remained, there was little sense of stability or permanence. Over the next several years, the justices followed the rest of the federal government to Philadelphia and then to Washington, where they took up residence in taverns, rented homes, and various rooms throughout the U.S. capitol. It was not until 1935—nearly 150 years after the inception of the republic—that the Supreme Court finally moved into its own home, a white marble building on Capitol Hill.[1]

Today, the U.S. Supreme Court is quite a different institution. Serving as a justice on the Court carries enormous prestige. Indeed, nominees are willing to undergo considerable professional and personal scrutiny in order to secure lifetime tenure on the bench. Those

[1]Henry J. Abraham, *The Judicial Process*, 7th ed. (New York: Oxford University Press, 1998), pp. 206–7; Joan Biskupic and Elder Witt, *Guide to the U.S. Supreme Court*, 3rd ed. (Washington: Congressional Quarterly, Inc., 1997), pp. 835–37; David M. O'Brien, *Storm Center: The Supreme Court in American Politics*, 5th ed. (New York: W.W. Norton, 2000), pp.105–16.

1

who are successfully elevated to the high court are hardly wanting for work. Literally thousands of cases seek the time and attention of the justices each year, yet only a few are granted full consideration by the Court. In that small group of cases, the justices' decisions generate considerable interest from a wide array of legal and political constituencies. It is not difficult to understand why, since the Supreme Court provides final and authoritative interpretation of the law relating to any number of prominent issues of public policy. In recent years, the justices have limited the ability of Congress to criminalize gun possession and sexual assault, upheld the right to sue the president of the United States, regulated police conduct and medical procedures, restricted religious activities in public schools, and effectively determined the outcome of a presidential election—just to name a few. Obviously, the business of the Supreme Court has consequences for both the nature of American government and its relationship to individual citizens. For that reason, it is especially important to understand the U.S. Supreme Court and its process of policy making.

In many respects, though, the Court remains a mystery. After all, most of what the Court does takes place behind closed doors, and the explanations for its decisions—its published opinions—are veiled in the seemingly cryptic canons of the law. Despite the obscurity of the justices and the puzzling nature of their policies, scholarly research has generated a good deal of insight into the Supreme Court. To that end, this book addresses itself to using that research to shed light on a number of related questions: Who is chosen to serve on the Supreme Court, and why? How do the members of the Court determine what issues to address? Why do the justices make the decisions that they do? What kinds of implications do the Court's policies ultimately have? These issues are the primary focus in the chapters that follow. Before exploring these questions, however, it is helpful to examine some of the Court's changing legal and political background.

HISTORICAL CHANGE ON THE SUPREME COURT

In drafting Article III of the Constitution, the founding fathers established the Supreme Court, but they made no provisions regarding its size, membership, or specific powers. Beyond outlining the types of cases that could be brought to the Court, the framers did remarkably little to define the structure and function of the nation's highest tribunal. Consequently, it has varied substantially over time in its composition, caseload, and influence.

One of the most basic changes in the Court has been its size. Originally pegged at six members, the Court's lineup has fluctuated a good deal. As the data in Table 1.1 show, the number of justices increased (albeit erratically) through the late nineteenth century. Part of the reason for this growth was administrative; at the time, the justices were responsible for serving on the federal appellate courts as well as the U.S. Supreme Court. So, as the nation expanded and new appeals courts were created, more justices were needed to help staff them. At the same time, the variation in size can also be explained by simple partisanship. In 1801, for example, the Federalists reduced the size of the Court from six to five, in order to deny an appointment to President Jefferson. Similarly, as a means of affording President Lincoln an appointment to the Court during the Civil War, the Republican Congress enlarged the Court to ten members in 1863. The norm of nine justices was not established until 1869 during the administration of President Grant.[2] Since then, there has been no serious attempt to change the size of the Court, with the exception of Franklin Roosevelt's proposal to enlarge the Court to fifteen after several of his leading economic initiatives were invalidated by a more conservative set of justices during the 1930s.

Just as the Court's size has varied over time, so too have its informal standards of membership. Although there is no requirement that a justice be a lawyer, virtually every member of the Court has been trained in the law.[3] Perhaps more surprising, though, is the absence of prior judicial experience among many of the justices. One might be inclined to suspect that the members of the Court bring a wealth of practical judicial expertise to the bench, but Table 1.1 reveals that, while it has certainly been common, experience as a lower court judge has hardly been an indispensable qualification. Before 1926, between 60 and 70 percent of the justices came to the Supreme

[2]O'Brien, *Storm Center*, pp.105–8, 364; Abraham, *The Judicial Process*, p.186.
[3]See Lee Epstein, Jeffrey A. Segal, Harold J. Spaeth, and Thomas G. Walker. *The Supreme Court Compendium: Data, Decisions, and Developments*, 2nd ed. (Washington: Congressional Quarterly, Inc., 1996), Table 4–4.

TABLE 1.1 Changing Characteristics of the U.S. Supreme Court

	Size	Standards of Membership		Policies	
Time Period	Number of Justices	Justices with Judicial Experience (%)	Justices with Political Experience (%)	Number of Decisions	Number of Major Decisions
1790–1825	6, 5, 6, 7	74	100	661	15
1826–1850	7, 9	67	89	1,143	22
1851–1875	9, 10, 7, 9	57	81	2,626	23
1876–1900	9	70	83	6,065	40
1901–1925	9	68	80	5,206	45
1926–1950	9	50	83	3,584	84
1951–1975	9	55	86	2,950	114
1976–2000	9	94	75	2,992	175

Note: Data assembled from Joan Biskupic and Elder Witt, *Guide to the U.S. Supreme Court*, 3rd ed. (Washington: Congressional Quarterly, Inc., 1997); Lee Epstein, Jeffrey A. Segal, Harold J. Spaeth, and Thomas G. Walker, *The Supreme Court Compendium: Data, Decisions, and Developments*, 2nd ed. (Washington: Congressional Quarterly, Inc., 1996).

Court after having served as judges elsewhere, but that figure fell to only 50 percent thereafter. Only recently has it become nearly universal. Since 1976, almost every person who has sat on the Supreme Court has had some prior experience as a judge.

Historically, the justices' professional credentials have also included political positions of one form or another, a tendency that was especially strong in the first days of the republic. Indeed, in the early 1800s, experience in elected or appointed office—as state legislator, governor, state attorney general, and the like—was widespread among the justices. Since then, previous work in public life has become less common on the Court, showing fairly steady decline over time. Of course, this decline is only relative; today, three out of every four justices have still spent at least part of their professional lives in politics.

These standards of membership on the Court have undergone noteworthy transformations, changes that make for an interesting contrast: Whereas virtually every justice on the early Supreme Court brought political experience to the bench, today almost all of the justices have judicial expertise. At the same time, both types of experience remain important.

Quite apart from the Court's composition, the justices' policies have evolved substantially as well. From humble beginnings, the Court has emerged as a leading institution of judicial policy making. In its earliest days, for instance, the Court had only a modest number of cases on its docket, and those that it did hear were typically not of any great consequence. As President John Adams's son wrote in a letter to his mother in 1799, "The Supreme Court of the United States adjourned this day—Little business was done, because there was little to do."[4] By the data in Table 1.1, the justices issued fewer than 700 opinions during the Court's earliest period, and of those, scarcely a dozen could be classified as landmark decisions. Moreover, the number of important policies remained meager, even as the Court's caseload grew. In fact, during the Court's first 100 years, the justices averaged only one major decision per year. To be sure, by establishing the power to declare laws unconstitutional and extending its supervisory authority over state as well as federal courts, the Court began to assume a more prominent political role; after all, it helped chart a course that gave constitutional validity to the actions of a newly created national government, even at the expense of states.[5] Still, decisions such as *Marbury v. Madison* (1803) and *McCulloch v. Maryland* (1819) were the exception rather than the rule.

Beginning in the mid-nineteenth century, the Court's caseload grew, but its influence continued to be limited, in part because the justices lacked the ability to avoid unwanted cases. Typically, the Supreme Court was legally bound to decide the cases that were appealed to it, no matter how unimportant, and it was not until 1891 that Congress began to give the Court some measure of discretion in deciding which cases to decide.[6] By the early twentieth century, the Court had become far more visible. Predominantly conservative in their orientation, the justices began arbitrating major disputes over Congress's power in economic affairs and its relationship to the states. Beginning in the 1950s, under the leadership of Chief Justice Earl Warren, the Court underwent a considerable transformation;

[4]Quoted in Bernard Schwartz, *A History of the Supreme Court* (New York: Oxford University Press, 1993), p. 20.
[5]*Marbury v. Madison* 1 Cr. 137 (1803); *McCulloch v. Maryland* 4 Wheat. 316 (1819); see also *Martin v. Hunter's Lessee* 1 Wheat. 304 (1816).
[6]O'Brien, *Storm Center*, p.156.

its more liberal membership began to shift the Court's attention to issues of civil liberties and rights, addressing such politically salient concerns as racial segregation, school prayer, and the rights of the accused. In more recent years, as the Supreme Court has begun to revisit issues long thought to be settled—the scope of national authority, federalism, and property rights, for example—the Court's impact has continued to increase.[7]

DECISION MAKING IN BRIEF

One of the noteworthy characteristics of the Supreme Court of the early nineteenth century was the absence of regular procedures for making decisions. With only a handful of cases to resolve, however, the lack of formal rules was not a major obstacle to its operations. As the Court began to mature and its caseload grew, it adopted more formal rules for handling the cases on its docket. Today, the justices have highly structured methods for handling their vast caseload, a set of procedures that are outlined in Figure 1.1.

Throughout the year, thousands of litigants bring cases to the Supreme Court, and in almost every instance, the justices have the discretion to decide whether to hear the case. Most frequently, parties who have lost in a lower court—usually a federal appellate court or a state supreme court—petition the justices for a writ of certiorari, the legal mechanism by which the Court agrees to consider a case. In a limited number of circumstances, however, formal consideration by the Supreme Court is mandatory. Some disputes, known formally as appeals, involve certain legal questions that Congress has thought to be so important that the Court must hear them when asked. Finally, as stipulated by the Constitution, a number of other cases can actually begin in the Supreme Court without having first been decided by a lower court. So, for example, under Article III conflicts between states (disputes over shared borders or water rights are typical examples) originate in the Supreme Court, and the justices are obliged to resolve them.

Once filed, these cases are placed on one of two lists at the Supreme Court. One list, the appellate docket, contains all appeals

---

[7]The number of important decisions from 1997 to 2000 is estimated based upon the annual figures from the preceding twenty-one years.

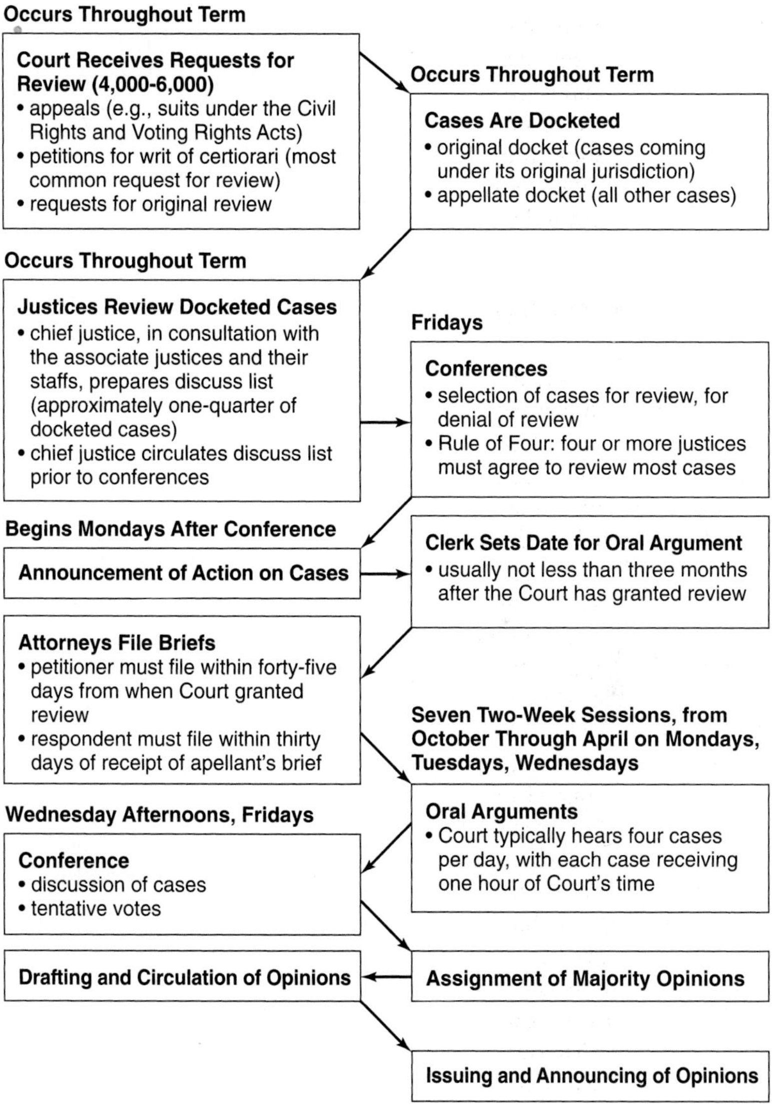

Occurs Throughout Term

Court Receives Requests for Review (4,000-6,000)
- appeals (e.g., suits under the Civil Rights and Voting Rights Acts)
- petitions for writ of certiorari (most common request for review)
- requests for original review

Occurs Throughout Term

Cases Are Docketed
- original docket (cases coming under its original jurisdiction)
- appellate docket (all other cases)

Occurs Throughout Term

Justices Review Docketed Cases
- chief justice, in consultation with the associate justices and their staffs, prepares discuss list (approximately one-quarter of docketed cases)
- chief justice circulates discuss list prior to conferences

Fridays

Conferences
- selection of cases for review, for denial of review
- Rule of Four: four or more justices must agree to review most cases

Begins Mondays After Conference

Announcement of Action on Cases

Clerk Sets Date for Oral Argument
- usually not less than three months after the Court has granted review

Attorneys File Briefs
- petitioner must file within forty-five days from when Court granted review
- respondent must file within thirty days of receipt of apellant's brief

Seven Two-Week Sessions, from October Through April on Mondays, Tuesdays, Wednesdays

Wednesday Afternoons, Fridays

Conference
- discussion of cases
- tentative votes

Oral Arguments
- Court typically hears four cases per day, with each case receiving one hour of Court's time

Drafting and Circulation of Opinions ← **Assignment of Majority Opinions**

Issuing and Announcing of Opinions

FIGURE 1.1 The Processing of Cases
Source: Epstein et al., *Supreme Court Compendium,* Figure 1–1.

and petitions for certiorari, while the other, the original docket, contains the very small number of cases that go directly to the justices for decision.[8] With the vast majority of filings on their appellate docket, the justices select from among this slate of candidates those cases that they believe to merit a hearing in the Supreme Court.

In order to winnow the caseload, the justices begin by preparing a list of cases from the current appellate docket that are judged to be worthy of further consideration. Although this list is assembled by the chief justice, any member of the Court may nominate a case for discussion by the full Court. Any case not on the weekly "discuss list" is rejected, while those on the list remain for closer scrutiny at the Court's Friday conference. At this conference, the justices deliberate over whether to grant review to the cases on the discuss list. If four or more justices support granting the petition for the writ of certiorari, then the Court will decide the case. Otherwise, review is denied.

After the Court announces its decision about the selection of a case, the clerk of the Court schedules a date for oral argument. In advance of that argument, the lawyers for both parties file written briefs in which they lay out the legal and policy grounds for their positions. These positions are then defended and elaborated during oral argument, a time during which each party is usually allowed thirty minutes to present arguments and answer questions from the bench.

Following a week's oral arguments, the justices convene to discuss the cases they have heard. During their conference, they cast preliminary votes to determine the outcome of a case, a decision made by majority rule. Thereafter, the most senior justice within the majority, often but not always the chief justice, selects one of the justices in that coalition to write an opinion announcing the Court's decision and articulating the legal rationale supporting it. Once drafted, it is circulated to the other members of the Court for their consideration. Often the justices in the majority will ask the opinion writer to make certain changes before they agree to join the opinion.

---

[8]This characterization refers only to paid cases, which are cases in which the party filing the case is able to pay the administrative fees and other expenses associated with litigating before the Court. Many cases are filed by indigents who certify to the Court that they cannot meet these financial obligations. Their petitions are placed on a third list known as the miscellaneous docket.

In addition, a justice in the majority might also want to supplement the opinion of the Court by expressing his or her distinctive views by writing separately in a concurring opinion. For their part, the justices in the minority prepare a dissenting opinion that explains why they would decide the case differently. Because no decision is final until the justices have completed their opinions, the members of the Court remain free to reconsider their initial conference votes until the decision is announced publicly.

Once the votes have been finalized and the process of opinion writing is concluded, the justices announce their decisions. Often, the justice who has written on behalf of the Court will read briefly from the opinion. Of course, the full text of the opinions is made immediately available, later published in both public and private sources.

Selecting cases, determining how to resolve them, and drafting opinions that advance both legal and policy goals are vital elements of the business of the Supreme Court, and a variety of individual and institutional variables potentially shape each one. Why do the justices make the decisions that they do? Exploring possible explanations for their choices is the primary focus of the chapters that follow.

PLAN OF THE BOOK

In examining the politics of the U.S. Supreme Court, this book adopts a somewhat different approach from other introductory texts. Whereas most books provide readers with a broad outline of judicial policy making that is punctuated with specific and concrete examples, this survey of the Court offers a detailed set of prototypical illustrations that embody the behavior of the justices and the principal actors who seek to influence them. Stated differently, it uses individual case studies as a means of gaining a firmer grasp on the systematic knowledge of judicial politics that is the product of scholarly research. The following chapters examine in detail individual illustrations that epitomize a current understanding of the U.S. Supreme Court.

Chapter 2, for instance, probes the politics of judicial selection. Who is selected to serve on the Supreme Court, and why? To answer this question, this chapter traces the events surrounding two nominations to the Court, Robert Bork and Clarence Thomas. Its primary attention is focused on explaining why, in the context of selecting justices for the Court, the president and members of the Senate make the decisions that they do. This chapter surveys the research on both presidential and congressional decision making to help explain why Thomas was ultimately elevated to the Court while Bork was turned away.

The third chapter begins an examination of decision making on the Supreme Court by investigating how the justices select cases. The Court has near total discretion to determine which cases it will hear and which cases it will reject, and this chapter describes what is known about the determinants of agenda setting on the Court. It does so by following the state of South Dakota's challenge to a federal program that made highway funds contingent upon raising its drinking age to twenty-one. It highlights some of the most conspicuous characteristics of the dispute, factors to which the justices often respond when choosing cases.

How do the justices resolve those cases they agree to consider? Deciding cases on the merits is at the heart of what the Supreme Court does, and Chapter 4 uses an intriguing challenge to Geogia's death penalty to illuminate this process and the forces that shape it. In this case, the justices were presented with statistical evidence that capital punishment in Georgia was being administered in a racially discriminatory way. Were those statistics sufficient to invalidate that state's death penalty? The justices disagreed sharply over the answer to this legal question, and this chapter examines the likely reasons why the members of the Court would come to such different conclusions.

The Supreme Court's work affects many interests in society, so it is not surprising that organized groups would work to influence its policies. The ways in which interest groups pressure the Court, and their effectiveness, are analyzed in Chapter 5. This chapter takes a close look at how and why different organizations responded to a New York law that tried to ensure that criminals could not benefit by later writing for profit about their unlawful behavior. The Court, it turns out, is actually very open to considering the voices of different constituencies within society. Not only that, the justices are in some respects quite responsive to these lobbying efforts.

Finally, Chapter 6 deals with the consequences of the Court's policies, the practical ramifications of its decisions. Obviously, the justices address legal issues that concern many Americans, but it is not clear what, if anything, happens after they speak to those issues. Do those who are presumably affected by a decision behave any differently? What difference does the Supreme Court make? To assess the impact of the Supreme Court's rulings, this chapter evaluates the effects of the justices' decision to invalidate a major portion of a federal law governing the financing of presidential and congressional campaigns. Chapter 6 considers the effectiveness of the Court's reforms and the responses of those who are affected by them.

SUGGESTED READING

Lawrence Baum. 2001. *The Supreme Court.* 7th ed. Washington: Congressional Quarterly, Inc.

Joan Biskupic and Elder Witt. 1997. *Guide to the U.S. Supreme Court.* 3rd ed. Washington: Congressional Quarterly, Inc.

Kermit L. Hall. 1992. *The Oxford Companion to the Supreme Court of the United States.* New York: Oxford University Press.

David M. O'Brien. 2000. *Storm Center: The Supreme Court in American Politics.* 5th ed. New York: W. W. Norton.

Bernard Schwartz. 1994. *A History of the Supreme Court.* New York: Oxford University Press.

Stephen L. Wasby. 1993. *The Supreme Court in the Federal Judicial System.* 4th ed. Chicago: Nelson-Hall Publishers.

CHAPTER 2

A Tale of Two Nominees

Robert Bork and
Clarence Thomas

Among the more important responsibilities of the president and the Senate is deciding who will serve on the U.S. Supreme Court. With lifetime tenure, justices can be expected to shape the debate over many of the nation's most pressing political issues. These choices, therefore, have significant consequences. This chapter follows the fate of two nominees, Robert Bork and Clarence Thomas. Bork, a highly respected legal scholar and judge, was turned away by the Senate, while Thomas, a less prominent and comparatively inexperienced member of the federal bench, was ultimately elevated to the Court. Why would one nominee, clearly qualified to serve, be rejected and another nominee, with more slender credentials, succeed? To answer this question, this chapter focuses on the factors that motivate the selection of nominees as well as the determinants of the vote within the Senate. It suggests that, rather than being based strictly upon merit, these decisions are influenced by a variety of sometimes competing considerations.

The 1980s were very good for the Republican Party. Less than ten years earlier, the party's reputation had been tarnished, almost irreparably, it seemed, under the administration of President Richard Nixon. During the 1972 election, several of Nixon's associates tried to sabotage the Democratic presidential campaign. Their various exploits—the most notable of which was a break-in at the Democratic Party's headquarters at the Watergate office building in Washington—and the willingness of the president to cover them up brought the GOP into considerable disrepute. By 1980, however, the American public was ready to put the scandal aside. In the face of a sluggish economy, the electorate showed its willingness to overlook the political and legal misdeeds connected with the Watergate affair by ousting Democratic President Jimmy Carter, who was seeking a second term. Voters returned to the Republican Party by electing Ronald Reagan, a charismatic Californian with highly conservative economic and social credentials.

Along with regaining control of the White House, the Republican Party enjoyed similar successes in the U.S. Congress. In the House of Representatives, the Republicans picked up thirty-three seats, their largest gain since the mid-1960s. Combined with the positions that the GOP had won in the previous mid-term elections, the Republicans' victories in the 1980 congressional elections completely recouped their devastating post-Watergate losses. On the other side of Capitol Hill, the Republicans reversed outright roughly thirty-five years of Democratic control of the U.S. Senate. By a slim ratio of 53 to 47, the Republicans became the majority party.

Thus began a sustained period of Republican national leadership. During his first term in office, President Reagan successfully promoted a number of noteworthy changes in federal policy, such as reducing taxes, and increasing the size and sophistication of the military. Four years later, Ronald Reagan would win reelection in a landslide with nearly 60 percent of the popular vote and become the first president since Dwight Eisenhower to serve two terms. Despite the typical congressional losses that are suffered by a president's party, Republicans retained control of the Senate for all but the last two years of his time in office. On balance, voters appeared to be quite satisfied with Republican leadership; by the end of the decade, George Bush would overcome the historical odds and become the first sitting vice president to be elected to the presidency since Martin Van Buren in 1836. Americans had not sent Republicans to the White House in three successive elections since the 1920s.[1]

What implications was this substantial Republican influence likely to have for the direction of policy making in the federal courts?

[1]These data are drawn from Harold W. Stanley and Richard G. Niemi, *Vital Statistics on American Politics* (Washington: Congressional Quarterly, Inc., 1998), Tables 1–8 and 1–9. See also Paul E. Peterson and Mark Rom. 1988. "Lower Taxes, More Spending, and Budget Deficits," in *The Reagan Legacy: Promise and Performance*, ed. Charles O. Jones, Chatham, NJ: Chatham House Publishers, Inc.

After the 1980 elections, the Republicans were poised to make a lasting imprint on the judiciary. In fact, Reagan's campaign had made much of the need to staff the federal courts with judges who were sympathetic to conservative ideals. Given the president's ideology, it was not difficult to understand why.

In 1953, the Supreme Court came under the leadership of Chief Justice Earl Warren. Although appointed by a Republican president, Warren quickly demonstrated that he could not necessarily be counted on to follow conservative ideology. Warren, it turned out, had quite different ideas, and together with a number of like-minded justices, he set the Court on a course of unprecedented liberalism. During his tenure as chief justice, the Court reshaped legislative districts, desegregated public schools, broadened the rights of the criminally accused, established a constitutional right to privacy, and expanded the protections of speech, press, and religion. To be sure, these ambitions were more restrained after Richard Nixon was elected in 1968 and reelected in 1972; as chief executive, Nixon was able to appoint Earl Warren's successor, Warren Burger, as well as three other more conservative jurists. By then, however, many of the Warren Court's precedents had firmly taken root in American law. That they had become so established made them difficult to undo. Not only that, a good many members of the Burger Court were holdovers from the earlier era, and several of them—Justices Brennan, Douglas, and Marshall, in particular—were actually interested in enlarging the scope of rights and liberties. With the occasional support of more moderate members of the Court, they were able to do just that.

In the wake of Watergate, the electorate was disenchanted with a Republican White House and elected Democrat Jimmy Carter over then-President Gerald Ford in the fall of 1976. As president, Carter was in the fortunate position of being able to name more members of the federal bench than any president in history, thanks in large part to congressional expansion of the judiciary.[2] As fate would have it, though, no vacancies occurred on the Supreme Court. Even President Ford, who had an abbreviated two-year tenure as chief executive, was given the chance to name John Paul Stevens to the Court after William Douglas resigned in 1975. Carter, by contrast, had no

---

[2]Sheldon Goldman, *Picking Federal Judges: Lower Court Selection from Roosevelt through Reagan* (New Haven: Yale University Press, 1997).

opportunities to leave his imprimatur on the nation's highest tribunal. Still, the Warren Court had left an impressive liberal legacy, one that remained relatively unchanged by the more moderate Burger Court.

To conservatives, much of the Supreme Court's handiwork was bad news. From their perspective, the Warren Court had sacrificed the rights of the community in order to protect criminals, unilaterally restricting the police and rewriting criminal courtroom procedures. It permitted the airing of unworthy, distasteful, and sometimes dangerous viewpoints. And it generally substituted its judgment for that of popularly elected decision makers. Not only that, the Burger Court, which built its doctrines upon many of the principles laid down by the Warren Court, left them equally dismayed. During the Burger era, the justices put their stamp of approval on affirmative action. They encouraged extensive busing of public school children for the sake of racial balance. They gave legal shelter to purveyors of pornography. They ruled that women had a constitutional right to abortion.

By 1980, Republicans had become greatly frustrated with the path of the Court's policy making, and they were ready for a change. Since the two leading institutions in the politics of judicial selection, the presidency and the Senate, were now in the hands of the GOP, the Republicans were prepared to reshape the Supreme Court and the nature of judicial policy making more generally. United—both institutionally and ideologically—the executive and legislative branches were anxious to set the Court on a new path of legal and political conservatism.

They did not have to wait long. In June 1981, shortly after President Reagan took office, Justice Potter Stewart announced his resignation after twenty-three years of service on the Supreme Court. As a presidential candidate, Reagan had vowed, "One of the first Supreme Court vacancies in my administration will be filled by the most qualified woman I can find, one who meets the high standard I will demand for all my appointments."[3] Making good on his campaign promise, the President nominated Sandra Day O'Connor, a state appeals court judge from Arizona. A conservative jurist with extensive experience as a legislative leader, she was precisely the

---

[3]Quoted in Henry J. Abraham, 1992. *Justices and Presidents: A Political History of Appointments to the Supreme Court* (New York: Oxford University Press, 1992), p. 338.

kind of person the president had wanted to elevate to the Court. Not surprisingly, she easily won confirmation in the Senate by a unanimous vote.

Three years later, Ronald Reagan handily won reelection, and midway through his second term in office, Chief Justice Warren Burger announced that he would retire from the Court. This gave the President a plum appointment, the chance to name the chief judicial officer of the U.S. government. It was, of course, an opportunity that came in the autumn years of the president's tenure, but it did give the administration the ability to ensure that the leadership on the high court would, at least for the foreseeable future, owe it origins to the Reagan presidency. Choosing a known quantity, the president decided to elevate Associate Justice William Rehnquist to the chief's position. A former official at the Justice Department who had been appointed to the Court by President Nixon, Rehnquist was an attractive choice: He was easily the Court's most conservative member, and as a sitting justice, he would be more likely to secure confirmation than an outsider with comparable ideological credentials.

Given that much of Rehnquist's record as a justice flew in the face of both Warren and Burger Court doctrine, many—especially the beneficiaries of the Court's policies—were anxious to see Rehnquist defeated. Various liberal interest groups, together with a number of sympathetic Democratic senators, actively sought to derail his candidacy. These efforts proved to be costly for Rehnquist's nomination; a third of the Senate voted against him. Ultimately, though, the administration's strategy succeeded, and Rehnquist was confirmed as chief justice.

With Rehnquist's seat as associate justice vacant, the president tapped a judge on the U.S. Court of Appeals for the District of Columbia Circuit named Antonin Scalia. A jurist with outstanding credentials, he had long been seen as a potential nominee. In addition to his service on one of the nation's most important appellate courts, Scalia had been general counsel in the White House Office of Telecommunications Policy as well as an assistant attorney general in the Justice Department. He was also a logical choice for ideological reasons; Scalia was formerly an associate at the American Enterprise Institute and a member of the law faculty of the University of Chicago, both of which are well known for their conservative orientations toward politics and the law. Certainly no less important to the White House, his record as a judge suggested that he would follow the Reagan administration's agenda in a number of leading policy areas, such as civil rights and church/state relations. For his part, Scalia had a stellar professional reputation, and the Senate and its Judiciary Committee—both exhausted from the prolonged and acrimonious battle over Rehnquist—quickly confirmed the nominee. On the floor of the Senate, Scalia's nomination was debated less than ten minutes.[4]

Notwithstanding the campaign and votes against him, Rehnquist was widely expected to win confirmation. Similarly, observers accurately forecast a warm reception for Scalia. At the time, the primary explanation was simple. "Neither Rehnquist's elevation from associate justice nor Scalia's appointment is expected to dramatically change the balance of power on a court that has been dominated by moderates for the last 15 years."[5] Since he was already sitting on the Court, Rehnquist's mere change of chairs would not introduce a new voice onto the bench, and, although technically he filled Rehnquist's vacancy, Scalia was really a replacement for Chief Justice Burger, who had been seen as Rehnquist's ideological kinsman. The proof was in their respective voting records. Burger and Scalia would end up voting together with Rehnquist with almost identical frequency—about 90 percent of the time.[6]

So, as the justices began their annual term in the fall of 1986, the Supreme Court had been only partially transformed by Ronald Reagan. After nearly six years as president, he had appointed just two new members to the high court. Neither altered appreciably the direction of its policies. Justice Stewart had been a moderating voice on the Warren Court. As his replacement, O'Connor did not depart radically from the positions taken by her predecessor. And as expected, the Court more or less marked time, as Scalia proved to be no more or less conservative than the former chief justice he replaced. Leaving aside the seemingly modest impact of the Reagan appointees, by

---

[4]Howard Kurtz, "Senate Panel Approves Rehnquist, 13 to 5; Judiciary Committee Unanimously Endorses Scalia for High Court," *Washington Post*, August 15, 1986, p. A1; Linda Greenhouse, "Senate, 65 to 33, Votes to Confirm Rehnquist as 16th Chief Justice," *New York Times*, September 18, 1986, p. 1.

[5]Al Kamen, "Rehnquist Confirmed in 65–33 Senate Vote; Scalia Approved as Associate Justice, 98–0," *Washington Post*, September 18, 1986, p. A1.

[6]See, for example, Lee Epstein, Jeffrey A. Segal, Harold J. Spaeth, and Thomas G. Walker, *The Supreme Court Compendium: Data, Decisions, and Developments*, 2nd ed. (Washington: Congressional Quarterly, Inc., 1996), Tables 6–6 and 6–7.

the time Scalia began his service as associate justice, three members of the Warren Court remained: liberal stalwarts William Brennan and Thurgood Marshall and the more mercurial Byron White. Together with the occasional support of the justices at the ideological center, the liberals tempered some of the Court's more conservative designs during that 1986 term. For example, these justices, by narrow majorities, turned back a state scheme that challenged the teaching of evolution in the public schools and upheld a gender-based program of affirmative action under federal civil rights law.[7] In short, the crop of veteran justices—combined with the replacements for recent retirees—had created a precarious ideological balance on the bench, one that left the Reagan legacy still unrealized. All that was about to change.

THE CASE OF ROBERT BORK

On the last day of the term, Justice Lewis Powell announced his retirement. Citing poor health and his advancing age, the 79 year-old, soft-spoken Virginian stepped down after more than fifteen years as a member of the Court. His unexpected announcement caught observers off-guard. The Reagan administration, however, wasted no time. Immediately, the White House declared its intention to replace Powell quickly with a nominee loyal to its policy agenda, someone who would support the president's principal goals, such as limiting abortion rights.[8]

Unlike the other high court vacancies that had occurred during Reagan's time in office, this one offered the president an extraordinary opportunity, a chance to alter in a significant way the direction of the Supreme Court. Recognizing that Powell's centrist views had served to counterbalance the liberal and conservative justices, "no commentator failed to report the ramifications for the tribunal's future direction." As one close student of the Court explained, "Powell had played a pivotal role as a tie-breaking vote in cases determining the Court's interpretation of constitutional law on such controversial

---

[7]*Edwards v. Aguillard*, 482 U.S. 578 (1987); *Johnson v. Transportation Agency, Santa Clara County, California*, 480 U.S. 616 (1987).
[8]Gerald M. Boyd, "White House Hunts for a Justice, Hoping to Tip Ideological Scales," *New York Times*, June 27, 1987, p.1.

issues as abortion, affirmative action, and separation of church and state."[9] Having become a swing vote on the bench, Justice Powell was someone whose moderate preferences often determined the outcomes of close cases. A new, more conservative justice would surely help solidify Reagan's control of judicial policy. The administration chose its nominee with precisely that goal in mind.

To no one's surprise, the president nominated Robert H. Bork. As a judge on the U.S. Court of Appeals for the District of Columbia Circuit, he had long been in the running for a spot on the high court. By objective standards, Robert Bork was certainly qualified to serve as a justice. A former professor of law at Yale University, he had served in the Nixon administration in the prestigious post of solicitor general, the lawyer whose job it is to argue the federal government's cases before the Supreme Court. As an appellate judge, his decisions were held in particularly high regard; in fact, not one of his opinions had ever been overturned by the Supreme Court.[10]

With an extensive record of legal writings and judicial opinions, he was also well known for his social and economic conservatism as well as his adherence to the doctrine of original intent. Believing that judges are bound to follow the intentions of the founders, he had been a strong critic of the constitutional activism of the Warren and Burger Courts. From his perspective, these justices wanted various liberties and rights—the right to privacy or the principle of "one person, one vote," for example—to enjoy legal protection. Not finding them explicitly safeguarded in the text of the Constitution, however, the Supreme Court had, in his view, simply decided to create them.[11]

After Justice Powell stepped down, Bork immediately became the leading candidate. For a White House so openly opposed to judicial liberalism, Bork was an ideal candidate; indeed, his qualifications and legal philosophy made him perfectly suited to serve on the Supreme Court. As President Reagan explained when he made the announcement, "Judge Bork, widely regarded as the most prominent and intellectually powerful advocate of judicial restraint, shares my view that judges' personal preferences and values should not be

[9]Abraham, *Justices and Presidents*, pp. 56–57.
[10]Ethan Bronner, *Battle for Justice: How the Bork Nomination Shook America* (New York: Doubleday, 1989).
[11]Robert H. Bork, *The Tempting of America: The Political Seduction of the Law* (New York: Free Press, 1990).

part of their constitutional interpretations. The guiding principle of judicial restraint recognizes that under the Constitution, it is the exclusive province of the legislatures to enact laws and the role of the courts to interpret them."[12] In short, Bork was exactly the kind of judge that the Reagan administration believed should be on the Court.

In the Senate, however, Bork's suitability for the Supreme Court was more of an open question. Within minutes of the announcement, Democratic Senator Edward Kennedy of Massachusetts denounced Bork's candidacy from the Senate floor. With fiery rhetoric, Kennedy attacked the nomination, claiming that "Robert Bork's America is a land in which women would be forced into back-alley abortions, blacks would sit at segregated lunch counters, rogue police could break down citizens' doors in midnight raids, schoolchildren could not be taught about evolution, writers and artists could be censored at the whim of government and the doors of the federal courts would be shut on the fingers of millions of citizens."[13] Whether these comments accurately characterized Judge Bork's views, they certainly highlighted the concerns that many organized interests had about his nomination to the Court. In light of Bork's philosophy, they feared that, if confirmed, he would work to roll back many of the victories that they had achieved during the Warren and Burger eras. Civil rights and women's groups were especially nervous.

Over the next 3½ months, both sides battled over Judge Bork's nomination. In the Judiciary Committee, senators pored over Bork's writing and questioned him extensively about his views on such legal esoterica as precedent and original intent, as well as more politically charged issues, such as privacy, freedom of speech, racial segregation, and the Watergate affair. At the White House, members of the Reagan administration worked closely with the Senate on Bork's behalf. Legal scholars, distinguished lawyers, and leading political figures lined up both in favor of and in opposition to Bork. Besides testifying at the confirmation hearings, interest groups of various stripes organized extensive grassroots campaigns to mobi-

---

[12]Gerald M. Boyd, "Bork Picked for High Court; Reagan Cites His 'Restraint'; Confirmation Fight Looms," *New York Times*, July 2, 1987, p.1.

[13]Lou Cannon and Edward Walsh, "Reagan Nominates Appeals Judge Bork to Supreme Court; Fierce Confirmation Battle Over Conservative Expected," *Washington Post*, July 2, 1987, p. A1.

lize public support for their positions on the nominee. After the hearings, the Judiciary Committee reported the nomination to the full Senate; voting largely along party lines, the panel recommended that Bork not be confirmed. This committee's decision provided a pessimistic forecast, but Bork, with the support of the White House, was determined to have a vote on the nomination. An acrimonious floor debate followed, and in the end the Senate voted against confirmation, 42–58.[14]

Though angered and frustrated, the administration was steadfast in its desire to see the Court's vacancy filled by a judicial conservative. Even when Bork's prospects had begun to dim, President Reagan was undaunted, vowing that he would send another candidate to the Senate "that they'll object to as much as they did to this one."[15] Soon after Bork's defeat, the president nominated Douglas Ginsburg, another conservative who sat with Bork on the D.C. Court of Appeals. Reports soon surfaced, though, of several legal and ethical improprieties, the most damning of which was the revelation that Ginsburg had occasionally smoked marijuana while on the faculty of the Harvard Law School. Such behavior did not sit well with the Reagan administration, which had maintained a very visible campaign against drug use, and Ginsburg's name was quickly withdrawn. A few days later, Reagan announced the nomination of a federal appellate judge from California named Anthony Kennedy. With an unblemished personal record and views that were perceived to be less extreme than Bork's, Kennedy quickly won a unanimous confirmation vote.[16]

THE CASE OF CLARENCE THOMAS

Despite the defeat of Robert Bork, the administration had reason to be pleased. President Reagan's second term was drawing to a close, and he had successfully filled three Supreme Court vacancies, one of which was the chief justiceship. More generally, Reagan was about to

---

[14]"Reagan Fills Court Vacancy on Third Attempt," *Congressional Quarterly Almanac: 100th Congress, 1st Session* (Washington: Congressional Quarterly, Inc., 1988).
[15]Lou Cannon, "Reagan Resumes Attack on Bork's Senate Foes; Ad-Libs Hurt Effort to Tone Down Rhetoric," *Washington Post*, October 14, 1987, p. A1.
[16]Bronner, *Battle for Justice*.

leave the White House with an impressive level of popular support; since Dwight Eisenhower, no president had ended his term in office with a higher job approval rating.[17] One measure of the electorate's satisfaction with the Reagan era was its decision to extend it. In the 1988 election, voters made Reagan's vice president, George Bush, the nation's next chief executive.

As president, Bush soon had the chance to make his mark on the Court. In July 1990, Justice William Brennan resigned. Brennan had been one of the most influential justices of the twentieth century, as well as one of its most liberal. To fill his seat, Bush named David Souter, an experienced appeals court judge from New Hampshire. Less than one year later, the president had a second vacancy to fill. With chronic health problems and advancing age, Thurgood Marshall announced his retirement from the Court after twenty-five years on the bench.

Marshall was the last of the Warren Court vanguard. Appointed to the Court by President Johnson, he had been a passionate champion for a variety of liberal concerns, most notably civil rights. Promoting the cause of equality was nothing new for Marshall. Even before coming to the Court, he had been a leading figure in the civil rights community. He was one of the principal organizers of the NAACP's litigation campaign that culminated in *Brown v. Board of Education* (1954), the decision that outlawed racially segregated public schools. In 1967, his elevation to the Court became a symbol of the civil rights movement; as the first African–American justice, he had broken the color barrier on the Supreme Court.

At the time of Marshall's retirement, the White House had been sparring with Congress over civil rights legislation. Congress, now back in the hands of the Democrats, was seeking to undo a number of conservative Supreme Court rulings on discrimination. As a result of recent Republican appointments, the Court had clearly moved to the right, and liberal legislators were now trying to minimize its influence. On Capitol Hill, Democrats sought to craft legislation that would reverse the Court while at the same time muffle conservative criticism. The president, though, denounced it as "a quota bill, no matter how its authors dress it up."[18] To some, this fight conveyed

---

[17]Stanley and Niemi, *Vital Statistics on American Politics,* Figure 3.4.
[18]Adam Clymer, "Bush Assails 'Quota Bill' at West Point Graduation," *New York Times,* June 2, 1991, p.32.

the impression that the president was hostile to civil rights. Conse-quently, there was considerable political pressure for Bush to fill Marshall's vacancy with another minority. The dilemma facing the president was obvious to political observers; with Marshall gone, "Mr. Bush will have to balance pressure to cement even further the conservative grip on the Court with equal pressure to appoint a black justice at a time when the President is . . . anxious to send a message of conciliation to blacks and other critics of his civil rights record."[19] How could the president demonstrate a concern for the liberal tradition of minority representation that had been established on the Court and yet, at the same time, appoint someone who would help advance a conservative agenda?

The answer: Clarence Thomas. Sitting on the Court of Appeals for the District of Columbia was a judge with great ideological sympathy for the GOP's agenda. As a black conservative, Thomas provided the Bush administration with an opportunity to name someone who would further Republican policy goals and yet, at the same time, continue the tradition of minority representation on the Court. The president announced his nomination on July 1, 1991.

Thomas was born into poverty in rural Georgia. Raised under the guidance of a strict, hard-working grandfather—and the stern discipline of the Irish nuns at the local Catholic school—Thomas de-veloped a strong sense of forbearance in the face of adversity. As he later explained, his upbringing "was far more conservative than many who fashion themselves conservatives today. God was central. School, discipline, hard work, and knowing right from wrong were of the highest priority. Crime, welfare, slothfulness, and alcohol were enemies. But these were not issues to be debated by keen intellectu-als . . . . They were a way of life: they marked the path of survival and the escape route from squalor."[20] To that end, he left Georgia to attend the College of the Holy Cross and Yale Law School. Deciding to pursue a career in public service, he went to Washington, where he moved from legislative aide, to assistant secretary of education, to chairman of the Equal Employment Opportunity Commission. In

---

[19]Andrew Rosenthal, "Marshall Retires from High Court; Blow to Liberals," *New York Times*, June 28, 1991, p.1.
[20]Timothy M. Phelps and Helen Winternitz, *Capitol Games: Clarence Thomas, Anita Hill, and the Story of a Supreme Court Nomination* (New York: Hyperion, 1992), p. 40.

1990, President Bush appointed Thomas to the D.C. Court of Appeals.

This story of self-reliance and hard work projected a perfect image for the White House. And his political views—such as his opposition to affirmative action—certainly met the administration's ideological standards for a spot on the high court. At the same time, though, his objective qualifications for the job were open to question. He had very little experience as a judge. In fact, when Bush announced his nomination, Thomas had only been sitting on the appeals court for fifteen months, scarcely enough time to become acclimated to the complex business of the federal judiciary. The American Bar Association, the nation's leading legal organization, provides an evaluation of all nominees to the high court, and it offered Thomas no better than its minimal "qualified" ranking. Most Supreme Court nominees, by contrast, garner a "well qualified" rating, the ABA's highest endorsement. Not only that, the ABA rating was not unanimous; at least two members of the evaluating committee regarded Thomas as "not qualified." Of course, members of the Senate would be under no legal obligation to consider the association's rating. Still, the nine justices appointed prior to Thomas were all considered to be well qualified. Confirmation of a nominee who could not muster minimum support from the entire committee was almost unheard of.[21]

As the hearings on the nomination began in September, members of the Judiciary Committee focused on the nominee's legal views.[22] For five days, Judge Thomas was peppered with questions on such topics as affirmative action, the death penalty, and civil rights. Senators were likewise anxious to have the nominee discuss his views on natural law, the interpretation of federal statutes, and the respect he would accord prior Supreme Court rulings. For his part, Thomas tried to avoid providing his specific opinions on delicate constitutional issues. The White House had learned important lessons from the Bork confirmation, among them that a conservative

---

[21]Neil A. Lewis, "Bar Association Splits on Fitness of Thomas for the Supreme Court," *New York Times*, August 28, 1991, p.1.

[22]My discussion of the Clarence Thomas confirmation is derived from "Clarence Thomas Wins Senate Confirmation," *Congressional Quarterly Almanac: 102nd Congress, 1st Session* (Washington: Congressional Quarterly, Inc., 1992), and Phelps and Winternitz, *Capitol Games*.

judge willing to discuss his views openly did so at his own peril. So at the strong urging of the Bush administration, Thomas skirted sensitive legal concerns and tried to emphasize his successful struggle to overcome poverty. This too proved to be a costly strategy. Almost all of the Democrats on the committee were unsatisfied with Thomas's testimony, and the result was a 7–7 split on whether to recommend his confirmation to the full Senate. Eventually, the committee voted, nearly unanimously, to send Thomas's nomination to the floor of the Senate with no recommendation.

Although the nomination had been marred by opposition on the Judiciary Committee, it seemed clear that Thomas would still have the necessary votes to win confirmation. Then, with only a few days before the scheduled vote in the Senate, media reports began to surface, suggesting that Thomas had sexually harassed one of his former employees. Anita Hill, a law professor at the University of Oklahoma, had provided information to investigators that alleged unwelcome sexual advances by Thomas while he was her supervisor at the Department of Education and later the Equal Employment Opportunity Commission. Senators had been privy to reports of these charges, and when the information became public, it immediately generated great public pressure on the Senate to reopen its examination of Thomas. Women in particular were concerned that the committee had not taken the allegations seriously.

When the hearings reopened, Hill made stunning accusations. Not only had Thomas repeatedly made romantic overtures toward her, he commented on various features of Hill's physique, bragged about his sexual prowess, and recounted the details of pornographic films. For his part, Judge Thomas was unequivocal in his denial. He had treated Hill as he had all of his employees—with support, consideration, and respect. In his view, the Judiciary Committee had irreparably damaged his professional reputation by airing Hill's false claims. Sorting out the truthfulness of their competing claims proved difficult for the committee. Both Hill and Thomas credibly acquitted themselves, and subsequent witnesses on both sides did little to settle the issue. The second round of hearings did create doubts serious enough for several wavering senators to vote against the nomination. In the end, however, the Senate decided to confirm, but only by the most slender majority in modern history, a vote of 52–48.

In retrospect, the events surrounding the nominations of Robert Bork and Clarence Thomas seem rather curious. Why did President

Reagan nominate Bork, a judge whose views were ultimately perceived to be too extreme? What motivated President Bush to select
Thomas, when clearly there were more capable candidates to whom
he might have turned? Why would members of the Senate reject
Bork, whose qualifications were outstanding? And paradoxically,
why would the Senate confirm Thomas, whose professional credentials were much more modest? How could a nominee accused of serious lapses in moral judgment be elevated to the Supreme Court
while another with an unblemished personal record be turned
away? However unpredictable they may seem, both presidential and
congressional decision making are not that mysterious.

WHO IS CHOSEN?

With lifetime tenure, justices typically outlast the presidential ad-
ministrations who appoint them. For that reason, Reagan and Bush,
like all presidents, had to consider with some care whom they would
nominate to the Supreme Court. What motivated their selection? Obviously, a number of different factors might well have shaped the selection process in the cases of Bork and Thomas. How did the White
House come to settle on these two nominees, and what do those
choices reveal about judicial selection more generally?

Ideology

Among the possible presidential motives, probably the central concern in selecting a nominee is a candidate's political views. In some
ways, the ideology of a potential justice might seem to be irrelevant;
judges, in the abstract at least, serve merely to give voice to the law's
commands. However, the precise meaning of the law is not always
clear, even to the most objective observers. With no clear legal answer and with no higher court to monitor their rulings, the justices
are free to allow their own predispositions to shape their judgment.
Presidents obviously would prefer to see judicial decisions that are
consistent with their own beliefs, and consequently they are especially anxious to name justices who share their views about law and
judicial policy making. Not surprisingly, since World War II, about

90 percent of all Supreme Court nominees have identified with the same political party as the presidents who appointed them.[23]

This was an especially important criterion for the Reagan White House. As much as any modern president, Reagan saw the federal courts as a source of potential political support and wanted to ensure that, if his programs were subject to legal challenge, they would be upheld. So staffing the judiciary with conservatives would become a way to extend his policy goals. Judicial appointments were, according to Attorney General Edwin Meese, a way "to institutionalize the Reagan revolution so it can't be set aside no matter what happens in future presidential elections."[24] Within the Justice Department, Meese and other officials developed a set of conservative criteria that their nominees to the Court would have to meet. Among them, as Table 2.1 illustrates, were principles of federalism and limited national government, opposition to policies like abortion and affirmative action, and a generally conservative legal and political philosophy.

In light of these considerations, Robert Bork became a leading contender for a seat on the Court, even before a vacancy occurred. Bork presented a very fine fit with the administration's ideological goals, as the comparisons in Table 2.1 reveal. During the course of his scholarly and judicial careers, he had clearly established the kinds of credentials that the Reagan administration considered necessary. Over the years, Bork had amassed an extensive written record that attested to his conservatism. Perhaps most important, he was a strong advocate of judicial restraint—an approach to judging in which courts adhere strictly to the law and defer to democratically elected decision makers.[25] From an ideological perspective, Bork was exactly what the Reagan administration had in mind.

Political conservatism was also a leading consideration when the Bush administration tapped Clarence Thomas for the Court. Although he did not have as lengthy a written record as Bork, his position on law and politics was no less conservative. Prior to being

---

[23]Epstein et al., *Supreme Court Compendium*, Table 4–12.
[24]Quoted in David M. O'Brien, "The Reagan Judges: His Most Enduring Legacy?" in *The Reagan Legacy: Promise and Performance.* Charles O. Jones, ed. (Chatham, NJ: Chatham House Publishers, 1998), p. 62.
[25]Bronner, *Battle for Justice,* pp. 88–89; Bork, *The Tempting of America,* p. 73; Yalof, *Pursuit of Justices,* pp.146–47.

TABLE 2.1 Comparison of Ideological Views of Reagan White House and Robert Bork

Reagan's Ideological Standard	Bork's Position
Conservative judicial role	
• Refusal to create new constitutional rights for the individual	"The Court [in *Roe v. Wade*] did not even feel obligated to settle the question of where the right of privacy or the subsidary right to abort is to be attached to the Constitution's text. The opinion seems to regard that as a technicality that really does not matter, and indeed it does not, since the right does not come out of the Constitution but is forced into it."
• Commitment to strict principles of "nondiscrimination"	"It makes little sense, or justice, to sacrifice a white or a male who did not inflict discrimination to advance the interest of a black or a female who did not suffer discrimination."
• Disposition toward criminal law as a system for determining guilt or innocence	"Criminal law was remade [by the Warren Court] as the constitutional rights of defendants were multiplied, including the requirement that persons arrested be given *Miranda* warnings. . . . *Miranda* reads more like the work of a legislative drafting committee than a judicial opinion."
Support for federalism	
• Recognition that the federal government is one of enumerated powers	"The Constitution does indicate that there are defined national powers and that they have limits. The fact that the powers of Congress are enumerated in article 1, section 8, demonstrates that Congress was not intended to have unlimited powers."
• Deference to states in their spheres	"There is little doubt that those who framed and ratified the Constitution enumerated the powers given the national legislature—and for good measure added the Tenth Amendment, 'The powers not delegated to the United States by the Constitution nor prohibited by it to the States, are reserved to the States respectively, or to the people'—so that federal government could not govern many aspects of life."

continued

TABLE 2.1 Comparison of Ideological Views of Reagan White House and Robert Bork (*Continued*)

Reagan's Ideological Standard	Bork's Position
Social conservatism	
• Respect for traditional values	"Victory over modern liberalism will require a robust self-confidence about the worth of traditional values. . . . Now that we have seen the catastrophes that the ideas of modern liberalism have produced and are producing, perhaps we will shed our guilt and forthrightly speak and act on the understanding that the evolution of traditional values will produce a far better society than the nihilism of the Left."
• Disposition toward "less government rather than more"	"As government spreads, bureaucracies get beyond the power of elected representatives to control. Government is too big, too complicated, there are too many decisions continually to be made. The staffs of both the President and Congress have been so enlarged in the effort to cope with the workload that both institutions have become bureaucratized. The result is a serious institutional overload for all branches of government."
Economic conservatism	
• Appreciation for the role of the free market in our society	"Antitrust defendants never won before the Warren Court, no matter what the facts, the law, or the rulings of the courts below. The government always prevailed over taxpayers, patents were routinely declared invalid, government regulations [of the economy] were upheld regardless of their rationality."

Source: Bork, *The Tempting of America;* Robert H. Bork, *Slouching Towards Gomorrah: Modern Liberalism and American Decline* (New York: Regan Books, 1996); David Alistair Yalof, *Pursuit of Justices: Presidential Politics and the Selection of Supreme Court Nominees* (Chicago: University of Chicago Press, 1999).

elevated to the federal appellate bench, he had been an outspoken advocate on behalf of the Republican agenda, criticizing civil rights leaders for not encouraging minorities to assume personal responsibility for their own advancement. "We must look to ourselves," Thomas argued, "admitting there are problems which antidiscrimination laws will not cure." By his reckoning, government support and affirmative action were not the answers to the racial disparities of society. As he explained before a group of fellow conservatives, "I marched. I protested. I asked the government to help black people. I did all those things. But it hasn't worked. It isn't working. And someone needs to say that."[26]

As chair of the Equal Employment Opportunity Commission, he took positions that further frustrated the civil rights community. In a change from how the EEOC had handled earlier cases involving allegations of discrimination, he preferred a more limited legal approach; he brought claims only on behalf of the individuals who had actually suffered discrimination, not the entire class of people who might fall under similar circumstances. Likewise, with the support of the Reagan Justice Department, he worked to reduce the federal government's emphasis on race-conscious hiring. As a voice of support for the White House, he remade the EEOC to fit a politically conservative agenda, and his efforts did not go unnoticed: when a seat became vacant on the Court of Appeals for the D.C. Circuit, President Bush quickly tapped Thomas to serve. "No one in Washington missed the significance of the move: Clarence Thomas was being groomed as the Republican replacement for Thurgood Marshall."[27]

Professional Qualifications

As important as ideological compatibility may have been, Presidents Reagan and Bush still demonstrated a great sensitivity to the objective qualifications of those whom they nominated to the Court. Merit

[26]Phelps and Winternitz, *Capitol Games*, p.88; Juan Williams, "Black Conservatives, Center Stage," *Washington Post*, December 16, 1980, p. A21.
[27]David G. Savage, *Turning Right: The Making of the Rehnquist Supreme Court* (New York: John Wiley & Sons, 1992), p. 428; Phelps and Winternitz, *Capitol Games*, p.118.

is clearly an important consideration when filling a vacancy on the Court, but the idea that any administration conducts an exhaustive inventory to find the most qualified person is simply not true. As one leading scholar of the Court puts it, "The Supreme Court is not a meritocracy."[28] At the same time, presidents certainly want justices who are up to the job of dealing authoritatively with the nation's most vexing legal problems. Clearly, Bork and Thomas were named with their professional qualifications in mind.

One measure of their intellectual aptitude is the high quality of their education. Both nominees had attended the nation's premier institutions of higher learning. Bork's undergraduate and law degrees were from the University of Chicago, an outstanding university whose law school is typically ranked among the best in the nation. Thomas was equally well trained; he attended one of the country's leading liberal arts schools, the College of the Holy Cross, and received his law degree from Yale University. In these respects, these two nominees were by no means unusual. In fact, the vast majority of nominees to the Court have been exceptionally well educated.

Perhaps more important, though, was the nature and extent of their professional experiences (see Table 2.2). Although there are no constitutional requirements that one must meet in order to serve on the Supreme Court, presidents have established certain norms that govern nominations. Aside from nominating members of the legal profession, modern presidents have almost always sought candidates who have had experience in public service. Franklin Roosevelt, for example, plucked Hugo Black from the Senate and William O. Douglas from the Securities and Exchange Commission. And Earl Warren was governor of California before he was named chief justice by Dwight Eisenhower. Presidents also value nominees with prominent reputations within the academic community. For that reason, those with experience as legal scholars—such as Felix Frankfurter or more recently Antonin Scalia and Ruth Bader Ginsburg—have often enjoyed an advantage in the selection process as well.

---

[28]David M. O'Brien, *Storm Center: The Supreme Court in American Politics,* 5th ed. (New York: Norton, 2000), p. 33.

TABLE 2.2 Professional Qualifications of Robert Bork and Clarence Thomas

Type of Qualification	Robert Bork	Clarence Thomas
Academic experience	• Law faculty, Yale Law School, 1962–72, 1977–80	—
State political experience	—	• Assistant Attorney General of Missouri, 1974–77
Federal political experience	• U.S. solicitor general, 1973–77	• Assistant Secretary of Education for Civil Rights, 1981–82
		• Chair, Equal Employment Opportunity Commission, 1982–90
Federal judicial experience 1982–87	• U.S. Court of Appeals for the D.C. Circuit, 1982–87	• U.S. Court of Appeals for the D.C. Circuit, 1990–91

Sources: Joan Biskupic and Elder Witt, *Guide to the U.S. Supreme Court*, 3rd ed. (Washington: Congressional Quarterly, Inc.); Bronner, *Battle for Justice.*

Since the 1950s, though, presidents have been increasingly keen to tap individuals with judicial experience. Since the Nixon presidency, roughly nine out of every ten nominees have been sitting judges at the time of their nominations.[29] Like Bork and Thomas, most have been judges on the federal appellate courts. Presidents give especially close attention to the judges on the Court of Appeals for the District of Columbia Circuit. Because a disproportionate share of its cases are eventually decided by the Supreme Court, this court is often seen as a stepping stone to the high court itself. Observers speculate over whether various judges on the D.C. Circuit will be named to the Supreme Court, and in the cases of Bork and Thomas those forecasts proved accurate.

Focusing on their judicial experience, however, actually hides a good deal of interesting variation in their careers. In fact, as Table 2.2 reveals, Robert Bork and Clarence Thomas had fairly substantial careers, mostly in public life, prior to their appointments to the federal

[29]Epstein et al., *Supreme Court Compendium*, Table 4–11.

bench. Like other nominees before him, Bork was a distinguished professor of law. As solicitor general, he also served as the voice of the U.S. government before the Supreme Court during the Nixon presidency. Similarly, after a stint in state politics, Thomas joined the ranks of the Reagan administration, serving first within the Department of Education and later as the nation's primary enforcer of employment discrimination law. In each case, their career paths led to the same proving ground from which potential justices are often selected.

Political Representation

By 1991, many people had come to believe that, regardless of ideological viewpoint, the justices on the Supreme Court should reflect the diversity of American society. As a result, after Marshall announced his retirement, the Bush White House set about trying to find a nominee who would satisfy its ideological goals yet at the same time uphold the precedent of a diverse bench. To that end, administration officials began to assemble a list of compatible candidates who would also demonstrate that the Supreme Court was open to qualified individuals, regardless of background. Since Justice Marshall had been the first African American on the Court, race naturally became the leading consideration. Several prominent Hispanics—such as federal judges Emilio Garza and Jose Cabranes— were in contention for the nomination, as well as the eventual nominee, Clarence Thomas.[30]

Outwardly, Marshall and Thomas shared a common racial background, but politically they had very disparate outlooks. As blacks, Marshall and Thomas had both experienced discrimination, but they had come to different conclusions about what government should do about it. For Marshall, merely outlawing discrimination was not enough; the effects of past discrimination were long lasting, and policies such as affirmative action were necessary to compensate for those lingering disadvantages. Thomas, by contrast, came to quite a different view: Blacks had secured legal equality, but he knew that many Americans harbored doubts about whether blacks were worthy of the rights they had won. To him, the solution was for blacks to

---

[30]Yalof, *Pursuit of Justices*, pp.194–96.

prove such people wrong by working twice as hard.[31] By replacing the liberal Marshall with the conservative Thomas, Bush was able to maintain minority representation among the justices while increasing the conservative stronghold on the Court.

This was hardly the first time that a president had been motivated by concerns over political representation. In fact, demographic factors have almost always played a prominent role in the politics of Supreme Court recruitment. Even in the earliest days of the republic, for example, George Washington was sensitive to such considerations, selecting his nominees with an eye toward a Supreme Court composed of justices from each region of the country.[32] In more contemporary times, presidents have chosen justices based, in part, on their religious affiliation. Indeed, beginning with the appointment of Louis Brandeis in 1916, five different Jewish justices occupied the same seat on the Court over a period of about fifty years. Similarly, William Brennan's Roman Catholicism seems to have been part of the calculus of President Eisenhower. Race and gender probably have become the most salient concerns, however. For Lyndon Johnson, race guided his choice of Thurgood Marshall, just as gender was a major motive for President Reagan in selecting Sandra Day O'Connor. Whatever the mix, these kinds of considerations are clearly at the fore of modern appointments to the Supreme Court.[33]

A survey of several justices currently on the Court testifies to the continued relevance of political representation. Historically, the personal backgrounds of the justices have been very similar—predominantly affluent white men from Protestant denominations.[34] Judged by the information in Table 2.3, however, presidents increasingly have sought to bring members of traditionally underrepresented groups onto the Court. In some ways, these data actually understate the importance of political representation, since the pool of leading contenders from which a president selects will often reflect a good many different demographic considerations. In the case of Robert Bork's nomination, for instance, the Reagan White House was also

---

[31]Phelps and Winternitz, *Capitol Games*, pp. 31–60.
[32]Abraham, *Justices and Presidents*, pp.78–79.
[33]Barbara A. Perry, *A "Representative" Supreme Court? The Impact of Race, Religion, and Gender on Appointments* (New York: Greenwood Press, 1991).
[34]See, e.g., Abraham, *Justices and Presidents*, p. 61.

TABLE 2.3 Political Representation Among Current Supreme Court
Justices

Justice	Demographic Factor	Characteristic
Sandra Day O'Connor	Gender	Female
Antonin Scalia	Ethnicity	Italian
	Religion	Catholic
Anthony M. Kennedy	Religion	Catholic
Clarence Thomas	Race	African American
	Geography	Southerner
Ruth Bader Ginsburg	Gender	Female
	Religion	Jewish
Stephen G. Breyer	Religion	Jewish

giving serious consideration to at least two female judges, one of
whom—Amalya Kearse—was black.[35]

To be sure, the qualifications of a nominee, both professional and
ideological, are the principal factors that govern who is nominated.
Still, presidents are well aware that their electoral and policy successes are tied to support from various constituencies. So one would
expect that presidents would try to strengthen such support by providing representation for those groups on the bench. In trying to decide whom to nominate to replace Marshall, for example, the
attorney general and White House chief of staff both "pushed hard
for consideration of a Hispanic nominee, arguing that President
Bush was much more likely to reap political rewards from the bur-
geoning Hispanic population than from blacks, who always voted
solidly for the Democrats."[36] But the president's leading Hispanic
candidate, Judge Emilio Garza, was considered too inexperienced.
At the same time, the administration was also concerned about securing the backing of southern Democrats in the Senate, most of
whom had voted against Robert Bork. Although traditionally conservative, these senators found that their black constituents were especially skeptical of the Bork nomination. By opting for Clarence
Thomas, Bush decided to use Marshall's vacancy to extend his appeal among blacks, especially those in the South.[37]

[35]Yalof, *Pursuit of Justices*, pp.156–57.
[36]Phelps and Winternitz, *Capitol Games*, p. 5.
[37]Mark Silverstein, *Judicious Choices: The New Politics of Supreme Court Confirmations*
(New York: W.W. Norton, 1994), p. 157.

For Clarence Thomas, then, race was clearly a major determinant of his nomination. Other candidates surely met the president's criteria for the Court, but since he was replacing the first and only black justice, it became especially important for Bush to be attentive to minority representation. In other nominations, obviously, such factors might be less central to the president's decision making. Whatever their relevance, these personal characteristics such as race, religion, and gender have played at least some part in virtually every nomination over the last twenty years.

WHO IS CONFIRMED?

The Senate's constitutional mandate in the process of judicial selection is to provide "advice and consent" on presidential nominees to the Court. As a practical matter, this means that the Senate's Judiciary Committee first holds hearings on a candidate; this committee assumes the responsibility of gathering information on a nominee's suitability for the Supreme Court and, in turn, making a recommendation to the full Senate. Typically that recommendation is that the Senate confirm the nominee, but it is by no means assured. After concluding its hearings on Robert Bork, the committee actually recommended against confirmation, and the committee sent Clarence Thomas's nomination to the Senate floor with no recommendation. Whatever the committee's judgment, the Senate then debates the nomination and decides, by simple majority vote, whether to confirm the nominee. Once the nomination is in the hands of the full Senate, what kinds of influences determine how members cast their votes?

Ideology

As a rule, members of Congress make decisions based upon their own political convictions, and voting on Supreme Court nominees is certainly no exception.[38] Senators, like most people in government,

---

[38]See, respectively, Keith T. Poole and Howard Rosenthal, *Congress: A Political-Economic History of Roll Call Voting* (New York: Oxford University Press, 1996); Charles M. Cameron, Albert D. Cover, and Jeffrey A. Segal, "Senate Voting on Supreme Court Nominees: A Neoinstitutional Model," *American Political Science Review* 84:525–34 (1990).

would like to see their preferences reflected in public policy. It makes sense, therefore, that they would vote to confirm those nominees who they believe have similar goals. Since Bork and Thomas were widely regarded as ideologically conservative, then they should have earned both the support of their fellow conservatives and the opposition of liberals.

A simple way to illustrate this is to compare the differences in voting along political party lines. Bork, for instance, won the votes of 87 percent of Senate Republicans, while only 4 percent of Democrats supported confirmation. The situation was much the same for Thomas. Virtually every Republican—some 95 percent—voted in favor of Thomas, while better than 80 percent of Democratic senators voted against him. Such clear partisan differences suggest that ideology is a dominant consideration.

Perhaps a better way to illustrate the relevance of political ideology is to rank the members of the Senate along an ideological continuum. Based upon certain roll call votes, different interest groups rate senators along a continuous scale from most liberal to most conservative, and political scientists often use these ratings to gauge a senator's political ideology.[39] Using these scores, the data in Figure 2.1 divide the members of the Senate into groups of ten, showing how the members of each group voted on each nomination. Judging by these data, it seems fairly clear that the political preferences of the Senate had a major impact on Thomas's success and Bork's failure. In Bork's case, none of the liberals voted in his favor, while by contrast he was strongly backed by the most conservative members of the Senate. Critical to the outcome, however, was his inability to convince a sufficient number of moderates to support him. In the case of Clarence Thomas, not only did the nominee have the overwhelming support of those on the far right, he also gained enough votes within

---

[39]Here, I use scores generated by Americans for Democratic Action (ADA), probably the most common set of ratings upon which scholars rely. For each nomination, I have used the average of the two annual scores (after standardizing them) for the congressional sessions in which the nominations took place, the 100th and 102d. Where, as in a few cases, only one year was available, I used the ADA score from the available year. Where no score was recorded for a particular congressional session, I used the score from the most proximate year. My data are taken from Michael Barone and Grant Ujifusa, *The Almanac of American Politics*, various editions (Washington: National Journal); and the ADA web site, http://adaction.org.

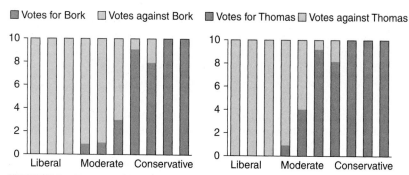

FIGURE 2.1 Impact of Senator Ideology on Confirmation Votes for Bork and Thomas

the Senate's ideological center to secure confirmation, if only by a narrow margin.

Professional Qualifications

Part of the rationale for requiring Supreme Court justices to pass first through the Senate is that it provides a check on the executive. By vesting the power to confirm in the legislative branch, the framers created an incentive for presidents to nominate those who are best suited to serve. As Alexander Hamilton, one of the Constitution's principal architects, explained, Senate confirmation "would be an excellent check upon a spirit of favoritism in the President, and would tend greatly to prevent the appointment of unfit characters . . . ."[40] Certainly, presidents search for candidates who have the necessary professional credentials. Merit is only one of several likely considerations, however, so inevitably there are trade-offs between legal competence and other competing factors.

Consistent with constitutional design, members of the Senate give a good deal of weight to a nominee's qualifications. Presidents from both parties who select capable candidates can typically expect to see their candidates confirmed. Among Republican appointees,

[40]Alexander Hamilton, "Federalist No.76," in *The Federalist Papers*, Alexander Hamilton, James Madison, and John Jay (New York: New American Library, 1788 [1961]), p. 457.

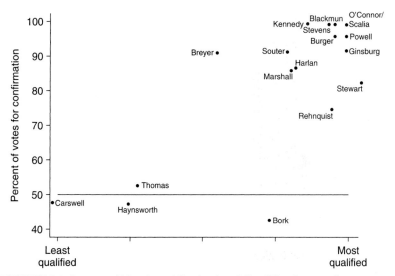

FIGURE 2.2 Impact of Nominees' Professional Qualifications on Support in the Senate

Antonin Scalia's "impeccable professional and personal attributes" surely contributed to his support in the Senate, just as for Democratic nominees, Ruth Bader Ginsburg's "competence, intelligence, and professional demeanor" helped to ensure a favorable reception.[41] When the Senate has reason to question the professional suitability of potential justices, their names are likely to be withdrawn before a vote can take place; in the ill-fated case of Douglas Ginsburg, for instance, the nominee bowed out amid revelations of his prior drug use. Those who have persevered in spite of dubious qualifications have suffered defeat. Clement F. Haynsworth and G. Harold Carswell, both Nixon nominees, were defeated in the Senate because of doubts about their lack of professional temperament.[42]

The importance that the Senate attaches to the credentials of potential justices is illustrated in Figure 2.2 Using a rating of the qualifications of nominees for the Court, this graph shows that the percentage of the vote that a nominee receives varies directly with

[41] Abraham, *Justices and Presidents*, p. 353; Silverstein, *Judicious Choices*, p.169.
[42] Abraham, *Justices and Presidents*, pp.13–23.

that candidate's competence.[43] As professional standards increase, so too do the number of senators voting to confirm. More often than not, presidents nominate highly qualified candidates, and those justices command anywhere from 90 to 100 percent of the vote, while the least qualified nominees have been defeated.

What impact did such professional standards have on the Bork and Thomas nominations? Leaving aside the allegations of sexual harassment made against him, Clarence Thomas was generally regarded as possessing a rather thin resume for a justice on the U.S. Supreme Court. His judicial experience amounted to no more than fifteen months on the federal bench, during which time he had written only eighteen opinions. At 43, he was also quite young to be serving on the high court. In light of these factors—and the perception that President Bush had chosen Thomas largely for ideological and symbolic reasons—many questioned whether Thomas had a record that merited confirmation as a justice.[44] Clearly, these qualifications did not help his chances; he was confirmed only by the narrow margin of 52–48.

In marked contrast, Robert Bork was at least as qualified as many other successful nominees; Justices John Harlan, Thurgood Marshall, William Rehnquist, and David Souter all brought fairly comparable levels of professional experiences to the Court. In Bork's case, his reputation as a brilliant legal scholar and his distinguished public service, both as solicitor general and as a federal judge, left little doubt that he had the necessary qualifications. As an obvious exception, Bork was rejected for reasons that must have had little to do with his objective merit. What might some of those reasons have been?

Policy Change on the Court

One of the factors that distinguished the Bork nomination was the justice whom he was named to replace. By the time he retired,

---

[43]The ratings are based upon newspaper evaluations of the candidates at the time of their nominations. These data, as well as the Senate votes, are taken from Epstein et al., *Supreme Court Compendium*, Tables 4–13 and 4–14.
[44]O'Brien, *Storm Center*, pp.89–90; John E. Yang and Sharon LaFraniere, "Bush Picks Thomas for Supreme Court; Appeals Court Judge Served as EEOC Chairman in Reagan Administration," *Washington Post*, July 2, 1991, p.A1.

Lewis Powell had come to occupy a precarious middle ground. When Powell retired at the end of the 1986 term, there was a clear ideological division on the Supreme Court, with liberals like Brennan and Marshall on one side and conservatives like Rehnquist and Scalia on the other. "A flexible conservative, Powell was the swing vote on a polarized bench. He provided the decisive fifth vote for the liberal wing on such issues as abortion, separation of church and state, and affirmative action. He was with the conservatives on the death penalty, protecting business interests, and aiding the prosecution in criminal cases."[45] Libertarian groups were especially concerned about the future direction of the Court's policies. According to the American Civil Liberties Union, Powell had been the crucial member of the majority in twenty notable civil liberties decisions during his final term, each one decided by a bare 5–4 vote.[46]

President Reagan was naturally anxious to move the Court in a more solidly conservative direction, and the replacement of Powell—upon whom the outcomes of cases often hinged—with Bork would have no doubt swung the Court in a more conservative direction. In this sense, the selection of Bork was a kind of critical nomination, one that "if successful . . . . would result in important shifts in partisan coalitions on the Court." These nominations are especially contentious, and historically they have been at least ten times more likely to fail than other nominations.[47]

At the time he was chosen, Robert Bork was generally seen as a jurist of highly conservative orientation. During his confirmation hearings, he spoke candidly and extensively about his views. Many in the Senate were worried that his ideological influence would produce a large-scale rewriting of constitutional law, and the hearings did little to dispel those concerns. Bork had been highly critical of Supreme Court decisions in such areas as civil rights, privacy, and freedom of expression. Rightly or wrongly, many feared that some of the established liberal precedents of the Warren and Burger Courts would be in jeopardy with Bork on the Court. Seen in this way, it is not hard to understand why the Senate rejected him. As a nomination that would have had the likely effect of significantly altering the

[45]Bronner, *Battle for Justice*, p.17.
[46]*Washington Post*, June 27, 1987, p. A1.
[47]P. S. Ruckman, Jr., "The Supreme Court, Critical Nominations, and the Senate Confirmation Process," *Journal of Politics* 55:793–805 (1993).

ideological balance on the Court, Bork's defeat in the Senate is consistent with a more general reluctance to confirm such nominees.

The rejection of Bork did little to forestall the Supreme Court's movement to the right, however. By the time Clarence Thomas was nominated in 1991, Byron White was the only remaining justice who was appointed by a Democratic president. Hence, the appointment of another conservative—even one that replaced one of the Court's historically most liberal members—would have far less impact in charting the Court's course of conservatism.

Senate Constituents

Another likely suspect is voter preferences. Motivated by a desire to secure reelection, members of Congress are remarkably attentive to the desires of their constituents.[48] Calculating how best to satisfy those respective constituencies, senators often follow the prevailing politics within their states when voting on Supreme Court nominees.[49] Certainly, satisfying constituents was foremost among the minds of many senators in the battles over Bork and Thomas.

An effective way to see how senators reflect the views of voters is to examine the ideology of their state electorates to see whether confirmation votes correspond to local preferences. If senators follow local mood, then the more conservative the voters in a state, the more likely its senators should be to vote for both Bork and Thomas. Since the candidates are the same in every state, the two-party vote in presidential elections provides a useful means of calculating liberalism across states.[50] Using that standard, Table 2.4 divides the states into groups of roughly equal size. As expected, it reveals that the more conservative a state's electorate, the more likely its senators were to support these two Republican nominees.

[48]See, e.g., Morris Fiorina, *Congress: Keystone of the Washington Establishment*, 2nd ed. (New Haven: Yale University Press, 1989); David R. Mayhew, *Congress: The Electoral Connection* (New Haven: Yale University Press, 1974).

[49]Jeffrey A. Segal, Charles M. Cameron, and Albert Cover, "A Spatial Model of Roll Call Voting: Senators, Constituents, and Interest Groups in Supreme Court Confirmations," *American Journal of Political Science* 36:96–121 (1992).

[50]State preferences, in this case, are based upon the Democratic percentage of the two-party vote in the election preceding each confirmation—1984 for Bork and 1988 for Thomas—as listed in Barone and Ujifusa, *The Almanac of American Politics*, 1990 and 1991 editions.

TABLE 2.4 Senate Voting on Bork and Thomas by State Preferences

State Preferences	Percentage of Senators Supporting Bork	Percentage of Senators Supporting Thomas
Liberal	28	39
Moderate	31	38
Conservative	69	83

In each case, senators from liberal and moderate states voted for confirmation in roughly equal proportions; Bork secured about 30 percent of their votes, while Thomas won approximately 40 percent. Senators representing the nation's more conservative voters backed Bork and Thomas by margins of about 70 and 80 percent, respectively. It is worth noting that, across all groups, roughly 10 percent fewer senators voted for Bork, which obviously helps to explain his defeat.

Senators were particularly sensitive to the ramifications that their votes would have for black voters within their states. Among other things, Bork had been critical of the Supreme Court's decisions that had struck down segregated schools, racial discrimination by homeowners, and voter qualifications that had been used to limit minority access to the voting booth. Fueled to action by such opinions, civil rights groups rallied in opposition, generating a grassroots movement that relied heavily upon African Americans in the South.[51] With their electoral fortunes tied to large numbers of black voters, the ordinarily conservative southern Democrats suddenly faced enormous organized pressure to vote against the nomination. As one of their ranks, Senator J. Bennett Johnston of Louisiana, explained to Alabama's Richard Shelby, "You're not going to vote for Bork. You know why? Because you're not going to turn your back on ninety-one percent of the black voters in Alabama who got you here."[52] In the end, Johnston's forecast proved accurate; some 14 of 16 southern Democrats voted against Robert Bork. Most of the Senate's 46 Republicans voted to confirm, but without the support of this group of Democrats, Bork's nomination was doomed.

Whereas black voters cost support for Robert Bork, they generated it for Clarence Thomas. After Thomas was nominated, civil

---

[51]Mark Gitenstein, *Matters of Principle: An Insider's Account of America's Rejection of Robert Bork's Nomination to the Supreme Court* (New York: Simon & Schuster, 1992).
[52]Bronner, *Battle for Justice*, p. 286.

rights leaders reacted cautiously, hinting that the conservative nominee's race would not, by itself, guarantee minority support.[53]
Among the black population at large, however, Thomas was received very favorably, and, just as in the case of Bork, members of
the Senate were well aware of the need to reflect the views of their
constituents. In light of Thomas's opposition to government programs to aid minorities, many Democrats were naturally disposed to
vote against him. At the same time, though, Democrats could not afford to disregard the preferences of their African–American voters,
and this was especially true for those Democrats who were going to
be facing reelection the following year. This, it turned out, is precisely what happened.[54]

With few blacks in their states and without fear of an upcoming
election, some Democratic senators would safely follow their ideology and oppose Thomas; in fact, among this group of senators, none
voted for confirmation. But other Democrats who depended upon
African–American voters felt a greater obligation to come out in favor of Thomas. Even among those without the worry of an impend-
ing reelection battle, for example, 18 percent voted to confirm Judge
Thomas. Most critically, the Democrats who knew that they would
soon have to ask large numbers of blacks for their votes found it
much more difficult to ignore the preferences of these constituents.
About 30 percent of these Democrats—senators who might otherwise have opposed the nomination—felt compelled to cast votes in
Thomas's favor. Combined with the virtually unanimous support of
Republicans, these Democrats made a crucial difference in this confirmation.

Interest Groups

Since members of the Senate are concerned with reelection, they
need to know what impact their decisions will have on their con-

[53]Maureen Dowd, "The Supreme Court; Conservative Black Judge, Clarence Thomas,
is Named to Marshall's Court Seat," *New York Times*, July 2, 1991, p.1.
[54]L. Marvin Overby, Beth M. Henschen, Julie Strauss, and Michael H. Walsh, "Courting Constituents? An Analysis of the Senate Vote on Justice Clarence Thomas," *American Political Science Review* 86:997–1003 (1992). Following their lead, I calculate (and
report below) support for Thomas among different Democratic senators, including
those who were facing reelection and those whose constituencies had a measurable
number of African Americans (i.e., at least 1 percent of a state's population).

stituencies. For that reason, senators often turn to interest groups to supply them with advance intelligence about how different segments of society will be affected by policy outcomes. When casting confirmation votes and calculating their consequences for reelection, senators can use the participation of interest groups as a barometer of likely voter sentiments.[55]

For their part, organized interests have incentives to provide this information to senators. Before the 1950s, groups of one kind or another were certainly involved in this process, but the activism of the Warren Court brought the political power of the judiciary into much sharper focus. As the Court began to exert greater influence over public policy, interest groups became much more anxious to express their views on nominees.[56] So, groups that are likely to be affected by the Court's decisions can usually be counted on to lobby in the Senate.

Frequently, interest group pressure takes the form of testifying at the nominee's hearings in the Senate Judiciary Committee. Over the last decade, some nominees have seen as many as thirty different organizations supporting and opposing confirmation. Some of those witnesses from the Bork and Thomas hearings are presented in Table 2.5. As one might expect, conservative interests, such as law enforcement groups, endorsed the nominees, while liberal groups, including various civil rights organizations, reacted against both candidates. A number of noteworthy legal scholars also weighed in. In Thomas's case, abortion rights groups and organized labor testified against his confirmation as well.

Looking only at congressional witnesses, however, actually understates the role that interest groups play in the politics of Supreme Court confirmations. Groups lobby senators in many ways. In Robert Bork's case, for example, "[e]very part of the liberal interest group community participated in some manner: environmentalists, consumers, civil rights activists, nonprofit organizations, mental health associations, the handicapped, women, gays and lesbians, and unions. This coalition used a wide variety of tactics, including advertising and grass-roots events, informed by focus groups, and

---

[55]Gregory A. Caldeira and John R. Wright, "Lobbying for Justice: The Rise of Organized Conflict in the Politics of Federal Judgeships," in *Contemplating Courts*, ed. Lee Epstein (Washington: Congressional Quarterly, Inc., 1995).
[56]Silverstein, *Judicious Choices*, pp. 62–71.

TABLE 2.5 Selected Witnesses Testifying at Confirmation Hearings for Bork and Thomas

Supporting Bork	Supporting Thomas
Academics Law professors from Columbia, Duquesne, Emory, Stanford, Villanova, and Yale Universities and Universities of Arizona, Chicago, Michigan, Pennsylvania, Virginia	*Academics* Law professors from Capital, George Mason, Seton Hall, and Yale Universities
Government officials Present and former public officials, including President Gerald R. Ford, Chief Justice Warren E. Burger, U.S. attorneys general, members of the U.S. House and Senate	*College administrators* Presidents of Elizabeth City State University, Holy Cross College, Lincoln University, Prairie View A&M University, Shaw University
Law enforcement organizations Fraternal Order of Police, National District Attorneys Association, National Law Enforcement Council, National Sheriffs' Association, National Troopers Coalition	*Government officials* Present and former officials, including member of the U.S. Senate, U.S. attorney general, staff of Equal Employment Opportunity Commission
Religious organizations Union of Orthodox Rabbis of the U.S. and Canada	*Law enforcement organizations* National Sheriffs' Association, National Law Enforcement Council, National Troopers Coalition, International Association of Chiefs of Police, Citizens for Law and Order

continued

polling." Conservative groups were more reluctant to enter the fray, but a number of business interests actively advocated confirmation. By some estimates, as many as three hundred organizations lobbied against confirmation, while roughly one hundred groups supported the campaign for Bork.[57] A whole range of groups felt that the future direction of judicial policy hinged on the outcome of the vote, and there was an unprecedented outpouring of activity.

Although the effort was not quite as extensive, organized interests also mobilized during the confirmation proceedings for Clarence Thomas. Even before the allegations of sexual harassment prompted the hearings to be reopened, a large number of groups had been involved. Having seen the apparent effectiveness of the anti-Bork campaign, conservative organizations—the Christian Coalition, the Coalition for Traditional Values, Concerned Women

[57]Caldeira and Wright, "Lobbying for Justice," p. 58.

TABLE 2.5 Selected Witnesses Testifying at Confirmation Hearings for Bork and Thomas (*Continued*)

Opposing Bork	Opposing Thomas
Academics Law professors from Duke, Georgetown, Harvard, New York, Northwestern, Stanford, and Yale Universities	*Abortion rights groups* National Abortion Rights Action League, Planned Parenthood Federation
Arts community PEN American Center	*Academics* Law professors from Georgetown, Harvard, New York, Stanford, and Yale Universities
Civil rights organizations Congressional Black Caucus, Mexican American Legal Defense and Educational Fund, NAACP Legal Defense and Education Fund, National Black Leadership Roundtable	*Civil rights groups* Congressional Black Caucus, Lawyers' Committee for Civil Rights Under Law, NAACP Legal Defense and Educational Fund, Leadership Conference on Civil Rights
Government officials Present and former public officials, including U.S. attorneys general, member of U.S. House, state attorneys general	*Government officials* Present and former officials, including members of U.S. House
Law enforcement organizations National Black Police Association, International Union of Police Associations	*Labor groups* AFL-CIO
Lawyers' organizations Association of the Bar of the City of New York	*Legal associations* Society of American Law Teachers, National Bar Association, National Conference of Black Lawyers
	Women's groups National Women's Political Caucus, National Organization for Women, Fund for the Feminist Majority, National Women's Law Center

for America, and the Family Research Council, among others—undertook a coordinated lobbying effort on behalf of Thomas. In the opposing camp, liberal groups launched their own appeals. The National Abortion Rights Action League, for example, directed its membership to contact their senators and express opposition to Thomas. In addition, this group devoted over $100,000 to a television campaign.[58]

---

[58]Phelps and Winternitz, *Capitol Games*, pp. 126–47.

Because these interest groups give senators important information about how different constituencies view a nominee, group participation often affects their decision making. Those that lobby in
favor of a nominee seem not to have a major impact on the members
of the Senate, but those in opposition certainly do. The sheer number
of interest groups that oppose a nominee indicates the likely political
fallout that would follow a vote to confirm. So, the larger the number
of interests that oppose a nominee, the more likely it is that a senator
will vote against confirmation.[59] While interest groups no doubt affected how senators viewed both nominees, in Bork's case in particular, it appears that the massive coalition of interests that mobilized
against him helped to derail his nomination.[60]

Presidential Term

Timing also helps to explain Senate voting on the Bork and Thomas
nominations. By the time he nominated Bork, Ronald Reagan was
well into his second term of office. Faced with any "lame duck" president, Congress has fewer incentives to come to terms with the
agenda of the executive branch. Having recently recaptured the Senate and knowing that Reagan would be in office for only another
twelve months, Democrats were reluctant to give him much ground.
When presidents are in such weak positions, their ability to muster
the political resources needed to secure confirmation are diminished.
Under these circumstances, nominees to the Court naturally stand to
lose votes.[61] Had Powell resigned earlier in the Reagan presidency,
the odds of Bork securing confirmation might have been much
better.

Thomas, by contrast, was nominated by a first-term president.
True, the Senate was still in the hands of the Democratic Party in
1991, but the Bush White House was already engineering a reelection campaign.[62] Consequently, senators who were otherwise inclined to oppose Judge Thomas had to make their decisions fully

[59]Segal, Cameron, and Cover, "A Spatial Model of Roll Call Voting."
[60]Norman Vieira and Leonard Gross, *Supreme Court Appointments: Judge Bork and the
Politicization of Senate Confirmations* (Carbondale, IL: Southern Illinois University
Press, 1998).
[61]Segal, Cameron, and Cover, "A Spatial Model of Roll Call Voting," p.111.
[62]John E. Yang and Ann Devroy, "Groundwork for Bush Campaign May Get Under-
way Next Month, Advisers Say," *Washington Post*, August 4, 1991, p. A11.

aware that a vote against the president might not be forgotten in the next four years. For members of Congress who often depend upon a president's good will for their own successes the possibility of Bush winning reelection surely made it more difficult to vote no. Although this by no means guaranteed Thomas's confirmation, it certainly created a strong incentive for members of the Senate to vote in his favor.

Public Opinion

Presidents are highly dependent upon public support for their policy successes. Presidents with strong public approval wield considerable political capital. As a result, they are much more likely to obtain legislative victories than are presidents whose popularity has waned.[63] Candidates for the Court who have the good fortune of being nominated by popular presidents, therefore, enjoy a considerable advantage in the Senate.[64] Having been nominated by presidents with very different levels of popular approval, Robert Bork and Clarence Thomas illustrate how critical public opinion can be.

During the Reagan administration, several Americans had been taken hostage in Lebanon, and national security officials were exploring possible solutions, including enlisting the aid of Iranian officials to broker their release. Meanwhile, in another part of the world, a group of rebels known as the Contras were trying to overthrow the socialist government in Nicaragua, and the White House, worried about the potential spread of communism, was anxious to aid their efforts. To achieve both ends simultaneously, administration officials developed a covert plan: to convince Iran to intervene on behalf of the hostages, military arms were sold to its government, and in turn the profits from that arms sale were used to provide support for the Nicaraguan Contras.[65] Unfortunately for the president, both actions were widely seen as contrary to U.S. foreign policy, and after the clandestine operation was revealed, President Reagan's approval rating took a precipitous plunge, dropping from more than 65 percent to less than 50 percent in the space of one month. Amid media

---

[63]Samuel Kernell, *Going Public: New Strategies of Presidential Leadership* (Washington: Congressional Quarterly Press, 1986).

[64]Segal, Cameron, and Cover, "A Spatial Model of Roll Call Voting."

[65]James P. Pfiffner, *The Modern Presidency* (New York: St. Martin's Press, 1994), pp. 214–19.

criticism and congressional investigations, Reagan's approval rating languished throughout 1987.[66]

As the data in Figure 2.3 show, by the time the Senate voted on Robert Bork's nomination, the Reagan administration was still reeling from the Iran-Contra affair. Having had his record criticized so severely in the Senate Judiciary Committee, Bork was anxious for the White House to throw its resources into a campaign on his behalf. Getting the nominee confirmed, however, had become much less of a priority. For White House Chief of Staff Howard Baker, the principal aim of the Reagan administration was to "survive the Iran-Contra hearings without impeachment proceedings."[67] Seen in this way, it is not hard to understand why it was relatively easy for an opponent of Bork's to vote against the nominee; because of flagging public approval, the president was in a very weak political position.

Clarence Thomas was nominated under very different circumstances. In the summer of 1990, Iraqi forces invaded Kuwait. Citing the importance of protecting the sovereignty of Arab nations, as well as the need to safeguard the United States' economic interests that were tied to the region's oil supplies, President Bush deployed thousands of American troops to the Persian Gulf. After weeks of economic sanctions, the president unleashed a military offensive against Iraq early in 1991. Congress rallied in support of the war, and Bush's popularity soared. By the end of January, nearly 80 percent of the public approved of the way he was handling his job.[68] The war was brought to a successful conclusion by early April, less than two months before Thurgood Marshall would announce his retirement.

As an opponent of affirmative action, President Bush provoked some skepticism for what seemed to be a desire to maintain minority representation on the Court. But his public support, as Figure 2.3 shows, was still enhanced from the Persian Gulf War, and this helped to quiet potential naysayers in the Senate. "In Congress," one observer noted, "there was a widespread feeling that . . . . most senators would find it hard to vote against a black nominee backed by a

---

[66]James W. Caesar, "The Reagan Presidency and American Public Opinion," in *The Reagan Legacy: Promise and Performance*, Charles O. Jones, ed. (Chatham, NJ: Chatham House Publishers, 1998), p. 201.

[67]Gitenstein, *Matters of Principle*, p.101; see also Bronner, *Battle for Justice*.

[68]Richard Morin, "War Boosts President's Popularity; Poll Finds Public Troubled by Bush's Handling of Economy at Home," *Washington Post*, January 29, 1991, p. A1.

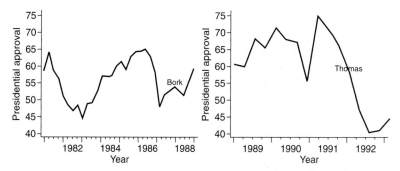

FIGURE 2.3 Presidential Approval at the Bork and Thomas Confirmation Votes

Source: Various survey items, Roper Center for Public Opinion Research.

popular President."[69] Following the nomination, Bush's popularity continued a decline that had begun several weeks earlier; nevertheless, when the Senate voted on Clarence Thomas in October, he still had an impressive approval rating of 60 percent, which surely helped to bolster his nominee.

CONCLUSION

The politics of appointments to the Supreme Court demonstrate that both presidents and members of the Senate are responsive to a variety of sometimes competing concerns. Presidents want to nominate people who are ideologically compatible and professionally capable, while senators want justices who will both share their policy views and satisfy their constituents.

In many ways, Robert Bork and Clarence Thomas reflected these tendencies. Both were well known for their skepticism of using government in general and courts in particular to generate social and economic change. Since Presidents Reagan and Bush wanted to elevate conservatives to the high court, their nominations made a good deal of sense. In Bush's case, having to replace the Court's only black would naturally make race an additional consideration.

In other respects, these two are seeming anomalies. Bork, an eminent judge and legal scholar, was denied a seat on the Court, while

[69]Dowd, "The Supreme Court; Conservative Black Judge," p. 1.

the considerably less qualified Thomas was successfully promoted. Yet with hindsight, it is not difficult to explain why Bork was defeated and Thomas was confirmed. Nominated by a lame-duck president suffering at a low-water mark in prestige, Bork had strongly conservative views that alienated key constituencies within the electorate and guaranteed the backing of only those senators on the far right. Since he was named to replace the more moderate Lewis Powell, he also would have altered the ideological balance of the bench; this too undercut his already fragile support. Thomas, by contrast, was nominated close to the height of a first-term president's popularity, and while concerns were raised about both his qualifications and his ideology, senators saw him as somewhat less conservative than Bork and less likely to affect the Supreme Court's now squarely conservative doctrines. Not only that, as an African American, Thomas was widely supported by the black community, a fact that was not lost on Democratic senators soon up for reelection.

Thus, the constitutional requirement that the president nominate justices with the advice and consent of the Senate actually understates the richness and complexity of the process of judicial selection. As these two cases vividly illustrate, presidents do not single-mindedly select only those most qualified to serve, and even when nominees are quite qualified, there are no assurances that the Senate will vote to confirm. This should not be surprising, given the prominent place the Supreme Court now occupies in American national politics. Because the Court plays such a leading role as a policy maker, decisions about who gets to serve naturally captivate the interest of a wide range of forces in the political environment.

QUESTIONS FOR DISCUSSION

1. Would the nature of the selection process change if presidents and senators placed more emphasis on a candidate's professional qualifications? Do the nominations of Robert Bork and Clarence Thomas suggest an answer?
2. Race seems to have been at least one of the factors that motivated President Bush to select Clarence Thomas for the Supreme Court. Should presidents try to ensure that the Supreme Court represents different segment's of American society?

3. When presidents nominate candidates for the Supreme Court, how confident can they be about their nominees' prospects for success in the Senate? To what extent do forces beyond the president's control affect a nominee's fate?

4. If the justices make decisions based upon the law and its application to the circumstances of each case, then their ideological views should presumably be irrelevant. Why, then, would presidents and senators place such importance on ideology as a basis for selecting justices?

5. In deciding how to vote on nominees for the Court, should members of the Senate rely upon the opinions of their constituents, or should they rely strictly upon their own judgments?

6. The nominations of Robert Bork and Clarence Thomas demonstrate the considerable extent to which interest groups can have input into the process of selecting members of the Supreme Court. Is that process well served by their participation?

7. What kind of role should the Senate play in selecting members of the Supreme Court? Should senators defer to a president's nominees for the Court unless there are exceptionally good reasons to reject them, or should the Senate scrutinize the president's choices more closely?

SUGGESTED READING

Henry J. Abraham. 1999. *Justices, Presidents, and Senators: A History of the U.S. Supreme Court Appointments from Washington to Clinton.* Lanham, MD: Rowman & Littlefield Publishers, Inc.

Gregory A. Caldeira and John R. Wright. 1995. "Lobbying for Justice: The Rise of Organized Conflict in the Politics of Federal Judgeships." In *Contemplating Courts,* ed. Lee Epstein. Washington: Congressional Quarterly, Inc.

John Anthony Maltese. 1995. *The Selling of Supreme Court Nominees.* Baltimore: Johns Hopkins University Press.

L. Marvin Overby, Beth M. Henschen, Julie Strauss, and Michael H. Walsh. 1992. "Courting Constituents? An Analysis of the Senate Vote on Justice Clarence Thomas." *American Political Science Review* 86:997–1003.

Barbara A. Perry. 1991. *A "Representative" Supreme Court? The Impact of Race, Religion, and Gender on Appointments.* New York: Greenwood Press.

Jeffrey A. Segal, Charles M. Cameron, and Albert Cover. 1992. "A Spatial Model of Roll Call Voting: Senators, Constituents, and Interest Groups in Supreme Court Confirmations." *American Journal of Political Science* 36:96–121.

Mark Silverstein. 1994. *Judicious Choices: The New Politics of Supreme Court Confirmations.* New York: W.W. Norton.

David Alistair Yalof. 1999. *Pursuit of Justices: Presidential Politics and the Selection of Supreme Court Nominees.* Chicago: University of Chicago Press.

CHAPTER 3

Setting the Court's Agenda

South Dakota v. Dole

Every year, thousands of cases are brought to the Supreme Court. Ultimately, the justices decide to hear only a very small number, usually less than one hundred. Because the Court has almost complete discretion to set its agenda, its members can focus on those legal questions that most interest them. Faced with so many choices, though, how do the justices identify those cases? This chapter offers several explanations by tracking South Dakota's challenge to a federal law that withheld highway funds from states that had not raised their drinking ages to twenty-one. It illustrates both the legal and political considerations that the justices take into account in the process of selecting cases.

Automobile accidents are one of the leading causes of death in the United States. Second only to such health problems as heart disease and cancer, motor vehicle accidents kill thousands of Americans each year. In 1998 alone, more than 43,000 people lost their lives in car crashes. Of that group, approximately four out of every ten involved the use of alcohol. Drunk driving accounts for more automobile fatalities than any other factor. Obviously, this problem exacts a heavy toll on society. By some estimates, the costs of alcohol-related crashes—damage to property, medical

55

bills, lost economic productivity, and the like—are as high $45 billion annually.[1]

Although drunk driving occurs in all age groups it is particularly prevalent among the young. Car crashes kill more people under the age of thirty-five than anything else, and a great many of them are alcohol-related. Among drivers between the ages of twenty-one and twenty-four, for instance, about 30 percent who are involved in fatal crashes are legally intoxicated, the highest death rate across all age groups. The data are also grim for people under twenty-one. In sheer numbers, they do not comprise a major segment of the driving population; they constitute less than 7 percent of the people on the road. Yet they are responsible for a disproportionately large share— some 14 percent—of the fatal crashes that involve alcohol. The consequences are quite severe; more than $1 billion dollars in medical costs occur each year as a result of drunk drivers under the age of twenty-one.

One reason why younger Americans are especially prone to driving while intoxicated is that they consume a good deal of alcohol. College students, who comprise a substantial proportion of sixteen- to twenty-year-olds, illustrate rather vividly this age group's drinking habits. On average, each college student drinks thirty-four gallons of alcohol each year. Collectively, "students spend $5.5 billion on alcohol, more than they spend on soft drinks, tea, milk, juice, coffee, and books combined. On a typical campus, per capita student spending for alcohol—$446 per student—far exceeds the per capita operating budget of the college library.[2] Since young people drink so often, their chances of being involved in alcohol-related accidents naturally increase.

Not surprisingly, drunk driving among America's youth, like the problems of drunk driving more generally, is a major issue of public policy for governmental decision makers. Legislators have considered a variety of mechanisms to reduce the very substantial and tragic effects of drinking and driving. Programs of increased public

[1]These statistics and those that follow are drawn from the following sources: National Vital Statistics Reports, Centers for Disease Control and Prevention, Vol. 48, No. 11, July 24, 2000; *Traffic Safety Facts* 1998, National Highway Safety Administration (DOT HS 808 950); Mothers Against Drunk Driving website (www.madd.org).
[2]"Rethinking Rites of Passage: Substance Abuse on America's Campuses," The National Center on Addiction and Substance Abuse, Columbia University, June 1994.

awareness, tougher penalties, stricter enforcement, roadside check-points, drug counseling for offenders, and the like have all been used, in one way or another, to help curb the rate of driving under the influence of alcohol. Given that drunk driving incidents are so heavily concentrated among the young, however, one of the principal ways that states have traditionally sought to reduce the problem is by raising the drinking age. The logic of the policy is simple; if young people appear to be particularly reckless in their use of alcohol, then the state simply revokes their right to consume it until they reach a more responsible age.

Whatever one might think about the wisdom or desirability of raising the legal drinking age, one fact does seem fairly clear: It works. Over the last twenty-five years, as states have increased their drinking ages, there has been a regular decline in drunk-driving fatalities among younger drivers. Specifically, the National Highway Traffic Safety Administration "estimates that these laws have reduced traffic fatalities involving drivers 18 to 20 years old by 13 percent and have saved an estimated 18,220 lives since 1975. In 1998, an estimated 861 lives were saved by minimum drinking age laws."[3] As the drinking ages have gone up, highway deaths among younger Americans have gone down.

At the same time, though, traffic fatalities that are associated with drunk drivers have dropped consistently across all age groups. So, raising the minimum drinking age cannot be solely responsible for the decline. Still, over the last decade, the group that has shown the greatest reduction has been those directly affected by these laws, Americans between the ages of sixteen and twenty. Higher drinking age laws surely deserve some of the credit.

Not all policy makers have agreed about the wisdom of raising the minimum drinking age. Some legislators have feared that many young adults will drink, no matter what the legal age, and that higher drinking ages only force underage drinkers to seek out alcohol illegally. Rather than visiting local establishments to drink legally, many young people take to the roads in search of the bars and convenience stores that will satisfy their thirst. For that reason, many believe that a blanket prohibition is unwise.[4] Not only that,

[3] "Traffic Safety Facts 1998," National Highway Safety Administration (DOT HS 808 950), p. 4.
[4] *South Dakota v. Dole*, Brief for the Petitioner, January 2, 1987, p. 19.

some evidence suggests that laws aimed at reducing the problem of drunk driving among teenagers have only temporary success. Instead, government should focus greater attention on programs of education and public transportation, as well as higher taxes designed to price alcohol out of the youth market.[5] Consequently, rather than support a prohibition on the sale of all alcohol to young adults, some have advocated allowing them to consume only certain types of alcohol, such as beer and wine. While these policies do not eliminate drinking by young people, they do give state governments some ability to regulate it.[6]

These debates intensified in the early 1980s, as the number of drunk driving deaths began to reach record numbers. Groups such as Mothers Against Drunk Driving mobilized to elevate public awareness of the thousands of fatalities caused by young drinkers on the nation's highways, and federal officials joined state legislators in the effort to combat the grim statistics.[7]

In Washington, policy makers set about studying ways in which the national government might help reduce the number of automobile accidents caused by alcohol-impaired drivers. At the White House, President Reagan created the Presidential Commission on Drunk Driving, a group whose purpose was to investigate the factors that contribute to this problem and to propose solutions. Established in the spring of 1982, the commission drafted a report, issued the following year, in which it concluded that "public officials at all levels of government must take action to eliminate or reduce the public health hazard of driving under the influence and should be primarily responsible for assuring legal and judicial innovation and program implementation."[8]

After examining the data on drunk driving, the presidential commission offered a number of policy recommendations. Most notable among them was the idea that a drinking age of twenty-one be

[5]Ralph W. Hingson, Jonathan Howland, and Suzette Levenson, "Effects of Legislative Reform to Reduce Drunken Driving and Alcohol-related Traffic Fatalities" (U.S. Department of Health and Human Services, *Public Health Reports* 103:659–67 [1988]); H. Lawrence Ross, "Social Control Through Deterrence: Drinking-and-Driving Laws," *Annual Review of Sociology* 10:21–35 (1984).
[6]*South Dakota v. Dole*, Brief for the Petitioner, January 2, 1987, p. 47–49.
[7]Hingson, Howland, and Levenson, "Effects of Legislative Reform to Reduce Drunken Driving and Alcohol-related Traffic Fatalities."
[8]*South Dakota v. Dole*, Brief for the Respondent, March 13, 1987, p. 2.

uniformly imposed across all the states. At the time of the report, some nineteen states had set their drinking ages at twenty-one, and in those states, people who were underage could easily drive to a nearby state where the drinking age might be lower. Once intoxicated, many of them would then die behind the wheel, often killing their passengers or other motorists in the process.[9] Thus, the motive behind this proposal was to eliminate the incentive to drive to neighboring states to obtain alcohol legally; if the drinking age were the same in every state, young people could no longer be tempted onto the roads to seek liquor outside their home states.

Of course, the commission might have suggested a lower drinking age, but the disproportionately high rate of alcohol-related accidents among eighteen- to twenty-year-olds would certainly have made that less feasible. Lives could be saved by a nationwide drinking age, and even more could be saved if that age were twenty-one.

On Capitol Hill, Congress responded quickly to the findings of the president's commission. Stimulated by its stark report on the consequences of drunk driving by younger Americans, members of Congress undertook to examine the problem for themselves. Several committees investigated the issue, and the evidence they produced came to substantially the same conclusion as the commission. Arguing in favor of nationalizing the drinking age, Senator John Heinz of Pennsylvania suggested that "this issue is truly a national one demanding congressional action because we are faced . . . with situations where a State has a 21-year-old drinking limit, but an adjacent State does not. The result is that we end up with blood borders where young people drive over the State line to get alcohol."[10]

By the spring of 1984, Congress was prepared to take action. In late June, both the Senate and the House of Representatives passed a measure known as the Uniform Minimum Drinking Age Law, an act that was designed to achieve a national drinking age of twenty-one. Rather than requiring states to raise their drinking ages—or simply imposing a national law outright—Congress sought to use its power of the purse to achieve the same end.

Each year, Congress appropriates money to the states to help them serve a variety of policy goals, and one of the categories for

---

[9]Douglas B. Feaver, "Panel Urges 21 as Nationwide Drinking Age," *Washington Post*, December 14, 1983, p. A1.

[10] *South Dakota v. Dole*, Brief for the Respondent, March 13, 1987, p. 5.

which Congress earmarks those funds is the construction and main-tenance of highways. In the early 1980s, Congress was allocating up-wards of $12 billion in highway funds in its annual budget, and a given state might receive tens of millions of those dollars. Thus, large amounts of federal tax revenue were being channeled into the hands of state governments to pay for one of the key components of a state's infrastructure—the development of its roads. Given the im-portance of these federal dollars to the states, Congress decided that it would attach a condition to its spending to create an incentive for states to raise their drinking ages. Under the legislation, which amended the Surface Transportation Assistance Act of 1982, states were given a two-year grace period during which they could in-crease their drinking ages. If a state had not raised its drinking age to twenty-one by the fall of 1986, the secretary of transportation was authorized to withhold 5 percent of its allotment of highway dollars. Any remaining states with a lower drinking age would lose 10 per-cent of their monies during the following fiscal year.[11] The federal law, therefore, did not actually require the states to take any action. It did, however, encourage compliance by making the higher drink-ing age a condition for receiving a full share of annual highway funds.

Lawmakers on Capitol Hill were not alone in their concerns. In fact, Congress's efforts to stem the tide of drunk driving among the young reflected a more general mood in the country. At the state level, legislators had begun to reassess their policies, and a good many had already elected to raise their drinking ages; by this time, nearly half of the states had drinking ages of twenty-one. Public opinion, too, seemed to be squarely in favor of the national drinking age. Gauging popular sentiment, members of Congress sensed strong support for the highway bill among the voters, as well. So even those legislators who might have been opposed to the bill were reluctant to vote against it. As one Senate insider explained, "The 21-year-old minimum drinking age is now seen as good public pol-icy, one you can't lose on, and this is an election year."[12] Similarly, at

---

[11]Feaver, "Panel Urges 21 as Nationwide Drinking Age"; Margaret Shapiro, "House Sends Reagan Bill on Drinking," *Washington Post*, June 28, 1984, p. A1; *South Dakota v. Dole*, Brief for the Respondent, March 13, 1987, pp. 3–4.
[12]Douglas B. Feaver, "Reagan Now Wants 21 as Drinking Age," *Washington Post*, June 14, 1984, p. A1.

the White House, Secretary of Transportation Elizabeth H. Dole announced the Reagan administration's support for the plan. As she
argued, the lack of a uniform drinking age led directly to drunk-
driving accidents. "The resulting checkerboard of different state
minimum drinking ages actually creates the 'blood borders,' where
young people drive across state lines to drink."[13] By a number of important indicators, then, there was broad support for the legislation.
Citing the "great national movement" to nationalize the drinking
age, President Reagan signed the bill into law in mid-July.[14]

In that summer of 1984, however, not everyone was solidly behind the congressional initiative. At the state level, some policy makers balked at what they considered to be the federal government's
intrusion into their sphere of authority. Traditionally, the regulation
of morality—setting drinking ages, regulating tobacco use, restricting gambling, and the like—had been left to the states. Congress, of
course, had considerable powers of its own, including the power to
tax and spend, but that authority was still limited. The national government, they argued, could not use the power of the purse to coerce
the states into adopting policies, however well-intentioned its actions might be. Rather than bend to the will of the federal government, some states defied the Congress.

One such state was South Dakota.[15] Faced with the loss of highway funds, it nevertheless refused to raise its drinking age to
twenty-one. In many ways, its resistance was quite predictable. The
state is far removed from the high-powered politics of Washington,
D.C. Still home to a significant Native American population, the
state is largely an untamed wilderness. "The land is punctuated, not
by roads meeting every mile at precise angles, but by buttes, gullies
and grasslands sweeping to the horizon with no sign of human habi-
tation. . . ."[16] With so much open land, its population is predictably
small; only about 730,000 people live in the entire state, a number

---

[13]Douglas B. Feaver, "House Bill Ties Highway Aid, Drinking Age," *Washington Post*,
June 8, 1984, p. A1.
[14]Steven R. Weisman, "Reagan Signs Law Linking Federal Aid to Drinking Age," *The
New York Times*, July 18, 1984, p. 15.
[15]Unless otherwise noted, the circumstances surrounding the case of *South Dakota v.
Dole* (1987) are drawn from the U.S. Supreme Court's opinions, as well as the written
briefs filed at the case selection stage and at the merits.
[16]Michael Barone and Grant Ujifusa, *The Almanac of American Politics 1998* (Washington: National Journal, 1997), p. 1291.

roughly equal to the size of Syracuse, New York. Those residents, however, maintain a sense of rugged independence, and many would naturally bristle at the prospect of having Washington law-makers—who probably have little appreciation of their local culture and concerns—dictate the state's public policy. Reflecting this senti-ment, a member of the state attorney general's office complained, "'We know South Dakota better than the federal government. This is blackmail. To states like South Dakota, with a lot of highways, this [the withheld highway funds] is a lot of money."[17]

Actually, by the time the federal government became involved, South Dakota's drinking age was already twenty-one for a good many types of alcohol. At least since 1939, though, the state main-tained a policy of allowing certain people under the age of twenty-one to consume beer that had a relatively modest alcoholic content. Low-point beer—that is, beer, whose total weight was composed of less than 3.2 percent alcohol—could be purchased and consumed by those who were eighteen or older. Meanwhile, the state's legal age for the purchase of liquor and wine was established at twenty-one. Over the years, the state modified its policy toward low-point beer, raising the drinking age to nineteen and then later returning it to eighteen.

In July 1984, as Congress and the president were acting on fed-eral legislation to promote a higher drinking age, state legislators in South Dakota decided to raise the legal drinking age for low-point beer, returning it to age nineteen. Why didn't the state simply raise its drinking age to twenty-one for all alcoholic beverages? The ratio-nale, according to Roger A. Tellinghuisen, South Dakota's attorney general, was that, by allowing nineteen- and twenty-year-olds to drink a less potent alcoholic beverage legally, the state was discour-aging drinking and driving among its younger citizens. As he later explained, "It was reasonable, as shown by scientific studies, for the State Legislature to find that controlled drinking by nineteen and twenty year olds promotes temperance to a greater degree than pro-hibition. Prohibition does not reduce drinking by nineteen and twenty year olds. Rather, it forces them to drink in cars, or in remote areas to which it is necessary to drive."[18] Since South Dakota legisla-

---

[17]Nicholas C. McBride, "A Few States Hold Out on Drinking Age," *The Christian Sci-ence Monitor*, October 16, 1986, p. 3.

[18] *South Dakota v. Dole*, Brief for the Petitioner, January 2, 1987, p. 19.

tors believed that many people under twenty-one were bound to drink, no matter what the drinking age, it was preferable to have them drinking something less intoxicating.

In Washington, the secretary of transportation did not see the matter in quite the same way. During the spring and summer of 1986, Secretary Dole notified South Dakota, along with seven other states, that they were not in compliance with the Uniform Minimum Drinking Age Law and that consequently they were scheduled to have a combined total of nearly $70 million withheld from their upcoming allocation of highway funds. For the most part, then, the law had its intended effect: When Congress enacted the law, less than half of the states had drinking ages of twenty-one. It had been only two years since the measure went into effect, and nineteen states with lower drinking ages had quickly conformed to the law, rather than face the loss of federal support. Now, the grace period was nearly over, and this remaining handful of states—Colorado, Idaho, Louisiana, Montana, Ohio, South Dakota, Tennessee, and Wyoming—was about to be subjected to the budgetary penalty.[19]

By this time, however, South Dakota had long been at work to undo the federal government's policy. Back in 1984, just two months after President Reagan signed the minimum drinking age bill, the state had gone to court, seeking to have the law declared invalid. Arguing that the federal government did not have the authority to use its spending power to compel states to raise their drinking ages, the state had sued Secretary Dole, challenging her withholding of highway dollars.

To this point, its efforts had been unsuccessful. Lower federal courts had twice rejected the state's arguments and upheld the congressional spending plan. The state legislature in South Dakota still had not raised its drinking age for low-point beer, and as the federal law's deadline approached, the state made one final attempt to block the national government. In August 1986, it asked the U.S. Supreme Court to hear its case. Some three months later, the justices agreed to consider it.

That year, the Supreme Court had more than four thousand similar requests. For South Dakota, of course, the case represented the

---

[19]McBride, "A Few States Hold Out on Drinking Age"; Reginald Stuart, "7 More States Face Loss of Some Funds Over Drinking Age," *The New York Times*, July 16, 1986, p. A14.

last chance to vindicate its right of self-determination and to be free from unwarranted federal intrusion. For the justices, however, it was merely one of the thousands of cases that seek the Court's attention each year. With limited time and resources, the Court can afford to hear only a very small proportion; during its 1986 term, for example, the Supreme Court agreed to decide only about 150 of those cases— and *South Dakota v. Dole* was one of them. Faced with so many requests for review, how do the justices go about selecting such cases? What factors determine which cases get heard and which cases do not? What made the case of *South Dakota v. Dole* distinctive enough to merit resolution by the nation's highest tribunal?

THE ROAD TO THE SUPREME COURT

On September 21, 1984, the state of South Dakota filed its lawsuit in federal court against Elizabeth Dole, the U.S. Secretary of Transportation. Its primary assertion was that Congress simply had no power to dictate its drinking age. From the state's perspective, the Constitution clearly entrusted the states, not the federal government, with the responsibility of establishing these policies. Turning to the text of the Constitution, it found supporting language in both the Twenty-First and the Tenth Amendments.

In 1933, Prohibition was repealed by the Twenty-First Amendment. Eliminating the United States' total ban on alcoholic beverages, the amendment gave explicit legal authority for regulating alcohol to the states by providing that "[t]he transportation or importation into any state . . . for delivery or use therein of intoxicating liquors, in violation of the laws thereof, is hereby prohibited." By its terms, states were given the explicit power to regulate the terms and conditions regarding the sale of alcohol, not Congress.

The Tenth Amendment, by contrast, does not deal with regulating alcohol but with the more general balance of power between the national government and the states. It guarantees that "[t]he powers not delegated to the United States by the Constitution . . . are reserved to the states respectively. . . ." In other words, if the Constitution does not grant a particular power to the Congress, then that power is to be exercised by the states. Setting a national age for the consumption of alcohol is not among the powers given to Congress; it must, therefore, be a matter for states to decide.

On this basis, South Dakota argued that the Uniform Minimum Drinking Age Law, which authorized the withholding of highway funds, was unlawful. In its complaint, the state argued that "Congress is without jurisdiction to enact any law which affects the power of the State of South Dakota to allow or prohibit the sale of alcoholic beverages [and] that Congress' enactment of [the drinking age law] is beyond its power granted by the . . . Constitution, which power is reserved to the State of South Dakota and other states, and is therefore unconstitutional." Clearly, the Constitution entrusts the Congress with the power to tax and spend, but, in South Dakota's view, Congress could not use this power of the purse to interfere with the states' control over alcohol.

All of these issues—the meaning of the Twenty-First and Tenth Amendments and the extent of Congress's spending power—involved questions about the proper interpretation of federal law. For that reason, it was the federal courts that had the authority to consider South Dakota's claim against Elizabeth Dole. Suing her in her capacity as the U.S. Secretary of Transportation, the state filed its complaint in the U.S. District Court for South Dakota.

In this case, Judge Andrew W. Bogue heard South Dakota's claim against Secretary Dole. Bogue was one of several trial court judges for the South Dakota District. Some states, such as Texas and California, have as many as four district courts with dozens of judges; less populous states, like South Dakota, have only a single district court staffed by considerably fewer.

In May 1985, Bogue issued his decision, ruling that the state had no legitimate claim against the federal government. In his written opinion, he concluded that, since Congress had the power to spend to promote the nation's general welfare, it was free to attach conditions to that spending as a means of advancing that welfare. Stated differently, if Congress wanted to reduce drunk driving by making highway funds contingent upon a state's higher drinking age, it was free to do so. Furthermore, South Dakota was still perfectly free to keep its lower drinking age for low-point beer; all the federal law did was make it attractive for South Dakota to change that policy. Since South Dakota still had the legal right to set its drinking age, neither the Tenth nor the Twenty-First Amendment was offended by the law.

Having lost initially, South Dakota decided to appeal Judge Bogue's decision. As illustrated by Figure 3.1, its next step was to ask

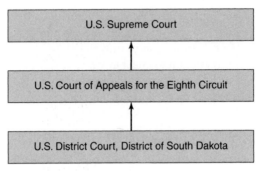

FIGURE 3.1 *South Dakota v. Dole*'s Route to the U.S. Supreme Court

a federal appellate court to review the decision of the district judge. Under the federal judicial system, the nation is divided geographically into eleven groups of states, known as circuits, and the appellate court for each circuit considers appeals from the district courts within its jurisdiction.[20] South Dakota and several other midwestern states comprise the Eighth Circuit, so it was to the U.S. Court of Appeals for that circuit to which the state brought its challenge.

Unlike trial courts, which consider evidence and testimony, appellate courts are concerned only with the correct application of the law. In reviewing a criminal conviction, for example, an appellate court does not determine whether the person is innocent or guilty. Rather, its responsibility is to determine whether the trial court responsible for that conviction applied the appropriate laws and procedures. Thus, in its appeal in *South Dakota v. Dole*, the state argued that Judge Bogue had misinterpreted the Constitution by upholding the congressional spending scheme. The legally correct understanding of the Tenth and Twenty-First Amendments, it maintained, barred Congress from interfering with a state's drinking age laws, a matter of purely local discretion.

[20]In addition, there is a U.S. Court of Appeals for the District of Columbia Circuit, which hears a number of important cases, including cases involving federal agencies. There is also a U.S. Court of Appeals for the Federal Circuit, a specialized appellate court in Washington that resolves, among other things, issues of international trade, veterans' affairs, and patents. For a more extensive treatment of the importance of federal courts of appeals, see Stephen L. Wasby, *The Supreme Court in the Federal Judicial System*, 4th ed. (Chicago: Nelson-Hall Publishers, 1993).

A panel of three judges from the Eighth Circuit considered these arguments, but concluded that the trial court had indeed made the correct decision. In May 1986, the appeals court concluded that "South Dakota has failed to demonstrate how [the federal law] forces the state to restructure its governmental system . . . or impairs the state's . . . ability to function effectively in the federal system. Further, South Dakota can hardly claim either a vested right in the federal funds being offered or the right to set the conditions on which the money will be provided. Rather . . . South Dakota is entirely free to reject Congress's offer of federal highway funds and exercise in any way it chooses its authority to establish a minimum drinking age."[21] Supporting Judge Bogue's decision, the court of appeals noted that Congress was not required to offer any highway money to the states. Since Congress was only encouraging states to raise their drinking ages, South Dakota was still free to set its own policies.

South Dakota's claims had now twice been rebuffed in the federal courts. At this point, as Figure 3.1 illustrates, only the U.S. Supreme Court could rule otherwise. Still hoping for final vindication, South Dakota asked the justices to consider its challenge to the Uniform Minimum Drinking Age Law.

THE PROCESS OF SELECTING CASES

On August 18, 1986, South Dakota officially filed papers with the Supreme Court, requesting a hearing from the justices. For its part, the U.S. government, acting on behalf of Secretary Dole, was likewise given the opportunity to submit a written statement, outlining the reasons why a hearing in the Court should be denied. In early November, the Court received the federal government's submission and began its process of internal review, a series of steps in which the justices decide what to decide. By December, that process was completed, and the case of *South Dakota v. Elizabeth H. Dole, Secretary, United States Department of Transportation* was slated for oral argument in April of the following year. What were the stages in that process?[22]

---

[21] *South Dakota v. Dole*, Petition for Certiorari, August 18, 1986, pp. A22–23.
[22] My discussion of the process of case selection is drawn from H. W. Perry, Jr., *Deciding to Decide: Agenda Setting in the United States Supreme Court* (Cambridge: Harvard University Press, 1991).

Petition for Review

The Supreme Court is not required to hear the vast majority of cases that are brought to it each year. With an almost completely discretionary agenda, the justices have near total control to decide which cases they will review and which cases they will not. As a result, litigants like South Dakota who hope to have their day before the justices must first overcome a substantial hurdle: They must convince the members of the Court that, out of literally thousands of cases, theirs is among the very few that are worthy of the Court's attention. If the Court agrees to take a case and render a decision on the merits of the legal dispute, the justices will consider both written and oral arguments and issue a written opinion. If the Court refuses—as it almost always does—then the losing party must abide by the lower court's ruling.

For at least the past three decades, the justices have had to contend with roughly four thousand new filings each year.[23] Challenging the ruling of both federal and state courts,[24] these requests for review by the Supreme Court typically come in the form of a petition for a writ of certiorari.[25] (*Certiorari* is a Latin term, meaning "to be informed of.") South Dakota was challenging the decision of the judges from the Eighth Circuit, and its petition was simply a legal request

---

[23]See Lee Epstein, Jeffrey A. Segal, Harold J. Spaeth, and Thomas G. Walker, *The Supreme Court Compendium: Data, Decisions, and Development* (Washington: Congressional Quarterly, Inc., 1996), Table 2-2.

[24] *South Dakota v. Dole* came to the justices through the federal court system, but the justices may also hear cases brought from state courts, provided that those cases raise issues of federal law. For example, a criminal case that involved the violation of a state's drug laws could be considered by the Supreme Court if there were some question as to whether the state police, say, violated the accused's right to be free from unreasonable searches and seizures, a right guaranteed by the U.S. Constitution.

[25]Although much less common, cases can also come to the Court via its original and appeal jurisdictions. Under the Constitution, there are certain cases that may begin in the Supreme Court. There are, however, very few cases that actually go directly to the Supreme Court before being heard by a lower court, and most involve disputes between states over shared boundaries, water rights, and the like. New Jersey and New York's conflict over the ownership of Ellis Island is one recent example (see *New Jersey v. New York* 523 U.S. 767 [1998]). Appeals, by contrast, come to the Court after having been decided by a lower court, and these are cases that Congress, by law, requires the Court to hear. While there have historically been a fair number of such cases, Congress has eliminated most of these instances of mandatory review. A small number of cases, such as the voting rights dispute presented by *Shaw v. Reno* 509 U.S. 630 (1993), still persist.

that the justices review the opinion of that federal appellate court. On behalf of South Dakota, its attorney general Mark V. Meierhenry filed the petition for certiorari, and as required by the Court, he began by identifying the legal issues at stake in the case, followed by his arguments as to why the case was worthy of review. U.S. Solicitor General Charles Fried—the lawyer whose job it was to represent the federal government before the Supreme Court—also filed a *brief in opposition,* a submission designed to persuade the Court to reject the petition. In it, Fried described the legal stakes from Secretary Dole's vantage point. In short, one party—known as the petitioner—makes the case for granting review, while the other party—the respondent—argues against it. Comparing their respective arguments in Table 3.1, one can easily see that the two parties had quite different views about the case. To South Dakota, the federal law posed a serious threat to the exercise of fundamental state power. As far as the solicitor general was concerned, however, the issue was merely whether Congress could attach conditions to federal spending.

Given that South Dakota sought to have the case placed on the Court's agenda—and given that the federal government wanted to keep it off—these two litigants naturally chose to frame the same

TABLE 3.1 Legal Questions in *South Dakota v. Dole*

Petition for Certiorari	Brief in Opposition
South Dakota	Elizabeth Dole (U.S. Government)
I. Does . . . the National Minimum Drinking Age . . . unconstitutionally displace the state's core power, under the Twenty-First Amendment, United States Consitution, to set minimum drinking ages?	Whether the Twenty-First Amendment bars Congress from conditioning a grant of federal highway funds to a state upon the state's adoption of a minimum drinking age of twenty-one.
II. Does . . . the National Minimum Drinking Age violate the Tenth Amendment, United States Constitution, by displacing the state's core power to set drinking ages, granted to the state by the Twenty-First Amendment?	

Source: South Dakota v. Dole, Petition for Certiorari, August 18, 1986, p. i.; Brief for Respondent in Opposition, November 7, 1986, p. i.

conflict quite differently. According to South Dakota's brief, the issues seem fairly critical to state autonomy and, as such, might be more prone to capture the Court's interest. By the solicitor general's reckoning, though, the case raises a more modest concern about how the federal government distributes its money, a question the justices might be less likely to examine more closely.

Pool Memorandum

As petitions are filed throughout the Court's term, they are distributed to the chambers of each of the justices. With thousands of cases to consider, however, the justices usually delegate the responsibility of reviewing these petitions to their law clerks. Under Chief Justice Burger, the justices began the practice of regularly dividing the filings among their chambers. In each case, a law clerk drafts a memorandum outlining the background and legal issues. In turn, that memorandum is then distributed to each of the justices. With the exception of Justice John Paul Stevens, every justice on the Court participates in this collective effort, known as the certiorari pool, or cert pool.[26] As one former clerk explains, "Rather than each Justice considering every case independently, a clerk for one Justice in the 'cert pool' circulates an advisory memo to all Justices in the pool. This 'pool memo' summarizes a case and assesses whether it is 'certworthy'—that is, whether it raises a sufficiently important and controversial issue to merit the Supreme Court's attention."[27]

The pool memorandum in *South Dakota v. Dole* was about ten pages long.[28] It began with a simple summary of the issue presented: "Petitioner challenges, on Twenty-First Amendment grounds, [federal law] which requires the Secretary of Transportation to withhold a percentage of federal highway funds from those states which fail to raise their drinking age to 21." It then described the facts of the case and the decision from the Eighth Circuit. After presenting the

[26]Stevens is not the only one who has elected not to join the cert pool. At the time *South Dakota v. Dole* was being considered, Justices William J. Brennan and Thurgood Marshall did not participate, either. Instead, each of these three justices bore the responsibility of reviewing all of the filings within his own chambers.

[27]Edward Lazarus, *Closed Chambers: The Rise, Fall, and Future of the Modern Supreme Court* (New York: Penguin Books, 1999), p. 31.

[28]Lewis F. Powell, Jr., Papers, 86–260, Washington and Lee Law School, Lexington, Virginia.

arguments made by both South Dakota and the solicitor general, the memorandum provided a balanced analysis of the case, discussing it in the context of other Supreme Court decisions related to Congress's spending power and the Twenty-First Amendment. Noting that the Eighth Circuit "may have interpreted the scope of powers granted the states under the Twenty-First Amendment too narrowly," the memo turned to the text of the amendment granting states the authority to regulate alcohol and emphasized that "[d]rinking-age laws certainly 'regulate the sale or use of liquor,' and it is clear that petitioner's drinking-age law is within its core powers." At the same time, the pool memo underscored that this case, like another recent Supreme Court decision, "involves the Spending Clause, and it is well-established that 'Congress may impose conditions on the receipt of federal funds, absent some independent constitutional bar.' . . . The Twenty-First Amendment may, however, be one of those 'rare exceptions.' "

True, the Supreme Court had already ruled that Congress could attach conditions to its spending, but whether it could do so in a way that interfered with the autonomy of states was a novel question that the justices had not addressed. In closing, the advice to the justices was straightforward: "I think the case presents an important cert-worthy question, and I recommend that the petition be granted." Since law clerks want to help the justices identify the few cases that deserve attention by the nation's highest court, pool memos can only endorse a few likely candidates each year. Based on this preliminary examination, *South Dakota v. Dole* appeared to be one of those cases.

Like all pool memos, this one was then sent to the office of Chief Justice William H. Rehnquist, where it was copied and distributed to the other justices who participated in the cert pool. Each of these justices then asked a law clerk to review the pool memo and to make an additional assessment. In the chambers of Justice Lewis F. Powell, for example, the clerk examining the pool memo came to much the same conclusion.[29] His recommendation was written by hand on the memo itself. Perhaps revealing how he believed the case should be decided, this clerk suggested that this case presented an issue that was worthy of the Court's time and resources:

[29]Powell Papers, 86–260.

I agree with the memo writer that this is important. Although the Court has not interpreted the 21st Amendment broadly, I do not believe it has upheld laws with so intrusive an effect as this one. Moreover, I think it would be important to recognize some boundary on the Fed's ability to use the spending power to coerce states in areas where the Fed cannot legislate directly. Grant — Ronald

Like Powell, the remaining justices in the cert pool did likewise, distributing the case's pool memorandum for additional review within their chambers. Those outside the cert pool—Justices Brennan, Marshall, and Stevens—reviewed *South Dakota v. Dole* on their own. Each member of the Court now had a general overview of this conflict between federal spending and state power. The justices' next step was to decide whether they would hear it.

Discuss List

Decisions about selecting cases are made at a weekly conference, where the members of the Court vote to grant or deny review. In preparation for that conference, the chief justice reviews the pending petitions and drafts a list of cases that he considers serious candidates for review by the Court. It is then circulated to the other justices, any one of whom can request that a case not identified by the chief justice be included for discussion. Once finalized, the Court's Special List I—known more informally as the discuss list—becomes the slate from which the justices will select their cases. All remaining cases are placed on the Court's Special List II, the set of petitions that no justice believes to be important enough to warrant the Court's attention. Appropriately enough, this roster is called the dead list, and any case on it is denied review without any further consideration. Since the Court is so selective about its agenda, the vast majority of petitions end up on the dead list; in only about forty to fifty cases do the justices actually discuss whether to grant the writ of certiorari.[30]

In late November 1986, just before Thanksgiving, the justices began to assemble their weekly discuss list, and in its final form it

---

[30]Gregory A. Caldeira and John R. Wright, "The Discuss List: Agenda Building in the Supreme Court," *Law & Society Review* 24:807–36 (1990); see also David M. O'Brien, *Storm Center: The Supreme Court in American Politics* (New York: W.W. Norton, 2000), pp. 201–2.

contained a number of interesting legal questions.[31] Among the cases for consideration that week was *California v. Superior Court of California, San Bernardino County*, a dispute over whether courts from one state could block the return of a fugitive to another state. Also on the discuss list was *Greer v. Miller*, a criminal case that asked the justices to consider if a defendant's right to a fair trial was violated when the prosecuting attorney asked why the defendant had remained silent at the time of his arrest. Could federal courts require the losing party in a trial to reimburse the winning party for the cost of its expert witnesses? That was the issue in *Crawford Fitting Co. v. J.T. Gibbons, Inc.*, another petition that the justices regarded as worthy of further consideration. The discuss list also contained *Agency-Holding Corp. v. Malley-Duff and Associates, Inc.*, which asked the Supreme Court to clarify how long one party had to sue another for fraudulent business practices.

That week, the case of *South Dakota v. Dole* also caught the Court's attention. Pitting, as it did, the power of the national government against the autonomy of the states, it too was placed on the discuss list and thus became one of the cases that would potentially be chosen for the Supreme Court's agenda.

Conference

On November 26, 1986, the justices met to evaluate the cases on the discuss list. Sitting around a large conference table, the justices considered each case, expressing their views and voting on whether to grant or deny review. As is the Court's custom, the most senior member of the Court—the chief justice, by definition—spoke first, followed by each of the associate justices in order of seniority. One by one, the members of the Court offered their opinions on each case on the discuss list and formally cast votes supporting or opposing the writ of certiorari.

When the conference discussion turned to *South Dakota v. Dole*, therefore, Chief Justice William Rehnquist began by stating his views on formally deciding the case. In turn, from the most senior associate

---

[31]Each of the following cases was granted review on the same day as *South Dakota v. Dole*. The cases on the discuss list are typically not public information, but it is a safe assumption that any case in which the Court grants review on a given day was on the discuss list for the previous conference.

justice, William Brennan, to the Court's junior member, Antonin Scalia, the remaining members of the Court likewise assessed whether they should consider the federal government's attempt to impose a national drinking age through its spending power.

In deciding which cases to select, the justices follow an internal norm known as the Rule of Four. By this standard, as the name implies, at least four justices must vote to grant certiorari in order for the Supreme Court to hear a case. In *South Dakota v. Dole*, that standard was easily met; six of the justices supported review of the Eighth Circuit's decision. As the Court's records reveal in Figure 3.2, Chief Justice Rehnquist, along with Justices William Brennan and Byron White, voted to grant certiorari. By contrast, Justices Thurgood Marshall and Harry Blackmun opposed hearing the case. Justice Lewis Powell provided the crucial fourth vote and thus ensured that the case would, in fact, be heard. Of the remaining justices, John Paul Stevens voted against granting the writ of certiorari, while Sandra Day O'Connor and Antonin Scalia voted in favor.

It was nearly two years after South Dakota brought its case against the secretary of transportation. The U.S. Supreme Court had formally decided to consider the constitutionality of the Uniform Minimum Drinking Age Law, and in a brief order on December 1, the justices announced that they had granted certiorari.

EXPLAINING CASE SELECTION

As with most cases, accounting for why the Supreme Court decided to grant review to *South Dakota v. Dole* is a perplexing task. The reason is that the justices usually do not specify why they select and reject petitions for review. Unlike the Court's written opinions, which ostensibly describe and justify the outcomes of legal disputes, the decisions about the process of agenda setting are almost never explained. Instead, the Court simply issues a list of cases, announcing which ones have been granted certiorari and which ones have been denied.

In the cases the Court ultimately agrees to hear, the justices will, from time to time, actually explain the factors that motivated them to select a particular case, but there is no formal requirement that they do so. In fact, in its written opinion in *South Dakota v. Dole*, the Court failed to offer any reason why, out of the thousands of cases from

	November 26, 1986
	No. 86-260

SOUTH DAKOTA

vs.

DOLE, Sec. of Transportation

	CERT.	
	G	D
Rehnquist, Ch. J.	✓	
Brennan, J.	✓	
White, J.	✓	
Marshall, J.		✓
Blackmun, J.		✓
Powell, J.	✓	
Stevens, J.		✓
O'Connor, J.	✓	
Scalia, J.	✓	

FIGURE 3.2 Docket Sheet in *South Dakota v. Dole.* A docket sheet is an internal record of the disposition of a case on which a justice records his or her vote. For votes on certiorari, columns marked *G* and *D* represent the votes to grant or deny, respectively.
Source: Powell Papers, 86-260.

which it might have chosen, it selected this dispute over the spending authority of Congress and the autonomy of states. Still, research has generated a number of important insights into the reasons behind case selection, many of which shed light on the decision to docket this case.

Conflict

The justices devote considerable attention to ensuring that the U.S. Constitution, as well as federal laws and regulations, have consistent meaning across the country. Without guidance from the U.S. Supreme Court, lower court judges faced with interpreting the same law may well come to different conclusions about its meaning. Even when the justices have issued a prior decision clarifying the law, judges in subsequent cases may not apply that precedent in a manner in which the Court intended. Thus, when lower courts disagree among one another, or when lower courts deviate from an earlier ruling by the Supreme Court, there is a conflict over the proper interpretation of the law. Quite often, the justices will grant review to resolve these disagreements that exist between courts.

Conflict is one the most important factors that affect the decision to grant review to a case, as the Court itself explains in its published guidelines. Under Rule 10 of the Court, certiorari is more likely to be granted when "a United States court of appeals has entered a decision in conflict with the decision of another United States court of appeals on the same important matter; has decided an important federal question in a way that conflicts with a decision by a state court of last resort; [or when] a state court or a United States court of appeals has decided an important question . . . in a way that conflicts with relevant decisions of this Court."[32] Although the justices are generally reluctant to explain their motives in selecting cases, they are explicit in expressing their interest in resolving disparate interpretations of the law.

Lawyers who are interested in getting their cases on the agenda seem to take this admonition to heart. One study of case selection over a thirty-year period (1947–76) found that in roughly 60 percent of all petitions for certiorari, litigants claimed that their cases

---

[32]Rule 10, Rules of the Supreme Court of the United States, January 11, 1999.

TABLE 3.2   Allegations of Conflict in Petitions for Certiorari

Type of Case	Number of Conflicts Claimed in Petition for Certiorari			
	0	1	2	3 or More
All cases (%)	38.6	17.3	13.2	30.8
U.S. Court of Appeals cases only (%)	46.4	18.3	12.1	23.3

Source: S. Sidney Ulmer, "The Supreme Court's Certiorari Decisions: Conflict as a Predictive Variable," *American Political Science Review* 78:901–11 (1984), p. 905.

presented conflicts for the justices to resolve. As the data in Table 3.2 suggest, parties routinely assert that the lower court decisions they are challenging are at odds with at least one other judicial opinion. In cases coming to the Court from one of the U.S. courts of appeals, allegations of conflict are made somewhat less often. Still, in both instances, petitions for certiorari often maintain that there is a conflict—or sometimes several conflicting decisions—that the justices should reconcile.

Without question, the justices give these cases close scrutiny. Simply asserting that a case presents a conflict makes it likely that a case will be placed on the discuss list.[33] There is likewise a high probability that the justices will grant review when conflict is alleged, regardless of whether one actually exists.[34] After all, it is not always apparent when there are genuine disagreements between lower courts, so to some extent the justices must rely upon the parties to identify them. As a result, the Court takes these claims very seriously. In cases of real conflict, the odds of review are even better; the justices grant certiorari in as many as 70 percent of these petitions.[35] Considering that the Court usually agrees to hear as little as 5 percent of all filings, the rate of review for such cases is extraordinarily high.

Obviously aware of the Supreme Court's desire to ensure a uniform interpretation of the law, South Dakota argued that the

[33]Caldeira and Wright, "The Discuss List."
[34]Gregory A. Caldeira and John R. Wright, "Organized Interests and Agenda Setting in the U.S. Supreme Court," *American Political Science Review* 82:1109–27 (1988).
[35]Caldeira and Wright, "The Discuss List"; S. Sidney Ulmer, "The Supreme Court's Certiorari Decisions: Conflict as a Predictive Variable," *American Political Science Review* 78:901–11 (1984).

principal reason for granting review was that two federal appeals courts had interpreted the Twenty-First Amendment in contradictory ways. Under the amendment's repeal of Prohibition, states were given the explicit authority to regulate the sale and distribution of alcohol. Reading this language, the Fifth Circuit ruled in a related case that this grant of power to the states was meant to deny any similar power to the national government. By contrast, the Eighth Circuit in *South Dakota v. Dole* had ruled that the amendment actually left Congress's regulatory power over commerce unchanged. As a practical result of these rulings, Congress could regulate alcohol in South Dakota but not in, say, Mississippi.

In addition, South Dakota urged the justices to grant review, because the Eighth Circuit's decision was contrary to a number of prior decisions of the U.S. Supreme Court. Citing numerous precedents, South Dakota argued that these decisions "have recognized that the Twenty-first Amendment is an affirmative grant of power to the states to regulate liquor more extensively than they may regulate other items or products in commerce."[36] By ruling that Congress had the power to induce states to raise their drinking ages, the appeals court had gone against a number of Supreme Court policies that seemingly gave preference to state laws over federal laws related to the control of liquor.

Claiming that the Eighth Circuit's ruling conflicted with both a federal appeals court and the U.S. Supreme Court, South Dakota's petition caught the attention of the justices. The preliminary memorandum prepared for the justices in the certiorari pool featured this issue prominently. As it emphasized, South Dakota "argues that CA8's [Court of Appeals for the Eighth Circuit] view that the Twenty-first Amendment did not decrease Congress' power to regulate intoxicating liquors conflicts with the view of CA5. CA8's view is also inconsistent with the decisions of this Court."[37] When lower courts disagree with one another or with the Supreme Court, the justices have an obvious interest in providing guidance to others in the legal system. Under such circumstances, it is easy to see why the justices would have been eager to use *South Dakota v. Dole* as a means of clarifying the law.

---

[36]*South Dakota v. Dole*, Petition for Certiorari, p. 12.
[37]Powell Papers, 86–260.

Importance of the Issue

Because the Supreme Court can hear only a small number of cases each year, the justices are obliged to choose cases that will have significant implications for both legal and public policy. As the leading treatise on Supreme Court litigation explains, "The Court does not have the time to give full consideration to all cases which present novel or interesting issues. It must necessarily confine itself to those which reflect the more important legal problems. . . ."[38] Consequently, the members of the Court try to identify cases with issues that matter to some broad segment of society. The justices have formalized this preference in Rule 10, declaring that the Court is inclined to grant certiorari when "a state court or a United States court of appeals has decided an important question of federal law that has not been, but should be, settled by this Court."[39] There is, though, an obvious problem for the Court: How does it identify important cases?

In some instances, the importance of a case may be obvious. For example, when the Supreme Court was asked to address the constitutionality of the legislative veto—whether Congress could engage in lawmaking without giving the president the opportunity to sign the legislation—all nine justices voted to grant certiorari.[40] That case, *Immigration and Naturalization Service v. Chadha* (1983), had considerable implications for the separation of powers. Later, in its written opinion, the Court noted that it had granted certiorari in order to "address the important question of the constitutionality of the [legislative] veto."[41] Indeed, that issue alone had consequences for some two hundred other federal laws.[42] Little wonder that all of the justices would recognize the significance of this case.

Amicus Curiae Briefs. More often than not, however, it is not clear that the issues in a case will have broad ramifications. In those instances, the justices often rely upon various indicators to guide their

[38]Robert L. Stern, Eugene Gressman, and Stephen M. Shapiro, *Supreme Court Practice,* 6th ed. (Washington: Bureau of National Affairs, Inc., 1986), p. 212.
[39]Rule 10, Rules of the Supreme Court of the United States.
[40]Powell, Papers, 80–1832.
[41]*Immigration and Naturalization Service v. Chadha* 462 U.S. 919 (1983), p. 929.
[42]Joan Biskupic and Elder Witt, *Guide to the U.S. Supreme Court,* 3rd ed. (Washington: Congressional Quarterly, Inc., 1997), p. 87.

judgment. One of the most important is the participation of organized interests. When a case is submitted at the agenda-setting stage,
interest groups are permitted to file briefs that either encourage or
discourage full review by the Supreme Court. These filings—known
as amicus curiae or "friend of the court" briefs—are designed to give
an opportunity for interested parties who are not directly involved
in a case to offer the justices additional information not provided by
the litigants. Regardless of the specific arguments it presents, "an
amicus curiae brief establishes at least one thing: someone other than
the parties considers the decision below an important one."[43] If an
outside interest is willing to take the time and effort to present arguments on whether certiorari should be granted, it lets the Court
know that someone other than the litigants cares about the issue in a
case. In a case involving health care policy, for example, a brief from
the American Medical Association would suggest that the case could
affect a large segment of the medical community. Similarly, in a criminal case, an amicus brief filed by several state attorneys general
might indicate that a decision will have consequences for law enforcement across the country. In another case, a business organization, such the U.S. Chamber of Commerce, might file a brief urging
the Court to grant certiorari, while a labor group, such the AFL-CIO,
might file another brief opposing it.

Knowing that a case matters to some large social or economic
constituency can be critical information for the justices. For a justice
or a law clerk in search of major legal conflicts, "amicus curiae participation by organized interests provides information, or signals—
otherwise largely unavailable—about the political, social, and
economic significance of cases on the Supreme Court's [agenda]."[44]
It is no wonder that, in cases with amicus briefs, the Supreme Court
grants review at such an impressive rate, nearly 40 percent of the
time.[45]

Evaluating the importance of the issues in *South Dakota v. Dole*
was therefore made easier by the participation of several different
sets of interests, each of which filed an amicus brief encouraging
the justices to grant certiorari. Listed in Table 3.3, there were three

---

[43]Stewart A. Baker, "A Practical Guide to Certiorari," *Catholic University Law Review*
33:611–32 (1984), p. 626.
[44]Caldeira and Wright, "Organized Interests and Agenda Setting."
[45]Caldeira and Wright, "Organized Interests and Agenda Setting," p. 1116.

TABLE 3.3 Amicus Briefs Filed in *South Dakota v. Dole*

Amici Curiae	Position Taken
National Beer Wholesalers' Association	Supporting certiorari
States of Colorado, Hawaii, Louisiana, Montana, Ohio, South Carolina, Vermont, and Wyoming	Supporting certiorari
Administrators of liquor laws from the States of Arizona, Hawaii, Kentucky, Louisiana, Nebraska, New Mexico, New York, and the City of Baltimore, Maryland	Supporting certiorari

amicus curiae briefs filed, each of which urged the Supreme Court to grant review. Outside parties can also file amicus briefs opposing certiorari—to persuade the justices to deny review—but most organized groups know that such briefs have the opposite of their intended effect: They only draw the justices' attention to a case.[46] Just as in *South Dakota v. Dole*, amicus briefs typically urge the justices to grant certiorari. In the pool memorandum, the arguments of these friends of the Court were sketched for the justices:

> There are three briefs filed by amici supporting petitioner. One was prepared by the Wyoming Attorney General and represents the views of that state and the states of Colorado, Hawaii, Louisiana, Montana, Ohio, South Carolina and Vermont. The states argue that the Twenty-First Amendment acts as an independent constitutional bar to Congress' spending power. The states argue that CA8's opinion did not adequately consider the states' interests. Wyoming, for example, . . . has adopted a program to prevent drunk driving that is far more substantial than [the federal law].
>
> Amicus National Beer Wholesalers' Association argues that this Court [has] made it clear that states enjoy "virtually complete control" in areas lying at the core of their Twenty-First Amendment power, and drinking-age regulation is part of this core power. A number of people responsible for administering their respective states' liquor laws have filed a brief underscoring the points already discussed.[47]

Through these three briefs, then, the justices learned that several different constituencies—the alcoholic beverage industry, state governments, and state and local regulators of alcoholic beverages—all

---

[46]Caldeira and Wright, "Organized Interests and Agenda Setting."
[47]Powell Papers, 80–1832.

regarded the decision in *South Dakota v. Dole* as important to their respective interests. In effect, these briefs informed the Court that the case presented an important issue of federal law that would have implications for a segment of the economy, as well as states and their regulatory power over alcohol. Considering the presence of these amici curiae, it is easy to understand why the justices concluded that this case presented an issue worthy of consideration by the nation's highest court.

Litigants. Of course, the voices of outside interests are not the only measure of importance. Quite often, simply knowing who is seeking certiorari offers potential clues about the significance of a case. A wide variety of litigants petition the Supreme Court, and some have a stronger likelihood than others of being involved in substantial legal questions. Chief among them is the United States government. Every year, the federal government is involved in scores of cases, and the solicitor general must screen them carefully, deciding which ones it will ask the justices to hear. Because that office sifts out all but the most worthy, the justices know that when the solicitor general does petition the Court, it represents one of the few instances where the government believed the legal questions to be important enough for the Court to consider. For their part, the justices reward this selectivity by granting certiorari to a substantial proportion of the government's cases.[48]

Like the solicitor general, state governments are prone to offer substantial issues to the Court. States are typically involved in a great number of noteworthy legal questions, including issues of criminal procedure, civil rights and liberties, business regulations, and federalism. States too must decide which conflicts are worth litigating in the Supreme Court, selecting the most crucial cases from

---

[48]Christopher J. W. Zorn, *On Appeal: United States Government Litigation in the Federal Appellate Courts* (Ann Arbor: University of Michigan Press, forthcoming). See also Caldeira and Wright, "Organized Interests and Agenda Setting." By contrast, some litigants raise significant issues only rarely, and the justices have traditionally viewed their claims with considerable skepticism. Many parties, for example, cannot afford to pay the administrative costs needed to bring a case before the Supreme Court. Thousands of such cases are filed each year, most of which are brought by prisoners whose cases affect few people except themselves. Since they rarely have relevance for national legal policy, virtually all of these petitions are denied. See Perry, *Deciding to Decide*, pp. 102–4.

among many possible petitions. The result is that states are more successful than most other litigants in securing space on the justices' agenda. Analyzing the success rate of various parties, one scholar found that states "were accepted at much lower rates than the U.S., but at rates substantially higher than for individuals. Of course, this may be highly correlated with importance." In other words, the petitions presented by institutional players, like the federal government and individual states, "are ones where it would be more likely to find issues of societal importance."[49]

This may be part of the explanation for the Court's decision to grant review in *South Dakota v. Dole*. Seeking certiorari, South Dakota would have sent a signal to the justices through its petition: a large political entity regards the constitutionality of the federal drinking age law to be one of the most pressing issues of public policy it can bring to the Supreme Court. Seen in this way, a petition brought by the state would have been a flag to the justices that the case contained issues worthy of closer scrutiny.

Lower Courts.   Often, the treatment of a case by lower courts can help the justices to evaluate its potential significance. If a case is simply routine—and therefore less important—then, as it makes its way to the Supreme Court, the case should pose few difficulties for judges to resolve. More important cases, by contrast, raise interesting legal questions whose answers are not immediately obvious from the written law or Supreme Court precedent. As a result, one measure of a potentially important case is whether the lower court judges reach the same conclusion about how to resolve it. For instance, if a trial court's decision is overturned on appeal, or if the judges on a lower appellate court disagree among themselves, then the case is probably out of the ordinary. Disagreements, either between different courts or between judges on the same court, "signal ferment in the lower courts and suggest a problematic outcome, one perhaps worthy of a closer look."[50]

---

[49]See Perry, *Deciding to Decide*, pp. 136–37.
[50]Caldeira and Wright, "Organized Interests and Agenda Setting," p. 1115. See also D. Marie Provine, *Case Selection in the United States Supreme Court* (Chicago: University of Chicago Press, 1980); Joseph Tanenhaus, Marvin Schick, Matthew Muraskin, and Daniel Rosen, "The Supreme Court's Certiorari Jurisdiction: Cue Theory," in *Judicial Decision-Making*, ed. Glendon Schubert (New York: Free Press, 1963); Ulmer, "Conflict as a Predictive Variable."

As it happened, however, *South Dakota v. Dole* had neither of these factors in its favor. The Eighth Circuit's opinion only supported Judge Bogue's decision, and unanimously so. In other words, all of the lower court judges who considered the case were of a single mind on how to resolve it: Each one favored allowing Congress to place conditions on its highway monies. Still, the justices had good reason to think that the case raised significant issues. Given the identity of the petitioning party and the input offered by outside interests through their amicus briefs, there were clear signals that the case was important enough to merit the Court's time.

Issue Area

One plausible explanation for why the Supreme Court was interested in *South Dakota v. Dole* was its subject matter. Over time, the justices have varied significantly in the substantive issues to which they have addressed themselves, and knowing the types of issues raised by a case often provides good information about whether the Court will hear it. Since the mid-1900s, the Court has devoted a sizable proportion of its attention to cases involving civil liberties and civil rights.[51] Consequently, if the justices are interested in making policy on particular subjects, then petitions raising those types of issues will naturally be advantaged in case selection.

When William Rehnquist was promoted to chief justice, one of the issues that soon became a focus of the Supreme Court was federalism—the relationship between the national and state governments—and since then the Court has come to show considerable interest in such cases.[52] During the 1960s, only about 6 percent of the cases on the justices' docket concerned federalism, but by the end of the 1980s that percentage had nearly doubled.[53] Inasmuch as the Rehnquist Court was keen to focus more of its attention on issues of

[51]Richard L. Pacelle, Jr., *The Transformation of the Supreme Court's Agenda: From the New Deal to the Reagan Administration* (Boulder, CO: Westview Press, 1991); Tanenhaus et al., "The Supreme Court's Certiorari Jurisdiction."
[52]Linda Greenhouse, "Justices Step In as Federalism's Referee," *The New York Times*, April 28, 1995, p. 1.
[53]Lawrence Baum, *The Supreme Court* (Washington: Congressional Quarterly, Inc., 1998), p. 196.

federalism, this conflict over drinking ages between the Congress and the states would have been a natural candidate for review.

Preferences of the Justices

Like other policy makers, the justices of the Supreme Court have goals that influence their decisions. Chief among them is the desire to develop legal policy that is consistent with their own views. The justices have preferences about the content of the Court's policies—they have preconceived ideas about how a case ought to be decided—and those preferences shape their selection of cases for review.[54]

The impact of those preferences is revealed, in part, by the justices' tendency to review cases that they believe to be wrongly decided by the lower courts. As one member of the Court explains, an important motive that governs voting on certiorari "is the fact that an error has been committed, because no one feels the obligation to correct something that has been correctly decided."[55] Lower courts often reach decisions that the justices find to be disagreeable, and with limited space on the docket, the justices evidently prefer to take cases in which they believe that lower courts were in error in their interpretation of the law. As a result, the Court usually overturns the lower courts whose judgments it reviews.[56]

That, it turns out, was not the case in *South Dakota v. Dole*. On June 23, 1987, the Supreme Court announced its 7-2 decision upholding the court of appeals' interpretation of the Surface Transportation Assistance Act. Like the lower courts, the Supreme Court determined that, despite the Twenty-First Amendment's grant of regulatory authority to the states, Congress could use its spending power to encourage states to raise their drinking ages to twenty-one. In the end, the Court's view of the federal law actually corresponded with that of the lower courts; the preferences of the justices were the

---

[54]See generally Jeffrey A. Segal and Harold J. Spaeth, *The Supreme Court and the Attitudinal Model* (Cambridge: Cambridge University Press, 1993).

[55]Perry, *Deciding to Decide*, p. 269.

[56]Saul Brenner and John F. Krol, "Strategies in Certiorari Voting on the United States Supreme Court," *Journal of Politics* 51:828–40 (1989); Donald R. Songer, "Concern for Policy Outputs as a Cue for Supreme Court Decisions on Certiorari," *Journal of Politics* 41:1185–94 (1979); S. Sidney Ulmer, "The Decision to Grant Certiorari as an Indicator to Decisions 'On the Merits'," *Polity* 4:429–47 (1972).

same as the other judges who had considered *South Dakota v. Dole.* That does not mean, however, that the justices' preferences were irrelevant in the process of selecting this case.

As a collegial body, the Supreme Court decides whether to grant certiorari to cases, but its decisions are actually the product of nine individual votes. Obviously, each justice will have goals in case selection—to grant review and uphold a precedent, to deny review to avoid making undesirable legal policy, and so on. Consequently, a justice who would like to see her goals realized must consider whether those preferences will command the support of a majority of her fellow justices. Stated differently, the justices should approach case selection strategically, considering their own views in light of the preferences of the rest of the Court.

Members of the Court who care about how a case will be decided if review is granted must ask themselves a simple question: Will I win on the merits? That is, if the Court grants certiorari, will the outcome that I prefer ultimately be adopted by the Court? A justice might see a particular petition as an ideal case for establishing a new legal policy, but if no other justices will support such a policy, then that justice would have little to gain by voting for review. On the other hand, justices who estimate that their view of a case will be shared by other members of the Court have good reason to vote in favor of certiorari.[57]

If the justices behave in this strategic fashion, then those who vote to grant certiorari ought to be on the winning side on the merits. Here, *South Dakota v. Dole* provides at least some evidence that the justices were acting in a strategic fashion. As Table 3.4 shows, nearly 60 percent of justices who were members of the Court's final majority voted to grant review. Interpreting this voting pattern, one might conclude that Chief Justice Rehnquist along with Justices Powell, Scalia, and White—all of whom voted in favor of certiorari—accurately estimated that they could secure a fifth vote in favor of upholding the spending authority of Congress. To the extent that they made such predictions, their forecasts obviously proved

---

[57]Perry, "Deciding to Decide"; Gregory A. Caldeira, John R. Wright, and Christopher J. W. Zorn, "Sophisticated Voting and Gate-Keeping in the Supreme Court," *The Journal of Law, Economics, and Organization* 53:549–72 (1999); see also Saul Brenner, "The New Certiorari Game," *Journal of Politics* 41:649–55 (1979).

TABLE 3.4 Comparison of Votes on Certiorari and
Votes on the Merits in *South Dakota v. Dole*

Justice	Certiorari Vote	Merits Vote
Powell	Grant	Dole
Rehnquist	Grant	Dole
Scalia	Grant	Dole
White	Grant	Dole
Brennan	Grant	South Dakota
O'Connor	Grant	South Dakota
Blackmun	Deny	Dole
Marshall	Deny	Dole
Stevens	Deny	Dole

Source: Powell papers, 86-260; *South Dakota v. Dole*, 483 U.S. 203 (1987).

accurate; Justices Blackmun, Marshall, and Stevens each joined the
Court's majority in support of the federal government.

At the same time, though, it is not clear that the justices voted
strictly along strategic lines. Justices Brennan and O'Connor voted to
grant certiorari, yet they were the lone dissenters when the case was
decided. If they were able to predict how their brethren would vote
once the Court accepted the case, they should have seen that their
position would not prevail and therefore should have voted to deny
review. Likewise, if Justices Blackmun, Marshall, and Stevens fore-
saw that most members of the Court would vote in favor of the federal government, as they eventually would, then they ought to have
supported the grant of certiorari.

Still, most of those who were on the winning side favored hearing *South Dakota v. Dole*. Seen in this way, several members of the
Supreme Court appear to have engaged in strategic behavior, voting
to review a case in which, by their calculations, their preferred outcome would ultimately prevail.

CONCLUSION

On October 23, 2000, President Bill Clinton signed into law legislation designed to promote a more stringent standard for drunk driving. Threatened with the loss of federal highway funds, states were
required to set the threshold of legal intoxication at a blood-alcohol
level of no more than .08. At the time, thirty-one states had a more

lenient standard of .10, requiring more alcohol in the blood in order to be considered legally drunk.[58] Like the Surface Transportation Assistance Act, this law was an exercise of Congress's spending power, one designed to encourage states to change their laws. What made this legislative act possible, at least in part, was the U.S. Supreme Court. Through its willingness to address the issue of Congress placing conditions on its spending, the Court provided authoritative guidance to policy makers on this important issue of federalism. Deciding to decide, therefore, is a critical component of the business of the Supreme Court.

What explains the decision to grant review in *South Dakota v. Dole*? Several factors appear to have entered into the Court's calculus. Among other things, the case presented the justices with a need to resolve conflicting interpretations of federal law. Two federal appellate courts had come to different conclusions about the meaning of the Twenty-First Amendment. Not only that, the decision of the Court of Appeals for the Eighth Circuit was seemingly at odds with earlier decisions by the justices. In light of the Court's interest in providing consistency in the law, the presence of lower court conflicts created a substantial incentive to take the case.

Quite apart from conflicts, the case raised an objectively important question of public policy. The issue of congressional influence over drinking ages, traditionally a matter of state discretion, had implications for state governments, their policy administrators, and the industries affected by their regulations. That these different interests filed amicus curiae briefs surely alerted the justices to that fact. Not only that, the case was brought by a state government, a frequent litigant in the Court that must make decisions of its own about which cases are important enough to bring to the justices' doorstep.

At the same time, the justices had interests of their own that they were pursuing. Federalism was an issue in which the Court was increasingly interested. So, a case such as *South Dakota v. Dole* would have naturally received greater attention within the pool of petitions. The justices' interest in federalism does not seem to tell the whole story, however. There is reason to believe that the justices acted strategically in selecting this particular case. Most of those who supported certiorari were probably confident that they would win once the Court agreed to decide the case.

[58]"Drunk-Driving Standard Toughened," *Los Angeles Times*, October 24, 2000, p. 15.

To an outside observer, the process of agenda-setting in the Supreme Court might seem to be somewhat arbitrary, providing no guarantee that cases will be given adequate consideration. After all, the justices delegate most of the critical reviewing to their law clerks and engage in little, if any, deliberation over the vast majority of petitions that are filed. In fact, there are clearly defined steps in the process of case selection through which the Court identifies the most plausible cases for review. Indeed, there are forces that systematically propel a small number of cases onto the Court's agenda. It is precisely these factors that explain why, out of thousands of possible choices, cases such as *South Dakota v. Dole* comprise the small slate of legal issues on which the justices will focus their attention.

QUESTIONS FOR DISCUSSION

1. In most cases, the justices deny certiorari without ever having personally examined the petitions for review. Should the justices look more closely at the cases that are brought to them?
2. Through the certiorari pool, much of the preliminary work is delegated to law clerks. Does this place too much responsibility in the hands of the justices' staff? Given the number of cases that the Court must consider, are there any practical alternatives?
3. In selecting the case of *South Dakota v. Dole*, the justices seemed more interested in addressing the legal question presented by the case and less interested in making sure that the state of South Dakota had its day before the Supreme Court. Is this the appropriate role of the Court—that is, to address important questions of legal policy—or should the justices be more concerned with safeguarding litigants whose rights may have been violated?
4. As in many cases, conflict within the lower courts seems to have been a primary motivation in selecting *South Dakota v. Dole*. What would be the consequences of the justices placing less emphasis on this consideration? Would there be benefits to allowing lower courts to experiment and try to work out sensible solutions to their conflicts?
5. The justices are concerned with finding cases that have significant consequences for public policy. How difficult is it for the Court to assess whether the issues presented by a case really do have major ramifications?

6. In the process of case selection, would a justice ever vote to deny certiorari in cases that he or she actually wanted to resolve on the merits? What would explain such voting?

SUGGESTED READING

Saul Brenner and John F. Krol. 1989. "Strategies in Certiorari Voting on the United States Supreme Court." *Journal of Politics* 51:828–40.

Gregory A. Caldeira and John R. Wright. 1990. "The Discuss List: Agenda Building in the Supreme Court." *Law & Society Review* 24:807–36.

Gregory A. Caldeira and John R. Wright. 1988. "Organized Interests and Agenda Setting in the U.S. Supreme Court." *American Political Science Review* 82:1109–27.

Richard L. Pacelle, Jr. 1991. *The Transformation of the Supreme Court's Agenda: From the New Deal to the Reagan Administration.* Boulder, CO: Westview Press.

H. W. Perry, Jr. 1991. *Deciding to Decide: Agenda Setting in the United States Supreme Court.* Cambridge, MA: Harvard University Press.

D. Marie Provine. 1980. *Case Selection in the United States Supreme Court.* Chicago: University of Chicago Press.

S. Sidney Ulmer. 1984. "The Supreme Court's Certiorari Decisions: Conflict as a Predictive Variable." *American Political Science Review* 78:901–11.

Christopher J. W. Zorn. Forthcoming. *On Appeal: United States Government Litigation in the Federal Appellate Courts.* Ann Arbor: University of Michigan Press.

CHAPTER 4

Making Decisions

McCleskey v. Kemp

Social science meets the death penalty. The case of McCleskey v. Kemp *asked the justices to consider whether statistical evidence of a race-conscious system of capital punishment violated the Constitution. What factors influenced their resolution of this case? As judges, the members of the Court are presumably guided by the law, but there is little to constrain them from making decisions based upon other factors. Forces both inside and outside the Court have the potential to shape the outcome of a case and the written opinions supporting it. This chapter explores several possible explanations for decision making on the Supreme Court and concludes that most of what the justices do is guided more by politics than by law.*

In 1983, an article appeared in the *Journal of Criminal Law and Criminology* entitled "Comparative Review of Death Sentences: An Empirical Study of the Georgia Experience." This study reported research findings related to the imposition of the death penalty in the state of Georgia during the 1970s. Conducted by two professors of law and a professor of statistics, the research systematically examined possible explanations for why some convicted murderers were sentenced to death while others were not. After examining a wide variety of factors that might contribute to the sentencing decision, these scholars came to an important conclusion: The death penalty in Georgia was being administered in a racially discriminatory way. Within a short time, this academic study would be propelled into the

91

U.S. Supreme Court, where it would help to establish the basis for a
major challenge to the constitutionality of capital punishment.

This challenge to the death penalty came in the form of a case
entitled *McCleskey v. Kemp*. The case itself began on May 13, 1978.[1]
On that day, four men in Marietta, Georgia—David Burney, Bernard
Dupree, Warren McCleskey, and Ben Wright—set out to commit an
armed robbery. Originally, they conspired to rob a local jewelry store
in Marietta. After canvassing the store that morning, though, they
abandoned their plan. Eager to find an alternative, they drove to
Atlanta in search of other possible targets. There they settled upon a
retail furniture establishment known as the Dixie Furniture Store.
Posing as a potential customer, McCleskey surveyed the store and
then left to meet his accomplices, who were waiting nearby in their
car. Quickly, they hatched a scheme. Shortly thereafter, armed with
several small firearms and a sawed-off shotgun, they raided the
store. From the front, McCleskey entered and ordered the customers
to lie on the floor. Meanwhile, the three other men appeared at the
back door. Finding several store employees, they began to secure
each one with tape. The men then held the manager at gunpoint,
forcing him to surrender the store's assets. This theft netted all of the
store's receipts, along with the manager's watch and a small amount
of cash.

The robbery did not go exactly as planned, however. A silent
alarm had been triggered within the store, and within minutes a police officer named Frank Schlatt arrived on the scene. Officer Schlatt
entered the store, and moments later, two gunshots were fired. The
initial bullet hit Schlatt in the chest, but it ricocheted off his cigarette
lighter and lodged in one of the store's sofas. The second shot,
though, hit the officer in the face and proved to be fatal.

Following the shooting, the four men escaped. Some weeks later,
however, Warren McCleskey was arrested in Cobb County, Georgia,
for his participation in another armed robbery, one unconnected
with the earlier crime. Under questioning from the Atlanta police,
McCleskey admitted to having participated in the robbery of the
Dixie Furniture Store, but he denied shooting Officer Schlatt.

---

[1]The factual description of *McCleskey v. Kemp* 481 U.S. 279 (1987) is adapted from various records from the case, including lower court opinions and briefs, as well as those
of the related case of *McCleskey v. Zant* 499 U.S. 467 (1991).

The evidence was largely to the contrary. It turned out that the deflected bullet from the Dixie Furniture Store shooting—the one recovered from the sofa—was fired from a .38 caliber Rossi revolver, a pearl-handled gun that police believed McCleskey had used in the course of the robbery. The police never found the Rossi revolver that had been used to kill Officer Schlatt, but two months earlier McCleskey had stolen exactly this type of gun in a holdup at a grocery store. Not only that, eyewitnesses had testified that they had seen someone fleeing the Dixie Furniture Store with a white-handled gun. In the store, no one had actually seen the shooting, but witnesses did identify McCleskey as the only one of the four men who was in the front of the store, which was where the shooting took place.

Perhaps most damaging to McCleskey was that two witnesses testified that he had confessed to—indeed, even bragged about—having killed the police officer. One of those witnesses was Ben Wright, one of McCleskey's fellow conspirators in the robbery who, by this time, had been arrested and agreed to testify against him. The other was an inmate in the Fulton County Jail whom the police recruited to help extract incriminating information against McCleskey. Placed in an adjoining cell, this informant successfully sought to win McCleskey's confidence. By his account, McCleskey confessed to the killing, boldly asserting that "he would have tried to shoot his way out [even] if it had been a dozen" police. To be sure, this evidence was largely circumstantial. Nevertheless, it provided every reason to believe that Warren McCleskey had indeed killed Officer Schlatt.

The jurors at McCleskey's trial evidently found the evidence to be persuasive. In October 1978, they convicted McCleskey of Officer Schlatt's murder. Once the jury returned its verdict, the trial court then conducted a sentencing hearing, as required by Georgia law. That is, the jury considered arguments by both the state and the defense regarding the appropriate punishment for the murder. In this instance, the prosecution asked the jury to impose the death penalty. Under the law, though, McCleskey could not be put to death unless the jury concluded that there was at least one "aggravating circumstance." In other words, were there—legally speaking—especially compelling reasons for putting McCleskey to death? These included such factors as whether the person had a prior record of serious crime, had escaped from custody, or had been hired to commit the murder.

In McCleskey's case, the jury determined that there were two aggravating circumstances. He had committed the murder during an armed robbery, and he had murdered an on-duty police officer. At the same time, the law also allowed the jury to consider mitigating circumstances—legitimate reasons for *not* imposing the death penalty—but McCleskey offered no arguments that might offset those aggravating factors. Accordingly, the jury officially recommended the death penalty, a sentence that the trial judge subsequently imposed.

Faced with the possibility of execution, McCleskey initiated a series of appeals over the next three years, challenging both the trial court's conviction and the sentence it imposed. These efforts were uniformly unsuccessful. The Georgia Supreme Court upheld the trial court, and the U.S. Supreme Court, in turn, refused to consider his case. Returning to the state courts of Georgia, he sought a new trial, a request that was later denied. This denial was likewise appealed, and again both the state supreme court and the U.S. Supreme Court rejected his claims.

Then, late in 1981, McCleskey asked a federal trial court in Georgia to reconsider his case. Technically, he sought a writ of habeas corpus; that is, he argued that he was being unlawfully held by Ralph Kemp, the superintendent of the state facility where he was imprisoned.

This time, McCleskey offered new arguments about why his case ought to be reexamined. Specifically, he had evidence that the death penalty in the state of Georgia was implemented in a race-conscious fashion. The evidence took the form of social scientific research conducted by three scholars. David C. Baldus was a professor of law at the University of Iowa, and George Woodworth was his colleague from the Department of Statistics. Together with another law professor, the University of Arizona's Charles Pulaski, they had conducted an extensive study of the death penalty in Georgia. It was a massive analysis of capital punishment in that state, systematically examining over two thousand cases that carried the possibility of a death sentence. Their research sought to answer a straightforward question: Why are some defendants sentenced to death while others are not? Their answer was that it had quite a lot to do with race.

With these data, they had undertaken a number of different studies, each of which suggested that, even when one took into account aggravating factors and other legitimate reasons for imposing

TABLE 4.1 Percentage of Convicted Murderers Sentenced to Death in Georgia

		Death Sentence Imposed?	
Race of the Victim	Race of the Defendant	Yes (%)	No (%)
White	Black	22	78
White	White	8	92
Black	White	3	97
Black	Black	1	99

Source: Research finding of Baldus, Woodworth, and Pulaski, cited in *McCleskey v. Kemp*, p. 286.

death sentences, racial considerations appeared to play a significant role in determining whether the defendant would live or die. Indeed, one of their primary findings was that juries appeared to place a greater value on the lives of whites than on the lives of blacks. It turned out, for example, that in capital cases in which the victim was white, the death penalty was imposed better than 10 percent of the time. By contrast, in cases involving the murder of African Americans, juries almost never sentenced the accused to death; only 1 percent of those convictions resulted in capital punishment.

Interestingly enough, this tendency could be especially pronounced, depending upon the race of the defendant. Their aggregate data, reproduced in Table 4.1, illustrate this effect. These data show that when black victims were involved, juries in Georgia rarely imposed the death penalty, whether the defendant was black or white; in both instances, the rate of death sentencing was quite low, 1 percent and 3 percent, respectively. When the murder victims were white, however, stark differences emerged. Not only did the number of death sentences increase, but the increase was greater for cases in which blacks had committed the crime. White-on-white murders produced death sentences 8 percent of the time, but in cases where blacks were convicted of killing whites, the defendant received the death penalty at a rate of 22 percent, nearly three times more often.[2]

Those who murdered African Americans almost never received the death penalty, regardless of their race. By contrast, those who murdered whites had a higher likelihood of receiving a sentence of death, especially if they were black. All things being equal, race—either the victim's or the defendant's—should not figure into the

[2]These data may be found in *McCleskey v. Kemp*, pp. 286–87.

calculus. Society should punish its offenders equally based upon legitimate legal considerations, not irrational considerations such as race. Here, though, it appeared that this was exactly what juries were doing; they were taking race into account, punishing most severely those blacks who took the lives of whites.

One possibility, of course, was that black-on-white crimes simply involved more aggravating factors. If a large number of the blacks who murdered whites had previously been convicted of similar offenses, for example, one would expect them to be sentenced to death more often. Such circumstances might give the appearance of race-conscious sentencing, but the comparatively higher rate of capital punishment would actually be explained by those aggravating factors. Once aggravating factors were taken into account, such racial disparities might well disappear.

To deal with this possibility, the researchers applied something known as multiple regression to their data. Multiple regression is a sophisticated statistical method that allows researchers to sort out the relative importance of such competing explanations. Invoking it to examine the possible causes of death sentences in Georgia, Baldus and his coauthors concluded that, even when a wide range of other factors were taken into account, cases involving white victims were still better than four times more likely to result in a death sentence than cases where blacks had been killed. In relative terms, the statistical impact of the race of the victim was more important than several other possible considerations, such as the defendant's history of substance abuse. Not only that, the victim's race—which theoretically should have been irrelevant—was just as important as several of the law's aggravating circumstances, including the defendant's record of prior felony convictions. Stated differently, juries were just as likely to impose the death penalty on someone whose victim was white as they were on someone who had a history of serious crime. Evidently, juries thought both issues to be equally relevant to deciding whether the defendant should live or die. Finally, as before, Baldus and his colleagues found that black-on-white murders were still among the most likely to receive the death penalty. Having statistically controlled for virtually every plausible basis for capital punishment in Georgia, these racial disparities persisted.

These findings were particularly relevant to McCleskey's case. McCleskey was African American, and the man whom he was convicted of shooting was white. Citing these findings, McCleskey argued that, if the jury system was biased against blacks—if the system operated so as to place a lesser value on their lives—then the implementation of the death penalty in Georgia violated the U.S. Constitution. The Fourteenth Amendment requires the states to guarantee the equal protection of the laws. Georgia could hardly be treating people equally, McCleskey claimed, if criminal punishments were administered in different ways, depending upon race. Likewise, pointing to the Eighth Amendment's prohibition of cruel and unusual punishment, he maintained that allowing juries to punish defendants so arbitrarily violated that constitutional provision as well.

Given the history of the death penalty in Georgia, McCleskey's arguments were quite plausible. The U.S. Supreme Court had issued two landmark decisions on the constitutionality of the death penalty, both of which originated in Georgia. In *Furman v. Georgia* (1972), the justices considered a similar challenge to the application of capital punishment in that state. Because there were virtually no standards governing when defendants could be sentenced to death, the Court concluded that the death penalty was imposed almost randomly and therefore violated the Eighth Amendment. Recognizing the potential racial undercurrent to the death penalty, Justice William O. Douglas wrote:

> The high service rendered by the 'cruel and unusual' punishment clause of the Eighth Amendment is to require legislatures to write penal laws that are evenhanded, nonselective, and nonarbitrary, and to require judges to see to it that general laws are not applied sparsely, selectively, and spottily to unpopular groups. A law that stated that anyone making more than $50,000 would be exempt from the death penalty would plainly fall, as would a law that in terms said that blacks, those who never went beyond the fifth grade in school, those who made less than $3,000 a year, or those who were unpopular or unstable should be the only people executed. A law which . . . reaches that result in practice has no more sanctity than a law which in terms provides the same. Thus, these discretionary statutes are unconstitutional in their operation. They are pregnant with discrimination and discrimination is an ingredient not compatible with the idea of equal protection of the laws that is implicit in the ban on 'cruel and unusual' punishments.[3]

[3]*Furman v Georgia* 408 U.S. 238 (1972), pp. 256–57.

Without sufficient guidance to juries, the death penalty was unpredictable and left open the possibility of potential abuse. States, therefore, would have to have strict guidelines that governed when capital punishment could be imposed.

Georgia dutifully followed the Court's mandate and rewrote its laws to reduce the potential for arbitrary sentencing. New rules provided guidelines for juries and required the state supreme court to review those decisions. These guidelines were challenged, and in 1976 the justices issued their second major ruling on the death penalty. This time, though, since Georgia had complied with the Court's mandate and provided for more systematic sentencing, its policy on capital punishment was upheld. As Justice Potter Stewart noted, "Georgia's new sentencing procedures require as a prerequisite to the imposition of the death penalty, specific jury findings as to the circumstances of the crime or the character of the defendant. Moreover, to guard further against a situation comparable to that presented in *Furman*, the Supreme Court of Georgia compares each death sentence with the sentences imposed on similarly situated defendants to ensure that the sentence of death in a particular case is not disproportionate."[4] Georgia had given specific guidance to juries and, as a safeguard, demanded supervision by the state supreme court. Through these procedures, Georgia had met its constitutional obligations. With careful legislation, it had minimized the danger of the death penalty being imposed arbitrarily or on a selective basis.

Or had it? The research of Professors Baldus, Woodworth, and Pulaski called Georgia's sentencing system into serious question. If the state's laws really guarded against juries considering such irrelevant factors as race, why did it appear that jurors were taking race into account? Examining cases decided after *Furman v. Georgia*, these scholars concluded that "Georgia is operating a dual system, based upon the race of the victim, for processing homicide cases. Georgia juries appear to tolerate greater levels of aggravation without imposing the death penalty in black victim cases; and, as compared to white victim cases, the level of aggravation in black victim cases must be substantially greater before the prosecutor will even seek a death sentence."[5]

[4]*Gregg v. Georgia* 428 U.S. 153 (1976), p. 198.
[5]David C. Baldus, Charles Pulaski, and George Woodworth, "Comparative Review of Death Sentences: An Empirical Study of the Georgia Experience," *Journal of Criminal Law and Criminology* 74:661–753 (1983), pp. 709–10.

A leading authority on the use of statistics in legal proceedings, David Baldus had written extensively about using statistical methods to demonstrate patterns of discrimination, and some of his work analyzing Georgia's system of capital punishment had already been published by the time McCleskey turned to the federal courts for help. So, to muster support for the argument that Georgia's juries were biased, McCleskey's attorneys asked Professor Baldus to provide testimony that described the results of his and his coauthors' research. In that testimony, he focused on the apparent racial bias and when it seemed to enter into the jury's decision. He noted that, as a result of considering aggravating and mitigating circumstances, jurors naturally faced some cases where the arguments for imposing the death penalty—or sparing the defendant's life—were exceptionally strong. In those cases, the sentencing decisions were made without regard to race.

Inevitably, however, there were cases where these aggravating and mitigating factors did not point overwhelmingly in one direction or the other; in those instances, the race of the victim appeared to explain why some defendants received the death penalty while others did not. He explained that "when the cases become tremendously aggravated so that everybody would agree that if we're going to have a death sentence, these are the cases that should get it, the race effects go away. It's only in the mid-range of cases where the decisionmakers have a real choice as to what to do. If there's room for the exercise of discretion, then the [racial] factors begin to play a role." Classifying cases along a scale, from "least aggravated" to "most aggravated," Baldus's research revealed that, within that middle range, only 14 percent of defendants who murdered blacks were sentenced to death. Those who murdered whites were given the death penalty at least twice as often, 34 percent of the time.[6] According to Baldus, McCleskey's case fell within that middle range. In other words, this was precisely the type of case in which Georgia's juries appeared to make race a determining factor when imposing the death penalty.

After weighing this evidence, however, Judge J. Owen Forrester was skeptical of McCleskey's claims. He concluded that errors were made in assembling the information used in Baldus's research and that important details relevant to death sentencing had not been

[6]*McCleskey v. Kemp,* p. 287, n. 2.

included. Since he questioned the reliability of the data and the conclusions derived from them, Judge Forrester rejected McCleskey's arguments.

Turning next to a federal appellate court—the U.S. Court of Appeals for the Eleventh Circuit—McCleskey again sought to use the statistical analyses to support his legal claims of discrimination. Unlike Judge Forrester, this court assumed that the Baldus research was valid and that it documented a genuine disparity in sentencing along racial lines. What these statistics did not show, said the appeals court, was that Georgia actually set out to discriminate against defendants, based upon the race of murder victims. All that the research demonstrated was that, after taking account of everything that Baldus and his colleagues believed juries *might* consider—not what juries actually *did* consider—there were sentencing disparities related to the race of the victim. These professors decided to label this as unlawful discrimination, but those results could just as easily have been the product of other factors that jurors considered but that the researchers never included in their study.

Warren McCleskey, twice denied by lower federal courts, decided to take his case to the U.S. Supreme Court. Still hoping to use the Baldus study to challenge the death penalty in Georgia, he petitioned the Court, and in July 1986 the justices granted review. When the Court began its new term in October of that year, one of the first cases on its docket was *McCleskey v. Kemp*.

AN OVERVIEW OF THE PROCESS

Did the Baldus study demonstrate that Georgia's system of capital punishment was unconstitutional? In making a decision on the merits of this issue, the justices began by considering the written arguments of both parties. As with most cases, lawyers for each side filed briefs outlining their arguments and the relevant laws and court decisions supporting them.[7] McCleskey's attorneys had filed their merits brief in early September, and Georgia followed with its brief

---

[7]The justices can dispense with these procedures. Occasionally, the justices will rely upon the petition for certiorari and the brief in opposition to render a decision. See Stephen L. Wasby, *The Supreme Court in the Federal Judicial System*, 4th ed. (Chicago: Nelson-Hall Publisher, 1993), pp. 206–8.

later that month. Thus, when the justices convened to hear oral arguments, they had already begun to consider the legal positions that were being staked out by both parties.

On October 15, 1986, the justices heard arguments in *McCleskey v. Kemp*, one of four cases that were argued that day.[8] The Court's new term had just begun the previous week, as federal law required, "on the first Monday in October," and the justices were concluding their regular cycle of hearing arguments on Mondays, Tuesdays, and Wednesdays of the first two weeks of the month. Two days later at the Court's Friday conference, the justices met to discuss and vote on the outcome of the case. Following their deliberations, the justices voted 5-4 to reject McCleskey's claims and to uphold the decision of the appeals court. Justice Lewis Powell was assigned the responsibility of writing an opinion on behalf of the Court, that is, a statement outlining the justices' decision and the reasons behind it. By the spring of the following year, he and his law clerks had drafted an opinion that was acceptable to the other members of the Court's majority. For their part, the four dissenting justices—those who disagreed with the majority's interpretation of the law—drafted opinions of their own in which they supported McCleskey and explained why they would have resolved the case differently. These opinions, excerpted in Box 4.1, would necessarily reflect the divisions over both law and policy that existed among the justices. On April 22, 1987, the Supreme Court announced its ruling that statistical evidence of racial disparities in death sentences violated neither the guarantee of equal protection of the laws nor the ban on cruel and unusual punishments.[9]

---

[8]Obviously, the number of cases that the justices resolve depends upon the number of cases they agree to hear, and in recent years, the justices have granted review to a smaller number of cases compared to earlier periods in the modern Court's history. During the 1986 term, for example, *McCleskey v. Kemp* was one of roughly 150 cases decided. Less than ten years later, however, that number had declined by almost half. As a result of its shrinking plenary docket, the current Court only hears about two cases per day. See Lee Epstein, Jeffrey A. Segal, Harold J. Spaeth, and Thomas G. Walker, *The Supreme Court Compendium: Data, Decisions, and Developments* (Washington, D.C.: Congressional Quarterly, Inc., 1996), Table 3-2.

[9]For more details on the Court's procedures for decision making, see Joan Biskupic and Elder Witt, *Guide to the U.S. Supreme Court*, 3rd ed. (Washington: Congressional Quarterly, Inc., 1997), pp. 788–89; and Wasby, *The Supreme Court*, pp. 224–35.

BOX 4.1

Excerpts of Written Opinions in McCleskey v. Kemp

McCLESKEY v. KEMP, 481 U.S. 279 (1987)

McCLESKEY v. KEMP, SUPERINTENDENT, GEORGIA DIAGNOSTIC AND CLASSIFICATION CENTER

CERTIORARI TO THE UNITED STATES COURT OF APPEALS

FOR THE ELEVENTH CIRCUIT

No. 84-6811.

Argued October 15, 1986

Decided April 22, 1987

POWELL, J., delivered the opinion of the Court, in which REHN-QUIST, C. J., and WHITE, O'CONNOR, and SCALIA, JJ., joined.

This case presents the question whether a complex statistical study that indicates a risk that racial considerations enter into capital sentencing determinations proves that petitioner McCleskey's capital sentence is unconstitutional under the Eighth or Fourteenth Amendment. . . .

Our analysis begins with the basic principle that a defendant who alleges an equal protection violation has the burden of proving "the existence of purposeful discrimination." . . . Thus, to prevail under the Equal Protection Clause, McCleskey must prove that the decision-makers in his case acted with discriminatory purpose. He offers no evidence specific to his own case that would support an inference that racial considerations played a part in his sentence. Instead, he relies solely on the Baldus study. McCleskey argues that the Baldus study compels an inference that his sentence rests on purposeful discrimination. McCleskey's claim that these statistics are sufficient proof of discrimination, without regard to the facts of a particular case, would extend to all capital cases in Georgia, at least where the victim was white and the defendant is black. . . . [But] a legitimate and unchallenged explanation for the decision is apparent from the record: McCleskey committed an act for which the United States Constitution and Georgia laws permit imposition of the death penalty. . . .

McCleskey's statistical proffer must be viewed in the context of his challenge. McCleskey challenges decisions at the heart of the State's criminal justice system. "[O]ne of society's most basic tasks is that of protecting the lives of its citizens and one of the most basic ways in which it achieves the task is through criminal laws against murder." Implementation of these laws necessarily requires discretionary judgments. Because discretion is essential to the criminal justice process, we would demand exceptionally clear proof before we would infer that the discretion has been abused. The unique nature of the decisions at issue in this case also counsels against adopting such an inference from the disparities indicated by the Baldus study. Accordingly, we hold that the Baldus study is clearly insufficient to support an inference that any of the decisionmakers in McCleskey's case acted with discriminatory purpose.

McCleskey also argues that the Baldus study demonstrates that the Georgia capital sentencing system violates the Eighth Amendment. . . . Because McCleskey's sentence was imposed under Georgia sentencing procedures that focus discretion "on the particularized nature of the crime and the particularized characteristics of the individual defendant," we lawfully may presume that McCleskey's death sentence was not "wantonly and freakishly" imposed, and thus that the sentence is not disproportionate within any recognized meaning under the Eighth Amendment.

. . . [H]e further contends that the Georgia capital punishment system is arbitrary and capricious in application, and therefore his sentence is excessive, because racial considerations may influence capital sentencing decisions in Georgia. We now address this claim.

To evaluate McCleskey's challenge, we must examine exactly what the Baldus study may show. Even Professor Baldus does not contend that his statistics prove that race enters into any capital sentencing decisions or that race was a factor in McCleskey's particular case. Statistics at most may show only a likelihood that a particular factor entered into some decisions. There is, of course, some risk of racial prejudice influencing a jury's decision in a criminal case. There are similar risks that other kinds of prejudice will influence other criminal trials. The question "is at what point that risk becomes constitutionally unacceptable." McCleskey asks us to accept the likelihood allegedly shown by the Baldus study as the constitutional measure of an unacceptable risk of racial prejudice influencing capital sentencing decisions. This we decline to do. . . .

Individual jurors bring to their deliberations "qualities of human nature and varieties of human experience, the range of which is unknown and perhaps unknowable." The capital sentencing decision requires the individual jurors to focus their collective judgment on the unique characteristics of a particular criminal defendant. It is not surprising that such collective judgments often are difficult to explain. But the inherent lack of predictability of jury decisions does not justify their condemnation. On the contrary, it is the jury's function to make the difficult and uniquely human judgments that defy codification and that "buil[d] discretion, equity, and flexibility into a legal system."

McCleskey's argument that the Constitution condemns the discretion allowed decisionmakers in the Georgia capital sentencing system is antithetical to the fundamental role of discretion in our criminal justice system. Discretion in the criminal justice system offers substantial benefits to the criminal defendant. Not only can a jury decline to impose the death sentence, it can decline to convict or choose to convict of a lesser offense. Whereas decisions against a defendant's interest may be reversed by the trial judge or on appeal, these discretionary exercises of leniency are final and unreviewable. Similarly, the capacity of prosecutorial discretion to provide individualized justice is "firmly entrenched in American law." As we have noted, a prosecutor can decline to charge, offer a plea bargain, or decline to seek a death sentence in any particular case. Of course, "the power to be lenient [also] is the power to discriminate," but a capital punishment system that did not allow for discretionary acts of leniency "would be totally alien to our notions of criminal justice."

At most, the Baldus study indicates a discrepancy that appears to correlate with race. Apparent disparities in sentencing are an inevitable part of our criminal justice system. The discrepancy indicated by the Baldus study is "a far cry from the major systemic defects identified in *Furman*." As this Court has recognized, any mode for determining guilt or punishment "has its weaknesses and the potential for misuse." Specifically, "there can be 'no perfect procedure for deciding in which cases governmental authority should be used to impose death.'" Despite these imperfections, our consistent rule has been that constitutional guarantees are met when "the mode [for determining guilt or punishment] itself has been surrounded with safeguards to make it as fair as possible." Where the discretion that is fundamental to our criminal process is involved, we decline to assume that what is unexplained is invidious. In light of the safeguards designed to minimize racial bias in the process, the fundamental value of jury trial in our criminal justice system, and the benefits that discretion provides to criminal defendants, we hold that the Baldus study does not demonstrate a constitutionally significant risk of racial bias affecting the Georgia capital sentencing process.

Two additional concerns inform our decision in this case. First, McCleskey's claim, taken to its logical conclusion, throws into serious question the principles that underlie our entire criminal justice system. The Eighth Amendment is not limited in application to capital punishment, but applies to all penalties. Thus, if we accepted McCleskey's claim that racial bias has impermissibly tainted the capital sentencing decision, we could soon be faced with similar claims as to other types of penalty. Moreover, the claim that his sentence rests on the irrelevant factor of race easily could be extended to apply to claims based on unexplained discrepancies that correlate to membership in other minority groups, and even to gender. Similarly, since McCleskey's claim relates to the race of his victim, other claims could apply with equally logical force to statistical disparities that correlate with the race or sex of other actors in the criminal justice system, such as defense attorneys, or judges. Also, there is no logical reason that such a claim need be limited to racial or sexual bias. If arbitrary and capricious punishment is the touchstone under the Eighth Amendment, such a claim could—at least in theory—be based upon any arbitrary variable, such as the defendant's facial characteristics, or the physical attractiveness of the defendant or the victim, that some statistical study indicates may be influential in jury decisionmaking. As these examples illustrate, there is no limiting principle to the type of challenge brought by McCleskey. . . . The Constitution does not require that a State eliminate any demonstrable disparity that correlates with a potentially irrelevant factor in order to operate a criminal justice system that includes capital punishment. As we have stated specifically in the context of capital punishment, the Constitution does not "plac[e] totally unrealistic conditions on its use."

Second, McCleskey's arguments are best presented to the legislative bodies. It is not the responsibility—or indeed even the right—of this Court to determine the appropriate punishment for particular crimes. It is the legislatures, the elected representatives of the people, that are "constituted to respond to the will and consequently the moral values of the people." Legislatures also are better qualified to weigh and "evaluate the results of statistical studies in terms of their own local conditions and with a flexibility of approach that is not available to the courts." Capital punishment is now the law in more than two-thirds of our States. It is the ultimate duty of courts to determine on a case-by-case basis whether these laws are applied consistently with the Constitution. Despite

McCleskey's wide-ranging arguments that basically challenge the validity of capital punishment in our multiracial society, the only question before us is whether in his case the law of Georgia was properly applied. We agree with the District Court and the Court of Appeals for the Eleventh Circuit that this was carefully and correctly done in this case.

Accordingly, we affirm the judgment of the Court of Appeals for the Eleventh Circuit.

It is so ordered.

Justice BRENNAN, with whom Justice BLACKMUN, MARSHALL, and STEVENS join, dissenting.

At some point in this case, Warren McCleskey doubtless asked his lawyer whether a jury was likely to sentence him to die. A candid reply to this question would have been disturbing. First, counsel would have to tell McCleskey that few of the details of the crime or of McCleskey's past criminal conduct were more important than the fact that his victim was white. Furthermore, counsel would feel bound to tell McCleskey that defendants charged with killing white victims in Georgia are 4.3 times as likely to be sentenced to death as defendants charged with killing blacks. In addition, frankness would compel the disclosure that it was more likely than not that the race of McCleskey's victim would determine whether he received a death sentence: 6 of every 11 defendants convicted of killing a white person would not have received the death penalty if their victims had been black, while, among defendants with aggravating and mitigating factors comparable to McCleskey's, 20 of every 34 would not have been sentenced to die if their victims had been black. Finally, the assessment would not be complete without the information that cases involving black defendants and white victims are more likely to result in a death sentence than cases featuring any other racial combination of defendant and victim. The story could be told in a variety of ways, but McCleskey could not fail to grasp its essential narrative line: there was a significant chance that race would play a prominent role in determining if he lived or died.

The Court today holds that Warren McCleskey's sentence was constitutionally imposed. It finds no fault in a system in which lawyers must tell their clients that race casts a large shadow on the capital sentencing process. The Court arrives at this conclusion by stating that the Baldus study cannot "prove that race enters into any capital sentencing decisions or that race was a factor in McCleskey's particular case." Since, according to Professor Baldus, we cannot say "to a moral certainty" that race influenced a decision, we can identify only "a likelihood that a particular factor entered into some decisions," and "a discrepancy that appears to correlate with race." This "likelihood" and "discrepancy," holds the Court, is insufficient to establish a constitutional violation. . . .

It is important to emphasize at the outset that the Court's observation that McCleskey cannot prove the influence of race on any particular sentencing decision is irrelevant in evaluating his Eighth Amendment claim. Since *Furman v. Georgia,* the Court has been concerned with the risk of the imposition of an arbitrary sentence, rather than the proven fact of one. *Furman* held that the death penalty "may not be imposed under sentencing procedures that create a substantial risk that the punishment will be inflicted in an arbitrary and capricious manner." . . . Defendants challenging their death sentences thus never have had to prove that impermissible considerations have actually infected sentencing decisions. We have required instead that they establish that the system under which they were sentenced posed a significant risk of such an occurrence. McCleskey's claim does differ, however, in one respect from these earlier cases: it is the first to base a challenge not on speculation about how a system might operate, but on empirical documentation of how it does operate. . . .

The statistical evidence in this case thus relentlessly documents the risk that McCleskey's sentence was influenced by racial considerations. This evidence shows that there is a better than even chance in Georgia that race will influence the decision to impose the death penalty: a majority of defendants in white-victim crimes would not have been sentenced to die if their victims had been black. In determining the guilt of a defendant, a State must prove its case beyond a reasonable doubt. That is, we refuse to convict if the chance of error is simply less likely than not. Surely, we should not be willing to take a person's life if the chance that his death sentence was irrationally imposed is more likely than not. In light of the gravity of the interest at stake, petitioner's statistics on their face are a powerful demonstration of the type of risk that our Eighth Amendment jurisprudence has consistently condemned. . . .

The Court next states that its unwillingness to regard petitioner's evidence as sufficient is based in part on the fear that recognition of McCleskey's claim would open the door to widespread challenges to all aspects of criminal sentencing. Taken on its face, such a statement seems to suggest a fear of too much justice. Yet surely the majority would acknowledge that if striking evidence indicated that other minority groups, or women, or even persons with blond hair, were disproportionately sentenced to death, such a state of affairs would be repugnant to deeply rooted conceptions of fairness. The prospect that there may be more widespread abuse than McCleskey documents may be dismaying, but it does not justify complete abdication of our judicial role. The Constitution was framed fundamentally as a bulwark against governmental power, and preventing the arbitrary administration of punishment is a basic ideal of any society that purports to be governed by the rule of law. . . .

The Court's decision today will not change what attorneys in Georgia tell other Warren McCleskeys about their chances of execution. Nothing will soften the harsh message they must convey, nor alter the prospect that race undoubtedly will continue to be a topic of discussion. McCleskey's evidence will not have obtained judicial acceptance, but that will not affect what is said on death row. However many criticisms of today's decision may be rendered, these painful conversations will serve as the most eloquent dissents of all.

Justice BLACKMUN, with whom Justice BRENNAN, Justice MARSHALL, and Justice STEVENS join, dissenting.

The Court today sanctions the execution of a man despite his presentation of evidence that establishes a constitutionally intolerable level of racially based discrimination leading to the imposition of his death sentence. I am disappointed with the Court's action not only because of its denial of constitutional guarantees to petitioner McCleskey individually, but also because of its departure from what seems to me to be well-developed constitutional jurisprudence.

Justice BRENNAN has thoroughly demonstrated that, if one assumes that the statistical evidence presented by petitioner McCleskey is valid, . . . there exists in the Georgia capital sentencing scheme a risk of racially based discrimination that is so acute that it violates the Eighth Amendment. . . . Yet McCleskey's case raises concerns that are central not only to the principles underlying the Eighth Amendment, but also to the principles underlying the Fourteenth Amendment. Analysis of his case in terms of the Fourteenth Amendment is consistent with this Court's recognition that racial discrimination is fundamentally at odds with our constitutional guarantee of equal protection. . . .

A criminal defendant alleging an equal protection violation must prove the existence of purposeful discrimination. . . . Under *Batson v. Kentucky* . . . McCleskey must meet a three-factor standard. First, he must establish that he is a member of a group "that is a recognizable, distinct class, singled out for different treatment." Second, he must make a showing of a substantial degree of differential treatment. Third, he must establish that the allegedly discriminatory procedure is susceptible to abuse or is not racially neutral.

There can be no dispute that McCleskey has made the requisite showing under the first prong of the standard. The Baldus study demonstrates that black persons are a distinct group that are singled out for different treatment in the Georgia capital sentencing system. . . . With respect to the second prong, McCleskey must prove that there is a substantial likelihood that his death sentence is due to racial factors. . . . The most persuasive evidence of the constitutionally significant effect of racial factors in the Georgia capital sentencing system is McCleskey's proof that the race of the victim is more important in explaining the imposition of a death sentence than is the factor whether the defendant was a prime mover in the homicide. Similarly, the race-of-victim factor is nearly as crucial as the statutory aggravating circumstance whether the defendant had a prior record of a conviction for a capital crime. . . . As to the final element of the prima facie case, McCleskey showed that the process by which the State decided to seek a death penalty in his case and to pursue that sentence throughout the prosecution was susceptible to abuse. . . .

The above-described evidence, considered in conjunction with the other record evidence outlined by Justice BRENNAN and discussed in opinions dissenting from the judgment of the Court of Appeals, gives rise to an inference of discriminatory purpose. McCleskey's showing is of sufficient magnitude that, absent evidence to the contrary, one must conclude that racial factors entered into the decisionmaking process that yielded McCleskey's death sentence. The burden, therefore, shifts to the State to explain the racial selections. It must demonstrate that legitimate racially neutral criteria and procedures yielded this racially skewed result. . . .

The State did not test its hypothesis to determine if white-victim and black-victim cases at the same level of aggravating circumstances were similarly treated. McCleskey's experts, however, performed this test on their data. They demonstrated that the racial disparities in the system were not the result of the differences in the average aggravation levels between white-victim and black-victim cases. The State's meager and unsophisticated evidence cannot withstand the extensive scrutiny given the Baldus evidence. . . .

One of the final concerns discussed by the Court may be the most disturbing aspect of its opinion. Granting relief to McCleskey in this case, it is said, could lead to further constitutional challenges. That, of course, is no reason to deny McCleskey his rights under the Equal Protection Clause. If a grant of relief to him were to lead to a closer examination of the effects of racial considerations throughout the criminal justice system, the system, and hence society, might benefit. Where no such factors come into play, the integrity of the system is enhanced. Where such considerations are shown to be significant, efforts can be made to eradicate their impermissible influence and to ensure an evenhanded application of criminal sanctions.

I dissent.

Justice STEVENS, with whom Justice BLACKMUN joins, dissenting.

In this case it is claimed—and the claim is supported by elaborate studies which the Court properly assumes to be valid—that the jury's sentencing process was likely distorted by racial prejudice. The studies demonstrate a strong probability that McCleskey's sentencing jury . . . was influenced by the fact that McCleskey is black and his victim was white. . . . This sort of disparity is constitutionally intolerable. It flagrantly violates the Court's prior "insistence that capital punishment be imposed fairly, and with reasonable consistency, or not at all."

The Court's decision appears to be based on a fear that the acceptance of McCleskey's claim would sound the death knell for capital punishment in Georgia. If society were indeed forced to choose between a racially discriminatory death penalty (one that provides heightened protection against murder "for whites only") and no death penalty at all, the choice mandated by the Constitution would be plain. But the Court's fear is unfounded. One of the lessons of the Baldus study is that there exist certain categories of extremely serious crimes for which prosecutors consistently seek, and juries consistently impose, the death penalty without regard to the race of the victim or the race of the offender. If Georgia were to narrow the class of death-eligible defendants to those categories, the danger of arbitrary and discriminatory imposition of the death penalty would be significantly decreased, if not eradicated. As Justice Brennan has demonstrated in his dissenting opinion, such a restructuring of the sentencing scheme is surely not too high a price to pay.

Like Justice Brennan, I would therefore reverse the judgment of the Court of Appeals. I believe, however, that further proceedings are necessary in order to determine whether McCleskey's death sentence should be set aside. First, the Court of Appeals must decide whether the Baldus study is valid. I am persuaded that it is, but orderly procedure requires that the Court of Appeals address this issue before we actually decide the question. Second, it is necessary for the District Court to determine whether the particular facts of McCleskey's crime and his background place this case within the range of cases that present an unacceptable risk that race played a decisive role in McCleskey's sentencing.

Accordingly, I respectfully dissent.

WHAT SHAPES JUDICIAL DECISION MAKING?

Why did the Supreme Court decide *McCleskey v. Kemp* as it did? Why did some members of the Court support Warren McCleskey and others vote in favor of the state of Georgia? Did legal considerations determine how the justices viewed the case, or did factors unrelated to the law affect the Court's outcome? What explains the substantive content of the Court's decision? Political scientists have spent a good deal of time trying to answer such questions. As a result, much is known about why the justices make the decisions that they do. In fact, considering the weight of the research on these issues, the outcome in this case is, in many respects, quite predictable.

Legal Factors

A good starting point for explaining the decisions of the justices is the law. Laws are crafted to embody certain principles, and it is the task of judges to identify those principles and apply them to individual cases. Naturally, the justices can and do disagree over how to identify those principles. The conclusions that they reach are often dictated by the particular methods of legal analysis that they bring to bear in a case.

Some members of the Court, for example, believe it necessary to turn to the intentions of those who framed the law for guidance in decision making, while others rely upon the literal text of the law to divine its meaning. Both of these influences—original intent and literalism—can be seen in the Court's treatment of the death penalty. In the earlier case of *Gregg v. Georgia*, where the constitutionality of capital punishment was at issue, Justice Potter Stewart noted:

> It is apparent from the text of the Constitution itself that the existence of capital punishment was accepted by the Framers. At the time the Eighth Amendment was ratified, capital punishment was a common sanction in every State. Indeed, the First Congress of the United States enacted legislation providing death as the penalty for specified crimes. The Fifth Amendment, adopted at the same time as the Eighth, contemplated the continued existence of the capital sanction by imposing certain limits on the prosecution of capital cases. . . . And the Fourteenth Amendment, adopted over three-quarters of a century later, similarly contemplates the existence of the capital sanction in providing that no State shall deprive any person of "life, liberty, or property" without due process of law.[10]

In Justice Stewart's view, the death penalty could not be considered cruel and unusual punishment since it was widely used at the time the Eighth Amendment was put into effect. If that amendment were supposed to eliminate capital punishment, then the laws allowing for capital punishment should have been repealed when that constitutional change was put into effect in the late 1700s. Not only that, reasoned Stewart, both the Fifth and Fourteenth Amendments explicitly recognize the constitutionality of the death penalty: The very words indicate that, in criminal cases, government can "deprive any person of life," provided it follows fair procedures when doing so.

While neither literalism nor original intent seems to have played a dominant role in the *McCleskey v. Kemp* decision, one method of legal analysis that was of greater relevance was the use of the Supreme Court's prior rulings as a basis for decision making. This is known more formally as "the doctrine of precedent, under which the judges refer to a previous decision or decisions in order to adjudicate the case at issue."[11] The idea is that, in order to provide a consistent interpretation of the law, comparable cases need to be resolved in a similar fashion. Thus, once a legal principle is established by the Court, the justices should apply the law in the same fashion across similar circumstances.

---

[10] *Gregg v. Georgia*, p. 177.
[11] Henry J. Abraham, *The Judicial Process*, 7th ed. (New York: Oxford University Press, 1998), p. 9.

Adhering to the standards of law derived from earlier cases is, as the Court puts it, "the means by which we ensure that the law will not merely change erratically, but will develop in a principled and intelligible fashion. That doctrine permits society to presume that bedrock principles are founded in the law rather than in the proclivities of individuals, and thereby contributes to the integrity of our constitutional system of government, both in appearance and in fact."[12] Precedent should, therefore, figure prominently in explaining how the justices make decisions.

Interestingly enough, the evidence that the justices base their decisions primarily upon precedent is not overwhelming. In fact, research suggests that prior decisions rarely, if ever, actually affect how the justices vote in a case.[13] The reasons are not hard to understand. Among other things, there is no higher court to ensure that the justices faithfully adhere to past decisions, so as a result, "the Court is much freer to reach what it regards as the correct or wise decision than any subordinate tribunal."[14] In addition, there is an enormous body of case law from which the justices can draw when making decisions. Even the most conscientious justices will inevitably find precedents to support both sides of a case. "Reliance upon precedent presents difficult problems to the judge, especially since the question to be resolved comes, normally speaking, to a *choice* of precedents," explains one scholar. "Precedents abound and not all precedents are of equal rank."[15] Whatever one's conclusion about a case, there is typically enough precedent to support it. Therefore, justices who write opinions will typically cite prior cases to *support* their decisions. But that is not the same as suggesting that those cases actually *affected* their decisions.

The difficulties in choosing from competing precedents is easily illustrated in *McCleskey v. Kemp*. Here, one of the central issues that the Supreme Court had to confront was whether the evidence from the Baldus study could be used to demonstrate that Georgia's system of sentencing violated the Equal Protection Clause of the Fourteenth

---

[12]*Vasquez v. Hillery* 474 U.S. 254 (1986), pp. 265–66.
[13]Harold J. Spaeth and Jeffrey A. Segal, *Majority Rule of Minority Will: Adherence to Precedent on the U.S. Supreme Court* (Cambridge: Cambridge University Press, 1999).
[14]Robert L. Stern, Eugene Gressman, and Stephen M. Shapiro, *Supreme Court Practice*, 6th ed. (Washington: Bureau of National Affairs, Inc., 1986), p. 560.
[15]Abraham, *The Judicial Process*, p. 361.

Amendment. Table 4.2 shows that, relying upon the Court's precedents, one could have made a legally persuasive case for either side.
On the one hand, *Gomillion v. Lightfoot* had established that one could
use statistical disparities to show that racial discrimination had occurred, and under *Bazemore v. Friday*, those disparities would only
have to suggest that, on balance, they were the result of illegal discrimination. This is precisely what the Baldus study did; it was a
quantitative analysis that documented racial disparities in Georgia's
system of capital punishment, and since it controlled for a great many
other possible explanations, the research suggested that those disparities were probably the product of race-conscious sentencing. Thus,
within the Court's prior decisions, there was clearly a legal foundation for deciding the case in McCleskey's favor.

On the other hand, the Court had also ruled in *Washington v.
Davis* that state policies that affected one race more adversely than
another were not constitutionally suspect, unless it could be shown
that the state actually set out to produce those differences. Based on
statistics, the Court was willing to infer that intentional discrimination had occurred, but the Court indicated in *Arlington Heights v.
Metropolitan Housing Corp.* that the supporting data would have to be
so strong that it could not be interpreted otherwise. Again, the circumstances in *McCleskey v. Kemp* seemed to fit these contradictory
precedents equally well. The Baldus study clearly showed that defendants were treated differently, depending upon the race of their
victims, but there was no evidence that either the state or its jurors
had actually used race as a basis for sentencing. And, since the data
also showed that some murders were so aggravated that the defendant was almost certain to be sentenced to death—no matter what
the victim's race—one could hardly claim that racial considerations
always determined who lived and who died. Based upon these
precedents, one could have made an equally compelling argument
that the state of Georgia should prevail.

Since there are usually competing precedents from which the
members of the Court can choose, it is not difficult to understand
why even the justices who disagree with one another can use precedents to justify their decisions.[16] In writing on behalf of the majority

---

[16]Glenn A. Phelps and John B. Gates, "The Myth of Jurisprudence: Interpretive Theory
in the Constitutional Opinions of Justices Rehnquist and Brennan," *Santa Clara Law
Review* 31:567 (1991).

TABLE 4.2 Sample of Precedents Available to the Justices in *McCleskey v. Kemp*

Can Statistics Be Used to Demonstrate Discrimination?	
In Support of McCleskey	In Support of Kemp
(Yes) A statistical pattern of racially discriminatory impact is sufficient to demonstrate a violation of the Equal Protection Clause. *Gomillion v. Lightfoot* (1960)	(No) Racially discriminatory impact is not sufficient to show a violation of the Equal Protection Clause. Proof of intent to discriminate is required. *Washington v. Davis* (1976)

Does the Evidence of Discrimination Have to Be Conclusive?	
In Support of McCleskey	In Support of Kemp
(No) The evidence need only show that it is more likely than not that unlawful discrimination exists. *Bazemore v. Friday* (1986)	(Yes) Unless discrimination is so stark that it can only be explained by race, additional evidence of intent to discriminate is required. *Arlington Heights v. Metropolitan Housing Corp.* (1977)

in *McCleskey*, Justice Powell could cite several dozen precedents that supported the majority's decision. At the same time, Justices Harry Blackmun, William Brennan, and John Paul Stevens each wrote dissenting opinions that likewise relied heavily upon the Court's prior cases. If precedent sufficiently supported a decision for either McCleskey or Georgia, then it is doubtful that it actually determined the votes of any of the justices. A more plausible interpretation is that precedent serves the useful function of justifying a decision that a justice has made for other reasons. What might those reasons be?

Ideology

Probably the best explanation for decision making on the Supreme Court lies in the personal policy preferences of its members. Given that the Constitution provides the justices with lifetime tenure and no higher court to overrule them, they are largely unconstrained in their behavior. Theoretically they are free to act on the basis of their own ideological views about how cases should be resolved. In fact, the evidence is quite strong that the justices do exactly that: Justices who have identifiably liberal values tend to vote in a liberal direction, while those who are more conservative, by contrast, tend to vote conservatively.[17]

In a number of different ways, political scientists have used the attitudes of the justices to illuminate their behavior. Some scholars, for example, have found that the justices display a great deal of ideological consistency in their voting. That is, the members of the Court vote either liberally or conservatively with considerable regularity—no matter what the written law, the Court's precedents, or other legal factors might seem to suggest.[18] Others have used materials available at the time of each justice's nomination to the Court to develop a measure of the nominee's policy attitudes. These ideological scores correspond quite closely to their actual voting behavior once they are on the Court.[19]

One way to see the relevance of the justices' attitudes in *McCleskey v. Kemp* is to identify their preferences in the area of criminal law and compare those preferences to their voting in that case. If ideology explains the choices they make, then the more liberal justices should have voted in favor of McCleskey, while the more conservative members should have supported the government. A straightforward indicator of the justices' attitudes is their votes cast in other cases involving criminal law. By this measure, some justices reveal their liberalism by frequently voting in favor of the accused, while other justices indicate their conservatism by more often siding with the state.

Following this approach, Figure 4.1 arrays the justices—and their respective votes—along an ideological continuum. The Court's more liberal members, such as William Brennan and Thurgood Marshall, appear at the left, while the more conservative justices, such as Sandra Day O'Connor and William Rehnquist, are to the

[17]Jeffrey A. Segal and Harold J. Spaeth, *The Supreme Court and the Attitudinal Model* (Cambridge: Cambridge University Press, 1993).

[18]David W. Rohde and Harold J. Spaeth, *Supreme Court Decision Making* (San Francisco: W. H. Freeman, 1976); Glendon Schubert, *The Judicial Mind* (Evanston, IL: Northwestern University Press, 1965).

[19]Jeffrey A. Segal and Albert D. Cover, "Ideological Values and the Votes of the U.S. Supreme Court Justices," *American Political Science Review* 83:557–65 (1989).

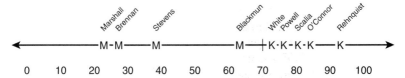

FIGURE 4.1 Justices' Ideology in Criminal Law and Votes in *McCleskey v. Kemp*. High ideological scores reflect greater conservatism. Each justice's ideology is marked on the line, denoted by either *M* or *K*. *M* indicates a vote for McCleskey, and *K* indicates a vote for Kemp.
Source: McCleskey v. Kemp (1987) and Lee Epstein, Jeffrey A. Segal, Harold J. Spaeth, and Thomas G. Walker, *The Supreme Court Compendium: Data, Decisions, and Developments,* 2nd ed. (Washington: Congressional Quarterly, Inc., 1996)

right. By this reckoning, their votes are perfectly consistent with their preferences: The five most conservative justices all voted in favor of the state of Georgia, while the Court's four most liberal members cast their votes in favor of McCleskey.

A reasonable interpretation of these data is that the justices voted on the basis of their policy preferences toward the rights of the accused. Some justices simply favored giving states the discretion to impose the death penalty, while others believed that capital punishment was not—or perhaps could never be—constitutionally administered. Stated differently, Georgia's argument against using statistics to demonstrate discrimination in death sentencing was closer to the preferences of the five justices in the majority, while Mc-Cleskey's argument in favor of permitting the use of the Baldus study was closer to the minority's preferences. If attitudes were irrelevant, then they would provide no basis for interpreting their behavior; Justice Brennan would be no less likely to vote to uphold Georgia's death sentences than Chief Justice Rehnquist. As it turns out, though, knowing something about the justices' ideological orientations provides a reliable basis for predicting their voting behavior on the Court.

Seen in this way, the votes of Justices O'Connor, Powell, Scalia, Rehnquist, and White do not reflect a shared interpretation of the Eighth and Fourteenth Amendments. Neither do the votes of Justices Blackmun, Brennan, Marshall, and Stevens indicate a mutual commitment to the Court's precedents. Instead, it appears that the justices arrived at their decisions by asking which party's policy position was closer to their own preferences and then casting their votes accordingly. Of course, this does not mean that legal factors were inconsequential and that the justices were motivated solely by their preferences, but those preferences do explain the vote of every justice on the Court.

Role Orientations

No matter what their personal policy preferences may be, justices have certain beliefs about the extent to which those attitudes should be permitted to affect their resolution of cases. Some may seek to practice judicial restraint, deferring whenever possible to popular majorities. Others may assume a more activist role, believing that it is their duty to consult their own consciences when making decisions, no less than the president, members of Congress, and state legislators. These views—judicial activism on the one hand and judicial restraint on the other—reflect competing orientations toward the role of Supreme Court justices. Accordingly, some "view restraintism as essential to the protection of the right of the majority to rule in a democratic polity. . . . Activists, on the other hand, believe that judges have the obligation to right the wrongs perpetuated by majoritarian institutions [in order] to achieve justice, not just legality."[20] Among lower courts, judges will often curb their personal policy ambitions, if they believe it is their duty to do so,[21] but do these competing notions of activism and restraint similarly affect the justices of the Supreme Court?

Justice Lewis Powell, who led the Court in *McCleskey* by authoring the majority opinion, clearly wanted to defer to Georgia's legislature. Adhering to a long-held view that the Supreme Court's foray into the death penalty had a "shattering effect" on both federalism

---

[20]James L. Gibson, "Decision Making in Appellate Courts," in *The American Courts: A Critical Assessment*, John B. Gates and Charles A. Johnson, eds. (Washington: Congressional Quarterly, Inc., 1991), pp. 262–63.

[21]James L. Gibson, "Judges' Role Orientations, Attitudes, and Decisions: An Interactive Model," *American Political Science Review* 72:911–24 (1978).

and judicial restraint,[22] he believed that the Court should defer to the judgment of elected officials on criminal punishments. As his internal memoranda and other private notes suggest, he was especially wary of using statistical analyses to second-guess the operation of law enforcement. According to Powell, "This case, if we agreed with McCleskey, would overrule *Gregg* and its progeny [and] end the imposition of death." Not only that, as Powell told the conference after oral argument, the "use of statistics could not be limited to blacks or to capital cases."[23] If the Court accepted the Baldus study as proof of discrimination, then the justices would be opening the door to any identifiable group to challenge all manner of criminal penalties with similar studies, each of which the justices—who were uneducated in the use of advanced statistics—would have to evaluate. Under the circumstances, Powell concluded, the justices should adhere to judicial restraint.

One should not be too quick to accept this evidence, however. After all, Powell was a conservative appointed by a Republican president, so he was ideologically disposed to support the state in criminal cases. His belief that the Court should give great weight to popularly elected legislators, therefore, could easily be explained by his personal policy preferences. In fact, recent scholarship on Justice Powell suggests that, despite a professed belief in judicial restraint, he was quite willing to uproot popular majorities if their decisions collided with his own conservative views.[24] Thus, a more complete test would require examining other cases to see if the conservative Powell, who advocated judicial restraint, voted to uphold popular policies that were more liberal in nature. If he and other members of the Court are actually affected by the role of judicial restraint, then they should support majoritarian policies, regardless of their personal preferences.

Here, the evidence in favor of role orientations is not terribly strong. Research shows that, across a wide range of cases, the justices who decided *McCleskey* rarely abandoned their policy attitudes for

---

[22]*Furman v. Georgia*, p. 417.
[23]Lewis F. Powell, Jr., Papers, 86-260, Washington and Lee Law School, Lexington, Virginia.
[24]John C. Jeffries, Jr., *Justice Lewis F. Powell, Jr.* (New York: Charles Scribner's Sons, 1994), p. 425. See also Gibson, "Decision Making in Appellate Courts," p. 264.

the sake of deferring to other decision makers.[25] To be sure, these members of the Court often voted in favor of majority rule, but they did so most often when the popular will coincided with their own political views. A simple way to see this is to examine their votes in cases where the Court actually considered overturning majority preferences and then compare those with the votes cast in other cases. By this test, the justices on the *McCleskey* Court show no meaningful differences. Powell, for example, voted conservatively about 60 percent of the time, regardless of whether the Court was assessing the constitutionality of a law. If anything, the more ideological justices, such as Brennan and Rehnquist, were actually more likely to vote against the majority will when the result would be consistent with their liberal or conservative preferences.[26] Evidently, the justices follow their attitudinal inclinations, whether that means supporting popular majorities or not. It seems likely, therefore, that the policy preferences of Powell and his brethren—not their role orientations—governed their votes in *McCleskey v. Kemp*.

Group Interactions

The story to this point has focused on explanations for the individual votes of the justices, but the members of the Supreme Court do not make their decisions in isolation. Rather, their votes, as well as the written opinions supporting them, are formulated in a collegial environment. Collectively, the justices deliberate over cases, cast votes, and draft opinions that contain the Court's interpretation of the law. For that reason, it is important to consider the extent to which the interactions that take place among the justices might affect their policy making. Do collegial interactions on the Supreme Court affect the behavior of its members?

A good place to begin examining the potential impact of group dynamics on the Court is in the conference that takes place following

---

[25]See Segal and Spaeth, *The Supreme Court and the Attitudinal Model,* pp. 305–18.
[26]These results are derived from the *United States Supreme Court Judicial Database, 1953–1995 Terms,* Harold J. Spaeth, principal investigator (Ann Arbor, MI: Inter-University Consortium for Political and Social Research, 1997).

oral argument.[27] Here, the justices discuss the cases that they have heard and cast preliminary votes on the outcomes of those cases. With the responsibility of leading and coordinating these deliberations, the chief justice begins by presenting an outline of the case and expressing an opinion on how it should be resolved. Then, in descending order of seniority, each justice does likewise, sketching his or her views on the case and casting a vote. The final outcome is determined by majority rule.

Vote Fluidity. Because of these interactions, one very real possibility is that some justices may be persuaded to change their votes. In some cases, members of the Court may have only tentative views, and the arguments of their fellow justices may affect their thinking, either during the conference or later as opinions are being crafted. Certainly, the votes in conference "provide an indication of the direction in which the Court is likely to rule, [but] the votes are nonbinding. Indeed, the justices' final votes do not necessarily resemble their initial conference votes."[28] On balance, though, the votes of the justices appear to be fairly stable; some justices occasionally recondsider their initial votes, but such voting fluidity is rare.[29]

Certainly, there was little change in the thinking of the justices in *McCleskey v. Kemp*. Their votes in conference were identical to their final votes when the opinion was announced. Taken from the papers of Justice Powell, Table 4.3 provides an overview of the justices' remarks during the conference, as well as a comparison of their

[27]For an extended discussion of the conference and the Court's decision-making process more generally, see Biskupic and Witt, *Guide to the U.S. Supreme Court*, pp. 788–805.
[28]Forrest Maltzman, James F. Spriggs II, and Paul J. Wahlbeck, *Crafting Law on the Supreme Court: The Collegial Game* (Cambridge: Cambridge University Press, 2000), p. 7.
[29]See Saul Brenner, "Fluidity on the United States Supreme Court: A Reexamination," *American Journal of Political Science* 24:526–35 (1980); J. Woodford Howard, "On the Fluidity of Judicial Choice," *American Political Science Review* 62:43–56 (1968); Forrest Maltzman and Paul J. Wahlbeck, "Strategic Policy Considerations and Voting Fluidity on the Burger Court," *American Political Science Review* 90:581–92 (1996).

TABLE 4.3 Summary of Conference Remarks and Votes in
McCleskey v. Kemp

Justices' Comments	Conference Vote	Final Vote
Chief Justice Rehnquist: Each jury decides the case before it. No reason to assume that [all juries] would discriminate.	Affirm	Affirm
Justice Brennan: Baldus study creates a strong inference of discrimination. It is more likely than not that race is the determinative factor.	Reverse	Reverse
Justice White: There is no showing that McCleskey's case falls within "middle range" where Baldus finds discriminiation. There is no showing that death was imposed arbitrarily.	Affirm	Affirm
Justice Marshall: Understandably, TM talked about the discrimination historically imposed on blacks.	Reverse	Reverse
Justice Blackmun: Passed on first vote. On his second vote, he agreed with JPS.	(Pass) Reverse	Reverse
Justice Powell: Petitioner relies solely on statistics, and criminal cases should not be decided on the basis of statistics alone.	Affirm	Affirm
Justice Stevens: Baldus study is sufficient to show that with respect to a particular class of cases, race is likely to be relevant.	Reverse	Reverse
Justice O'Connor: Baldus study is a concern to everyone, [but] jury discretion is essential.	Affirm	Affirm
Justice Scalia: Not impressed by statistics. We can't do anything more than try to guide a jury. We can't abandon the discretion of a jury in particular cases.	Affirm	Affirm

Source: Powell papers, 84-6811.

conference and final votes. Each of the justices who voted to uphold the decision of the Eleventh Circuit was, in one way or another, skeptical of interfering with the jury system by allowing statistics to prove discrimination, and none of these votes changed throughout the process of opinion writing.

Still, it is clear that at least one justice, Harry Blackmun, came to the conference uncertain about how to resolve the case, and when his turn came during the discussion, he passed rather than commit himself to any specific position. His ambivalence is not hard to understand, since it is clear from Figure 4.1 that his views placed him near the ideological center of the Court in criminal cases. Apparently, he was not willing to use the Baldus study to invalidate Georgia's sentencing system, but neither was he willing to dismiss its relevance. Justice John Paul Stevens then offered a moderate position that Blackmun found appealing: The Baldus study did not call into question the death penalty as a whole in Georgia; it was only in those middle-range cases where there was a good deal of jury discretion that race seemed to be a consideration. So the statistics did not invalidate capital punishment in Georgia, just that segment of it. On that rationale, Blackmun decided to vote to reverse the appeals court.

Of course, had Blackmun cast his lot with the more conservative majority, it would have made little difference for the outcome.[30] There were already five justices in favor of affirming the lower court. Nevertheless, the conference deliberations in *McCleskey* illustrate fluidity by demonstrating how the initial impressions of a justice can be changed through his interactions with other members of the Court.

Opinion Assignment. Having voted in favor of upholding Georgia's capital sentencing, the Court next set about drafting a written statement announcing its ruling and describing its rationale. By custom, the decision as to who will write the opinion of the Court is made by the most senior member of the majority. Since the chief justice—who, by definition, is the most senior member of the Court—voted with the majority, William Rehnquist had the responsibility of deciding who among those five justices would write on their behalf.

Who would write the majority opinion in the *McCleskey* case? Like all chief justices, Rehnquist had to consider a variety of factors. He would have to ensure that the justice designated to write the opinion was not already overly burdened with opinions assigned in other cases. Balanced against that consideration would be the relative expertise that a justice might have within the area of criminal law; through opinion assignments, justices can often specialize in

---

[30]In fact, when vote changes do occur between the conference and final vote, they rarely change the outcome of a case; see Brenner, "Fluidity on the United States Supreme Court."

certain legal questions, a practice that not only makes good adminis-trative sense but also enhances the legitimacy of the Court's decisions. Should he assign the case to himself? Cases dealing with the death penalty tend to be regarded by most observers as especially significant, and in important cases chief justices often use the authority and reputation of their office to strengthen an opinion.[31]

Perhaps the central issue that Chief Justice Rehnquist had to con-sider, though, was the narrow margin by which the case was to be decided. Since the justices' conference votes are not binding, any slim 5-4 majority has the potential to disintegrate. Under those cir-cumstances, if only a single justice can be persuaded to abandon the majority and vote with the minority, that would change not only the vote in the case but the outcome, as well. If any one of Justices O'Connor, Powell, Scalia, and White were to reconsider, the minority would become a majority. Thus, the Court's decision would then be to reverse the appeals court and allow the Baldus study to be used to limit or perhaps even invalidate the death penalty.

In order to ensure that the Court's decisions will reflect their own views, chief justices often assign opinions to themselves or to those with whom they most often agree.[32] By the data in Figure 4.1, then, if Rehnquist were to assign the opinion to anyone other than himself, Justice O'Connor would be the likely choice; she was the most conservative member of the Court on criminal issues, after Rehnquist himself. Still, the chief justice surely had to consider the possibility that the more moderate justices might be persuaded to defect from his slender coalition and vote in favor of McCleskey. What if those in the minority offered an alternative way to resolve the case that proved to be more appealing to, say, Powell or White? True, asking either of them to write on behalf of the Court might not

---

[31] See, e.g., Abraham, *The Judicial Process*, pp. 218–40; Sue Davis, "Power on the Court: Chief Justice Rehnquist's Opinion Assignments," *Judicature* 74:66–72 (1990); Maltz-man, Spriggs, and Wahlbeck, *Crafting Law on the Supreme Court*, pp. 29–56; Elliot E. Slotnick, "The Chief Justices and Self-Assignment of Majority Opinions: A Research Note," *Western Political Quarterly* 31:219–25 (1978).

[32] Forrest Maltzman and Paul J. Wahlbeck, "May It Please the Chief? Opinion Assign-ments in the Rehnquist Court," *American Journal of Political Science* 40:421–33 (1996); David W. Rohde, "Policy Goals, Strategic Choice and Majority Opinion Assignments in the U.S. Supreme Court," *Midwest Journal of Political Science* 16:652–82 (1972); Segal and Spaeth, *The Supreme Court and the Attitudinal Model*, pp. 262–90.

produce an opinion that matched Rehnquist's own preferences—it might leave too much legal room for future challenges to the death penalty—but it would at least ensure that Georgia's basic right to impose capital punishment would be upheld. Better to have a partial victory than a total loss.

Although it is not clear that it is effective, this strategy in opinion assignment is quite common on the Supreme Court.[33] It is hardly surprising, therefore, that Rehnquist decided to ask Justice Powell to take on the responsibility. It is worth noting that both Powell and White were apparently anxious to draft an opinion for the Court.[34] So it seems unlikely that the majority coalition was ever in serious jeopardy. Leaving aside its effectiveness, Rehnquist's choice of Powell suggests that strategic considerations played a role in deciding who would write the majority opinion in the *McCleskey* case.

Opinion Writing.   With the assignment in hand, Justice Powell's office immediately began drafting an opinion.[35] Two of Powell's law clerks worked closely with the justice in developing an initial draft, and by late October the opinion had begun to take shape. Like most majority opinions, it began by detailing the legal questions at issue as well as the case's factual circumstances and history in the lower courts. It then blended together a mixture of history, precedent, logic, and data to support the majority's decision—that the Baldus study, by itself, was not sufficient to show that capital punishment in Georgia was arbitrarily imposed or racially discriminatory. Justice Powell and his staff undertook careful and extensive editing, and by early November they had prepared a formal draft to be circulated to the other members of the Court. Before the opinion could be finalized, though, every justice in the majority would have to formally endorse its contents. How did the other justices in the majority respond to Powell's draft?

---

[33]Saul Brenner and Harold J. Spaeth, "Majority Opinion Assignments and the Maintenance of the Original Coalition on the Warren Court," *American Journal of Political Science* 32:72–81 (1988); Maltzman and Wahlbeck, "May It Please the Chief?"; Rohde, "Policy Goals."

[34]Edward Lazarus, *Closed Chambers: The Rise, Fall, and Future of the Modern Supreme Court* (New York: Penguin Books, 1999).

[35]My discussion of the process of writing the opinion in *McCleskey v. Kemp* is drawn from the materials available in Justice Powell's papers, 84–6811.

Once the draft of any majority opinion is distributed, the members of the majority have several options.[36] They might endorse it, suggest changes, or simply wait to see how other justices react before making a decision. Another alternative is to write an opinion of one's own. Known formally as concurring opinions, these represent independent views that are not reflected in the majority opinion. Of course, when justices find the majority opinion to be wholly unsatisfactory, they can change their votes and side with the minority.

By far, the most common reaction is to join the majority opinion after it is circulated. In most cases, the members of the majority simply endorse the draft. On the day that Justice Powell distributed his opinion, for example, Justice O'Connor immediately expressed her enthusiasm. In a personal memorandum to Powell, she wrote, "Dear Lewis, You have written a splendid opinion in *McCleskey*. No one could have done better. You grappled fairly and appropriately with all aspects. We owe you our thanks. Sandra." The following day, she formally signed on to Powell's opinion with a standard one-line reply: "Dear Lewis, Please join me in your excellent opinion."

In a good many cases, though, a justice will indicate an interest in writing a separate concurring opinion. Over the past few decades, roughly 40 percent of all cases have been decided with at least one concurrence.[37] At least initially, this is what Justice Antonin Scalia planned to do. He was especially concerned that the opinion seemed to suggest that McCleskey might have prevailed, if only the statistical evidence had been stronger, and he wanted to emphasize that view in a separate opinion. In a memorandum to the other justices, he wrote:

> I plan to join Lewis's opinion in this case . . . [but] I do not share the view, implicit in the opinion, that an effect of racial factors upon sentencing, if it could only be shown by sufficiently strong statistical evidence, would require reversal. Since it is my view that the unconscious operation of irrational sympathies and antipathies, including racial, upon jury decisions . . . is real, acknowledged in the decisions of this court, and ineradicable, I cannot honestly say that all I need is more proof. I expect to write separately to make these points, but not until I see the dissent.

[36]This discussion is drawn from Matlzman, Spriggs, and Wahlbeck, *Crafting Law on the Supreme Court*, pp. 62–72.
[37]See Epstein et al., *The Supreme Court Compendium*, Table 3-3.

In other words, Scalia conceded that racial prejudice enters into the minds of jurors when making decisions; he did not need statistical evidence to convince him of that. As far as he was concerned, however, there was really nothing that the law could do to purge the jurors of such irrational considerations. He intended, therefore, to write a concurring opinion expressing that sentiment. Later, he reconsidered and joined Powell's opinion; the planned concurrence was never written.

Chief Justice Rehnquist and Justice White sought only modest changes in the Court's opinion. So rather than write separate concurrences, they asked Powell to modify his opinion. The draft hinted that the death penalty could not be imposed without a jury considering mitigating circumstances, and both justices were troubled by the implications this might have for an upcoming case, *Sumner v. Shuman*, which raised the issue of whether the death penalty could ever be mandatory. Rehnquist and White were worried that the opinion, as written, could be interpreted to mean that it could not. The Court had not yet addressed that issue, and these justices wanted to make sure that the opinion in *McCleskey* clearly made that point. Accordingly, the Chief Justice wrote:

> You have written a very thorough opinion in this case, and I will be happy to join it if you will make one minor modification. We granted certiorari last month [to review] Nevada's mandatory death sentence. . . . I think some of the language in parts C and D, while not foreclosing the state's position [in that case], casts more doubt upon it than I would like to see. If you are willing to consider the sort of modification I have in mind, I would be happy to accept any suitable language which you propose, or would be happy to suggest some myself.

Although he shared the chief justice's misgivings, White did not demand changes as a condition for joining Powell's opinion; he merely suggested it. "I shall join your draft opinion in this case," wrote White "but in order not to preordain the result in the mandatory death case we have granted, perhaps the language . . . in the middle of p. 20 could be modified and a footnote dropped." White's memo went on to suggest a possible clarifying footnote, and Powell incorporated it into the opinion, almost verbatim.

Both reactions—suggesting changes and threatening not to join an opinion unless changes are made—"are neither rare nor ineffective."[38] They serve very useful strategic purposes for the justices in the majority, for they are devices by which justices can try to ensure that their views are reflected in the Court's opinion. By using these bargaining tools during the writing of an opinion, the justices inevitably shape its content.

Here, Rehnquist and White obviously cared about the policy that was being adopted in this case, and its possible implications for the future; they did not want the precedent being set in the *McCleskey* opinion to affect the upcoming case. The new footnote, which explicitly stated that the Court had not yet addressed the issue of mandatory capital punishment, seems to have allayed the fears of both Rehnquist and White. When Powell's second draft was circulated, the chief justice joined almost immediately, with White following shortly thereafter.[39]

Like the majority, the justices in the minority also began drafting their own opinions, known as dissents. Dissenting opinions express disagreement with the Court's official decision, so by definition they do not have the force of law. Still, they provide an important opportunity for those who believe the Court has erred to justify their objections and explain why they would come to a different result. Because disagreement occurs so often in the Court, the majority of cases—about 60 percent, in fact—are decided with one or more dissents.[40]

Who will write the opinion for the minority is also determined by the same seniority rule that governs the assignment of opinions for the majority, but since there is no need to maintain a cohesive voting bloc among the dissenters, there is nothing preventing other minority justices from taking up the pen at their own initiative.[41] So, for instance, Justice Brennan drafted a dissent that Justices Blackmun, Marshall, and Stevens joined. In addition, two of those justices, Blackmun and Stevens, each wrote a dissent of his own. Just as majority opinions are revised to accommodate the members of the majority, dissents likewise undergo revisions in order to address the concerns of the minority justices.

[38]Maltzman, Spriggs, and Wahlbeck, *Crafting the Law on the Supreme Court*, p. 65.
[39]Their objections are instructive, since they suggest a preference for allowing the mandatory death sentence. Later, when the Court decided the issue in *Sumner,* both justices voted in favor of the state (see *Sumner v. Shuman* 483 U.S. 66 [1987]).
[40]See Epstein et al., *The Supreme Court Compendium*, Table 3-2.
[41]See Abraham, *The Judicial Process*, p. 221.

In late January 1987, shortly after Justice Brennan circulated his dissent, Justice Scalia abandoned the prospects of writing a concurring opinion and signed on as the final member of the majority to endorse Powell's opinion. All that remained was for Justice Powell to finalize his opinion by responding to the criticisms of the dissenters. As the three dissents took form, Powell and his clerks read them and revised accordingly. When Justice Brennan, for instance, criticized the majority for upholding a system that gave jurors too much discretion in death sentencing, Powell responded that, since the Court's prior decisions actually required that jurors be given discretion, "it is difficult to imagine guidelines that would produce the predictability sought by the dissent without sacrificing the discretion essential to a humane and fair system of criminal justice."[42]

By late spring, both the majority and minority opinions were finalized, and on April 22, the Court publicly announced its decision. For its part, the majority opinion reflected the Court's refusal to accept the Baldus study as evidence of either purposeful discrimination or arbitrary sentencing. After all, as the excerpts in Box 4.1 highlight, McCleskey had killed a police officer during the course of an armed robbery, providing ample legal basis for imposing the death penalty; there was absolutely no evidence that he himself was the subject of discrimination. Concluding otherwise, the dissenters determined that the statistics were sufficient to establish both cruel and unusual punishment as well as a denial of equal protection of the laws; whereas Justice Brennan placed a strong emphasis on the Eighth Amendment in his opinion, Justice Blackmun's dissent focused more heavily upon the Fourteenth Amendment. Finally, Justice Stevens questioned only one segment of the system of capital punishment in Georgia; he advocated reducing the likelihood of race-conscious death sentences by restricting the range of cases in which jurors in Georgia had discretion.

As in so many instances, then, the substance of the Court's policy in *McCleskey* was affected by several different justices. From the conference votes cast in the case to the assignment and drafting of the written opinions, the decision was the product of interactions among the members of the Court. Such interactions underscore that policy making on the high court is a collective enterprise that takes place in a collegial environment.

---

[42]*McCleskey v. Kemp*, p. 314, n. 37.

The Court's Constituencies

Along with such factors as the justices' policy preferences and their group interactions, forces outside the Supreme Court can also affect judicial policy. Different segments of the legal and political community, as well as the public more generally, can exert pressures to which the justices may be attentive. For the most part, these constituencies seem not to have played prominent roles in resolving *McCleskey v. Kemp*. Nevertheless, the justices permitted some of them, at least, to inform their decision.

Legal Actors. It is tempting to believe that the members of the Supreme Court are influenced by the arguments presented by the parties. After all, the process of reading briefs and listening to oral arguments would suggest that the justices approach cases with an open mind and vote according to which side makes the more compelling case. If the members of the Court make decisions based largely upon their own policy values, however, that leaves little room for lawyers to affect their votes. That does not mean, of course, that legal argument can have no impact; it simply suggests that its influence will be limited.

In a typical case, arguments come to the Supreme Court from a variety of sources. The parties, obviously, stake out their respective legal positions, arguing over the proper interpretation of the law, the relative importance of different precedents, and the like. In this instance, McCleskey had secured the support of civil rights lawyers from the NAACP Legal Defense and Educational Fund, while Georgia was represented by lawyers from within the state attorney general's office.

In addition to the parties' lawyers, the Court also allows outside interests—governments, corporations, organized groups, and individuals—to participate as amici curiae, or "friends of the court," by filing briefs that provide the justices with additional arguments and information.[43] Here, the Congressional Black Caucus and the International Human Rights Law Group filed amicus briefs that challenged Georgia's death penalty. Urging the justices to uphold the state's sentencing system were the state of California and the conser-

---

[43]Gregory A. Caldeira and John R. Wright, "Amici Curiae before the Supreme Court: Who Participates, When, and How Much? *Journal of Politics* 52:782–806 (1990).

vative Washington Legal Foundation. The role of organized interests such as these is sufficiently important to merit a chapter of its own, and their participation and impact are discussed in greater detail in Chapter 5.

Oral arguments are one place to examine the influence of legal advocacy, since they provide the most direct opportunity for lawyers to present their cases to the Court. Limited to thirty minutes on each side, lawyers can use this time to reinforce their written arguments and to convince skeptical or ambivalent justices. Do these arguments matter? Some research compares the relative experience of lawyers who argue cases in the Court and concludes that legal advocacy makes a small but significant difference in the outcome. The logic is that the more often a lawyer appears before the Court, the more likely that lawyer is to develop the expertise necessary to convince its members.[44] By that gauge, it seems unlikely that the lawyers had any effect on the outcome of the *McCleskey* case, since both had similar records of experience. John Charles Boger, who argued on behalf of McCleskey, had made one previous appearance before the justices, and so too had Georgia's Assistant Attorney General, Mary Beth Westmoreland.[45] Without having the advantage of greater expertise before the Court, neither would be any more likely to persuade the justices, all else being equal.

Governmental Actors. Outside the Court's immediate legal community, there are prominent political institutions that may affect the justices' decisions. Congress and the president often take an active interest in the Court's policies, as do state-level policy makers. Some have argued that, because these officials can limit or even reverse the Court's decisions, the justices are constrained by the preferences of other governmental actors.[46]

Thus, there is some reason to think that, when interpreting federal statutes, the justices measure the preferences of Congress and the president. Since the Court can be overturned by new legislation,

---

[44]Kevin T. McGuire, "Repeat Players in the Supreme Court: The Role of Experienced Lawyers in Litigation Success," *Journal of Politics* 57:187–96 (1995).

[45]See *Zant v. Stephens* 456 U.S. 410 (1982) and *Waller v. Georgia* 467 U.S. 39 (1984), respectively.

[46]See, for example, William N. Eskridge, Jr., "Overriding Supreme Court Statutory Interpretation Decisions," *Yale Law Journal* 101-331-455 (1991).

the justices may not want to stray too far from the desires of the other two branches. The evidence, however, is far from conclusive.[47] By comparison, in cases involving constitutional questions, such as *McCleskey v. Kemp*, the members of the Court can almost always safely ignore the other branches; although it certainly has been done, amending the Constitution to overturn the Supreme Court is enormously difficult to do.[48]

When the Court decided *McCleskey* in 1987, the White House was in the hands of the Republican Party, as was the U.S. Senate. With Ronald Reagan as president and a strong conservative influence on Capitol Hill, the justices obviously had little fear that a "law and order" decision would provoke unfavorable reaction. If anything, the Court looked to Congress for support by noting that, like the state of Georgia, it too had sought to have consistent sentences in federal cases while ensuring that jurors had a measure of flexibility. The federal government's recent sentencing guidelines, the Court noted, "further an essential need of the Anglo-American criminal justice system to balance the desirability of a high degree of uniformity against the necessity for the exercise of discretion."[49] Far from limiting the Court's actions in *McCleskey*, popular policy makers actually helped to reinforce the majority opinion.

Public Opinion. Unelected judges with lifetime tenure need not respond to public pressures in the same manner as members of Congress, but the justices certainly do care about the perceived legitimacy of their decisions and the likelihood that they will be followed.[50] This occurs, according to Alexander Hamilton, by constitutional design; because the Court "has no influence over either the sword or the purse," it must enlist the support of the popular

[47]Eskridge, "Overriding Supreme Court Statutory Interpretation Decisions." For a skeptical view, see Jeffrey A. Segal, "Separation-of-Powers Games in the Positive Theory of Congress and Courts," *American Political Science Review* 91:28–44 (1997).

[48]Over the last quarter century, there has been only one serious attempt to override the justices' interpretation of the Constitution, and that involved the Court's enormously unpopular decisions upholding flag burning as protected expression. Even that effort, however, fell well short of generating the necessary congressional support. See Biskupic and Witt, *Guide to the U.S. Supreme Court*, pp. 726–31.

[49]*McCleskey v. Kemp*, pp. 312–13, n. 35.

[50]See, e.g., Walter F. Murphy, *Elements of Judicial Strategy* (Chicago: University of Chicago Press, 1964).

branches of government to put its policies into effect.[51] Consequently, even though the justices are insulated from popular opinion, they cannot afford to ignore it. Indeed, there is mounting evidence that their decisions are influenced by public preferences.[52]

In *McCleskey*, public opinion on capital punishment is unlikely to have affected the votes of the justices. Some of the Court's more liberal members, such as Brennan and Marshall, had long ago decided that the death penalty violated the Eighth Amendment, and conservatives, such as O'Connor and Rehnquist, had consistently voted in support of the state in such cases. Still, for those in the majority who had concluded, perhaps for other reasons, that McCleskey's death sentence should be upheld, public opinion certainly provided an important justification for that decision.

The Supreme Court's earlier conclusion that the death penalty was not cruel and unusual punishment was based, in part, on its general public acceptance.[53] So, in deciding whether the Baldus study showed that the jury's death sentence was excessive or arbitrary, the justices again turned to public opinion to help frame their rationale. As Powell wrote, "In assessing contemporary values, we have . . . sought to ascertain 'objective indicia that reflect the public attitude toward a given sanction' . . . [and] have been guided by the sentencing decisions of juries, because they are 'a significant and reliable objective index of contemporary values.' "[54] As a microcosm of public values, the jury in McCleskey's case had determined that, given the circumstances, he should be put to death. Consequently, the majority saw no reason to question its judgment. Seen in this way, public opinion did not determine the Court's policy, but it did help to shape it.

---

[51]Alexander Hamilton, James Madison, and John Jay, *The Federalist Papers* (New York: New American Library, [1787–88] 1961), p. 465.

[52]See Roy B. Flemming and B. Dan Wood, "The Public and the Supreme Court: Individual Justice Responsiveness to American Policy Moods," *American Journal of Political Science* 41:468–98 (1997); Kevin T. McGuire and James A. Stimson, "The Least Dangerous Branch Revisited: New Evidence on Supreme Court Responsiveness to Public Preferences," presented at the annual meeting of the Midwest Political Science Association Meeting, Chicago, IL (2000); William Mishler and Reginald S. Sheehan, "Public Opinion, the Attitudinal Model, and Supreme Court Decision Making: A Micro-Analytic Perpective," *Journal of Politics* 58: 169–200 (1996).

[53]See *Gregg v. Georgia*, pp. 171–73.

[54]*McCleskey v. Kemp*, p. 300.

CONCLUSION

Despite the Supreme Court's decision, Warren McCleskey continued to fight his conviction. Four years later, he returned to the Court, this time to challenge the testimony of the prison informant who had been in McCleskey's adjoining cell. Again, he was unsuccessful. That decision cleared the way for the state to do what, thirteen years earlier, it had sought—execute him for the murder of Officer Frank Schlatt. On September 25, 1991, McCleskey was electrocuted.[55]

As a means of illuminating the process of Supreme Court decision making, McCleskey's challenge to the death penalty provides a number of important insights. Interestingly enough, *McCleskey v. Kemp* suggests that legal considerations are, at best, an imprecise guide for resolving cases. Adherence to precedent is at the heart of the judicial process, and yet the availability of competing precedents makes it possible for the justices to use the Court's prior decisions as a basis for almost any outcome. In trying to determine whether statistical evidence could be used to establish illegal discrimination and, if so, how strong that evidence would need to be, the Court was confronted with several precedents that would plausibly justify a vote for either litigant. If the law supports both sides, it is somewhat problematic to suggest that it truly affects the justices' votes.

In the absence of clear legal rules, a more reliable predictor of the justices' votes is their policy values. It turns out that the justices base their decisions largely upon their own personal preferences. Thus, each of the five most conservative members of the Court voted in favor of Georgia's sentencing procedures, while the justices with more liberal attitudes all supported McCleskey's challenge to the death penalty.

It is possible, of course, that these votes were a function of varying degrees of judicial restraint. Perhaps Justice Powell and the other members of the majority supported the state of Georgia because they believed that, as judges, it was their responsibility to defer to the judgments of elected legislators. Their votes in other cases, however, suggest that they are much less willing to show restraint when restraint means supporting more liberal interests.

---

[55]Peter Applebome, "Georgia Inmate Is Executed After 'Chaotic' Legal Move," *The New York Times*, September 26, 1991, p. 18.

No less important than deciding who wins and who loses is crafting the rationale to support that outcome. By virtue of seniority, the chief justice is often in the position of assigning the written opinion. In close cases, such as *McCleskey*, this prerogative can be used as a strategic device to help foster agreement among the majority. As one of the more moderate members of that slender majority, Powell developed an opinion that easily won endorsement, but not without first having to make at least minor changes to satisfy White and Rehnquist. In the end, Powell's opinion reflected a sensitivity not only to the interests of his fellow justices but to broader forces within society as well. Although it is doubtful that the Supreme Court was affected by either congressional or public opinion, the Court's decision was certainly cognizant of both.

Like many cases, *McCleskey v. Kemp* brought to the Court an intriguing question that blended law and public policy. Faced with a complex issue, the members of the Supreme Court had to grapple with strong arguments on both sides. A close look at this case reveals that the justices consider those arguments in light of their own preferences, the views of their colleagues, and the legal and political environment. However they may weigh these individual factors, the members of the Court ultimately resolve cases with attention to both the legal soundness and the practical consequences of their decisions.

QUESTIONS FOR DISCUSSION

1. The evidence suggests that, in *McCleskey v. Kemp*, precedent did not determine the justices' decisions. Does that mean that it is unimportant? What might be some other ways in which precedent could affect how the justices think about cases without necessarily changing their views about how to vote?

2. Members of Congress appear to make many of their decisions based upon their personal policy preferences. Is there anything wrong with the members of the Supreme Court doing likewise? In those cases where legal factors provide no clear answers, upon what else should the justices base their decisions?

3. In *McCleskey v. Kemp*, the justices who had voted most liberally in previous criminal cases voted to invalidate Georgia's death sentence, while those with more conservative records voted to

support it. Is that necessarily evidence that the justices make decisions based upon their preferences? Are there other ways of interpreting this evidence that would suggest that legal factors played an important role?

4. What arguments—if any—might the lawyers for McCleskey have offered in order to convince, say, Justice Powell to vote against Georgia's death penalty?

5. Does the position of chief justice appear to offer significant opportunities to lead the Court? If so, how well did Chief Justice Rehnquist exploit those opportunities in *McCleskey v. Kemp*?

6. If public opinion had been strongly against the death penalty, is there any reason to think that *McCleskey* would have been decided any differently? Why or why not?

7. Short of reversing the Supreme Court through legislation or constitutional amendment, what other means are available to Congress to try to constrain the actions of the Supreme Court? How effective might they be?

8. The only component of Supreme Court decision making that is publicly visible is oral argument. Would there be benefits to televising this part of the process, or would it jeopardize the integrity of the Court? Is the Congress any better (or worse) for having cameras in its legislative chambers?

SUGGESTED READING

Lawrence Baum. 1997. *The Puzzle of Judicial Behavior*. Ann Arbor: University of Michigan Press.

Phillip J. Cooper. 1995. *Battles on the Bench: Conflict Inside the Supreme Court*. Lawrence: University Press of Kansas.

Lee Epstein and Jack Knight. 1998. *The Choices Justices Make*. Washington: Congressional Quarterly, Inc.

James L. Gibson. 1991. "Decision Making in Appellate Courts." In *The American Courts: A Critical Assessment*. John B. Gates and Charles A. Johnson, eds. Washington: Congressional Quarterly, Inc.

Edward Lazarus. 1999. *Closed Chambers: The Rise, Fall, and Future of the Modern Supreme Court*. New York: Penguin Books.

Forrest Maltzman, James F. Spriggs II, and Paul J. Wahlbeck. 2000. *Crafting Law on the Supreme Court: The Collegial Game*. Cambridge: Cambridge University Press.

David G. Savage. 1992. *Turning Right: The Making of the Rehnquist Court*. New York: John Wiley & Sons.

Jeffrey A. Segal and Harold J. Spaeth. 1993. *The Supreme Court and the Attitudinal Model*. Cambridge: Cambridge University Press.

Harold J. Spaeth and Jeffrey A. Segal. 1999. *Majority Rule or Minority Will: Adherence to Precedent on the U.S. Supreme Court*. Cambridge: Cambridge University Press.

CHAPTER 5

Interest Groups in Litigation

Simon & Schuster, Inc. v. New York State Crime Victims Board

Organized interests are a pervasive part of the political process, but they are also conspicuously active on the legal landscape. The Supreme Court is a major force in American national policy making, so it makes sense that interest groups would seek to influence its decisions. This chapter documents how different political constituencies lobby the justices when their interests are at stake. The context is a New York law that prevented accused or convicted criminals from profiting from published works in which they described their illegal activities. Although this case involved a single book about an organized crime figure and his exploits, it turned out to be important to national and state government as well as to some of the largest publishing and entertainment groups in the United States. Why did these various interests become involved in the case, and what difference did they make? This conflict between free expression and law and order highlights the methods, strategies, and consequences of group participation in the Court.

Richard Snyder and Michael Korda had an idea for a book. As executives at Simon & Schuster, one of the nation's largest and most distinguished publishers, they were responsible for finding talented writers, overseeing the development of their literary projects, and producing interesting and attractive titles to add to their company's list. Their idea, in this case, was to publish a story about life inside the Mafia. It certainly would not be the first book to explore the underworld; a wide variety of existing volumes testified to its popular appeal. Yet these books, they felt, often gave organized crime a mystique and an air of glamour, and Snyder and Korda—Simon & Schuster's president and editor-in-chief, respectively—were keen to market a book that told the tale of the sordid and seamier side of organized crime in the United States.[1]

To that end, they recruited a well-known author, Nicholas Pileggi, to write just such a book. In the fall of 1981 Pileggi agreed to undertake the project, and roughly four years later, Simon & Schuster published *Wiseguy: Life in a Mafia Family*. The story's protagonist is named Henry Hill. Set in Brooklyn, New York, during the 1960s and '70s, it opens with Hill's boyhood recruitment into the local mob and traces a twenty-five-year career as an insider in a powerful crime family. Throughout the book, the character of Hill describes his involvement in a wide variety of illegal activities. Among other things, it chronicles a point-shaving scheme involving the Boston College basketball team and a multimillion-dollar cash heist from Lufthansa Airlines at Kennedy Airport. In short, *Wiseguy* was a gripping saga of hijacking, arson, extortion, robbery, illegal gambling, and narcotics. But what made it so compelling was that, unlike other books on the Mafia, such as *The Godfather*, the story told in *Wiseguy* was absolutely true. Henry Hill actually provided muscle for the mob—torching businesses, smuggling cigarettes, running bookmaking. He dealt drugs. He witnessed murders. He orchestrated a basketball scam. And, he helped steal $6 million from the Lufthansa cargo terminal, the largest cash theft in U.S. history.

Henry Hill, it turned out, was a real person. His years in the Mafia had caught up with him, and faced with numerous federal and state prosecutions on the one hand, and his likely murder by his former associates on the other, Hill decided, in 1980, to enter the

---

[1]The information presented here is derived from *Simon & Schuster v. Members of the New York State Crimes Victims Board* 502 U.S. 105 (1991); *Briefs and Records of the U.S. Supreme Court*, 90–1059; and Nicholas Pileggi, *Wiseguy: Life in a Mafia Family* (New York: Simon & Schuster, 1985).

Federal Witness Protection Program. Through his testimony, he was able to help the United States secure convictions against a good many of the people with whom he had previously conspired. Not long thereafter, living in anonymity under an assumed name, Hill decided to sell his story. Federal authorities arranged for Pileggi to meet Hill, and over a period of two years they had almost daily conversations in which Hill detailed, at length, his extensive participation in organized crime. For its part, Simon & Schuster paid Hill an advance to work with Pileggi and subsequently brought the book to press. Following its publication, both men received a share of the royalties from its sale.

For its unflinching look at life inside the Mafia, *Wiseguy* earned wide acclaim. The *Washington Post* and the *Wall Street Journal* offered enthusiastic reviews. Prominent national magazines, including *Time* and *Newsweek,* applauded it as a frightening and fascinating tale of true crime. Columnist Jimmy Breslin, writing in the *New York Daily News,* went so far as to proclaim *Wiseguy* "the best book on crime in America ever written." Not surprisingly, the book was enormously popular, enjoying a lengthy stay on *The New York Times* Bestsellers List. The story again garnered similar praise upon the release of *Goodfellas,* a movie based upon the book. In light of *Wiseguy*'s enormous success, the money Hill earned was considerable. Indeed, by 1987, Hill's royalties were close to $125,000.

Unfortunately for Henry Hill, however, he was, by law, not entitled to this income. Several years earlier, New York had enacted a law designed to ensure that criminals could not profit from their wrongdoing by publishing books in which they describe their offenses. Under the law, any monies generated through the sale of such works, instead of going to the authors, would be placed in a state fund designed to provide financial compensation to the author's victims.

It is not difficult to understand why the New York legislature would pass such a law. In the summer of 1977, state lawmakers were concerned that David Berkowitz, a recently convicted serial killer known as the "Son of Sam," might seek to exploit the notoriety surrounding his case by selling the rights to his story. Berkowitz stood to generate a substantial profit from his criminal acts—while his victims would remain uncompensated—and the legislature enacted this statute to ensure that this would not happen. The sponsor of the bill argued, "It is abhorrent to one's sense of justice and decency that an individual, such as the forty-four caliber killer, can expect to receive large sums of money for his story once he is captured—while five people are dead, other people were injured as a result of his conduct. This bill would make it clear that in all criminal situations, the victim must be more important than the criminal." The state wanted to guarantee that, regardless of whether a person was formally convicted, an individual could not generate earnings by writing about past misdeeds. Accordingly, the New York State Crime Victims Board, which administered these funds, wrote to Simon & Schuster: "It has come to our attention that you may have contracted with a person accused or convicted of a crime for the payment of monies to such person." After having reviewed *Wiseguy*, as well as the publisher's financial arrangements with Pileggi and Hill, the Board ordered Hill to return to the Board all the royalties that he had received. It also ordered Simon & Schuster to deposit with the state any further royalties that it was scheduled to pay Hill. This money, in turn, was to be placed in an account from which the victims of Hill's offenses could draw compensation.

New York's literary community was well aware of the "Son of Sam" law. In fact, some publishers with works in progress were already working to avoid printing an author's references to past criminal conduct. Writers, too, were anxious to avoid entanglements with the law; several book projects that Pileggi himself had been considering went unwritten for fear of being embroiled in the state's policy. Because of the sensational nature of the activities described in *Wiseguy*, Simon & Schuster had reason to worry. The actions of the Crime Victims Board only confirmed that their apprehensions were indeed justified.

From Simon & Schuster's perspective, the law posed genuine problems for the publishing industry; if the Board could take the earnings of the people who created its books, it would compromise its ability to publish. After all, part of what made *Wiseguy* so successful was the willingness of Henry Hill to devote hundreds of hours of his time providing to Pileggi his knowledge of the details of the Mafia's operation. Compensating authors and their sources for their time and effort was a standard business practice; that was simply how the publishing business worked. As Editor-in-Chief Korda argued, by eliminating a basic economic incentive—payment for services—the state was, in effect, determining what books Simon & Schuster could and could not publish:

By forbidding payment to certain writers and sources, the statute necessarily results in some books not being published. In all my years in publishing, I have never seen an author, and rarely a primary source (one who will have to spend substantial time providing information to an author), who would be willing to undertake the necessary tasks without an enforceable promise that he will be paid, and paid promptly. Most authors and primary sources do not have the financial resources to write without promise of recompense; the hours they spend writing rather than at other work are hours for which they need to be remunerated. Yet the statute precludes us from promising to compensate certain authors or sources at all, and prohibits us from paying them advances or royalties on the standard timely basis—making it as a practical matter impossible to conclude an agreement with an author or source.

Since the law penalized writing and publishing about one specific topic—criminal activity—Simon & Schuster initiated a legal challenge to the "Son of Sam" law, arguing that it violated the First Amendment's guarantee of freedom of speech. The publishers began their case in a federal district court, asking the judge to declare that, since it tended to inhibit speech, the law was unconstitutional. The judge, acknowledging that the law did have a limiting effect on speech, determined that its effects on free expression were only incidental: "[T]he statute's reach is not prohibitive of the expressive activity. The effect is limited to the nonexpressive element of the activity: receiving a profit." In other words, there was nothing about the law that forbade Henry Hill from telling his story; all the law did was prevent him from earning income from doing so. After this initial loss, Simon & Schuster turned to a federal appeals court, but again it was unsuccessful. This time, the members of the appellate court were more skeptical of the law, concluding that the law placed a substantial burden on would-be authors who wanted to write about their criminal activities; the goal of compensating victims of crime, however, was so important that it simply outweighed the First Amendment interests. Again, the law was upheld. Its argument having been twice rejected in the lower federal courts, Simon & Schuster asked the U.S. Supreme Court to overturn the law.

Interestingly enough, when Simon & Schuster asked the Supreme Court to review the decision of the lower court and to pass judgment on New York's "Son of Sam" law, it did not do so alone. Even though they were not directly involved in the case, two prominent interest groups filed briefs with the Court, urging the justices to accept the case. One group, the Motion Picture Association of America, noted that the law had the similar effect of deterring the production of movies that were based upon firsthand criminal accounts. Another organized interest, the Association of American Publishers, also urged the Court to grant review. Among other things, this organization argued that stories of crime have been an important staple of the publishing industry and that New York's program of diverting profits from authors to crime victims would prevent comparable books from being published.

The input the Supreme Court received from interest groups scarcely ended there. To the contrary; once the justices slated the case for formal consideration, more than fifty separate interests quickly moved to provide information of their own for the Court to consider. Again, these organized groups were not connected to either Simon & Schuster or the state of New York. Nevertheless, through their own papers filed with the Court, they wanted to make sure that their views about how best to handle the "Son of Sam" law were available to the justices.

Some groups, like the American Civil Liberties Union, supported Simon & Schuster's argument that the law violated the guarantees of the First Amendment; other organizations, like the Washington Legal Foundation, backed New York's assertion that the law was appropriate because it regulated profits, not speech. Some organizations acted alone, others pooled their resources; so, for example, the Crime Victims Legal Clinic filed a brief on its own, while thirty-four state attorneys general worked together to present a unified front to the justices. A few interests, like the United States government, brought to light information not fully addressed by the parties. Other groups reinforced the parties' arguments as well as one another. And, perhaps most importantly, at least some of these interest groups appear to have shaped the Supreme Court's judgment in this case, affecting not only the decision to accept the case but the substantive content of the Court's policy itself.

The case of *Simon & Schuster, Inc. v. New York State Crime Victims Board* raises some intriguing questions regarding the participation of organized interests in the judicial process: In a decision-making setting theoretically governed by law, not politics, why would interest groups bother to try to influence the Supreme Court? What kinds of groups are most prevalent among those that do participate? What are the means by which they can pursue their goals? What impact, if any, does the involvement of outside interests have on the decisions the justices make? These issues are explored in this chapter.

EXPLAINING INTEREST GROUP ACTIVITY

If, as a means of compensating victims of crime, Congress were considering legislation that would make it difficult for publishers or moviemakers to produce true crime stories, representatives from the publishing and motion picture industries would almost certainly be dispatched to congressional offices. Pressing individual legislators, these lobbyists would make sure that members of Congress were fully aware of the adverse consequences that such a law might have upon books and films. Similarly, law-and-order groups would likely line up in support of the bill, providing data on the high costs of criminal activity and the importance of providing restitution. Being an elected political branch of the federal government, Congress is expected to be sensitive to the opinions of the constituent groups it represents.

But the U.S. Supreme Court is an unelected legal institution whose judgments are supposed to be based upon the law, not the politics of interest group advocacy. If the justices make decisions by applying the law to the factual circumstances that arise in a case, then what interest groups have to say certainly should not change that. Still, a variety of different interests went to the time and expense of expressing their views to the Court about how the "Son of Sam" law should be resolved. Why?

One answer is that, despite what distinguishes the justices from other governmental decision makers, the Court is very much a political institution. Many of the same issues that confront Congress, the executive, and state legislators inevitably arise in the Supreme Court as well, and its decisions—its interpretation of the Constitution, federal laws and regulations, and the like—become binding public policy for the nation. The justices have lifetime appointments, so they can base their decisions on whatever they deem most relevant for resolving cases. Under these circumstances, one might expect that interest groups would look for ways to affect the course of legal doctrine.

As a consequence, interest group activity in the Supreme Court is common. In fact, for some time now, different groups have followed closely the comings and goings of cases before the Supreme Court and have routinely expressed their views in any number of areas of the law. At least as far back as the 1950s, interest groups entered the judicial arena, drawn by clashes over leading issues of public policy.[2] Today, given the broad array of organized interests in the United States, conflicts over such salient concerns as abortion and school prayer can be assured of wide group participation, while even less visible legal disputes over patents or intergovernmental tax immunity are apt to spark the input of interest groups.[3]

Of course, thousands of cases are brought to the Supreme Court every year, of which the justices typically select less than one hundred for deliberation. Organized groups, therefore, usually have a great number of cases from which to choose. Many different interests became involved in the *Simon & Schuster* case; why, out of all these potential candidates, did they choose this one?

Most often, a group decides to devote its resources to a case because the constituency it represents will be affected by the Supreme Court's decision. These constituencies can assume many different forms: They could be corporations, unions, or businesses; they could be the members of public interest groups; still others might include state governments or indeed even the federal government. Whatever the interest, "the most frequently cited reason for participating . . . is the perceived economic, political, and social significance of the case to the organization's members."[4] In other words, interest groups participate in litigation before the Supreme Court because the issues at stake are likely to have consequences for them.

These consequences are easily illustrated by examining, in Table 5.1, some of the reasons why various groups became involved in the *Simon & Schuster* case. The Association of American Publishers, for example, was concerned that the New York law would affect a great many publishers by diminishing their capacity to produce books

[2]David Truman, *The Governmental Process* (New York: Knopf, 1951).
[3]Gregory A. Caldeira and John R. Wright, "Amici Curiae before the Supreme Court: Who Participates, When, and How Much?" *Journal of Politics* 52:782–806 (1990).
[4]Gregory A. Caldeira and John R. Wright, "Why Organized Interests Participate as Amici Curiae in the U.S. Supreme Court." Presented at the annual meeting of the American Political Science Association, 1989, p. 13.

TABLE 5.1 Why Did Interest Groups Participate in *Simon & Schuster v. Crime Victims Board?*

Selected Examples
In Support of Simon & Schuster:

[The] **Association of American Publishers** is the major national association of book publishers in the United States. AAP's more than 200 members include most of the leading commercial book publishers in the United States, as well as many smaller and nonprofit publishers, university presses, and scholarly associations.

Among the wide range of general and educational books produced by AAP members are diverse works dealing with the subject of crime. It is of particular importance to AAP's members that the decision below be reversed. New York is the center of the nation's publishing industry, and home to many of AAP's members. The legislatures of other states have patterned similar "Son of Sam" laws based on New York's "model." The Second Circuit's ruling in this case, if left undisturbed, will not only adversely affect publishing activities subject to the New York statute, but likely will have the effect of legitimizing more than 30 similar statutes in other states. The result will be to multiply manyfold the "chilling" effect on publication exacted by the New York law.

[The] **Motion Picture Association of America, Inc.** is a New York not-for-profit corporation that seeks to advance the interests of the American motion picture industry. MPAA's members are primarily engaged in the production and distribution of filmed entertainment, including theatrical motion pictures, television programs, and home videos.

New York's "Son-of-Sam" law, and similar laws in other jurisdictions, place significant and unjustified burdens on the MPAA's members and others who engage in film-making. These laws make it impossible or very difficult for film-makers to obtain the rights necessary to make films based on specific crimes from the persons accused or convicted of those crimes, or to obtain the assistance of such persons in the making of such films.

dealing with crime. Even though the case involved a book, not a movie, the Motion Picture Association of America entered the case because its members worried that the "Son of Sam" law would inhibit the production of movies that drew from the same types of sources as *Wiseguy*. Defending the law, the National Organization for Victim Assistance, a victims' rights group, saw the need to support and compensate those who had suffered from crime, and, since many states provided this compensation, the Council of State Governments recognized that this case would affect how their policies were financed.

Selected Examples
In Support of Crime Victims Board:

The National Organization for Victim Assistance, founded in 1975 and based in Washington, D.C., is a national nonprofit membership organization dedicated to improving the rights and services for victims of crime through national advocacy, victim counseling, professional education, and membership support.

[The] protection and enhancement of the rights of victims of crime need to be a major goal of the criminal and civil justice systems. One of these rights is the recovery of financial losses that crime imposes on victims. . . . [T]he New York Son of Sam law . . . and similar statutes in other states are an essential part of a societal interest in compensating victims for the losses they suffer from crime.

[The] Council of State Governments include[s] state, county, and municipal governments and officials throughout the United States. These organizations and their members have a compelling interest in legal issues that affect the powers and responsibilities of state and local governments.

This case presents questions concerning the constitutionality of state legislation designed to ensure that criminals do not profit from their crimes before their victims have had an opportunity to satisfy civil judgments out of such profits. Among other things, this legislation eases the burden of victim compensation that would otherwise fall on the State's treasury. The great majority of States have comparable legislation.

Although these groups expressed very different reasons for becoming involved in the case, the common theme was the effect the case would have upon the members of each organization. In this sense, the interest groups in *Simon & Schuster* are characteristic of a more general pattern in the Supreme Court. When cases come before the Court, organized interests recognize that those cases represent something more than simply a conflict between two parties. These are, in fact, disputes over the direction and scope of the nation's public policy. As with any governmental decision having a wide range of consequences, those who have a stake in the outcome want to ensure that their views are expressed and taken into consideration. Interest groups, then, lobby the Court for much the same reason that they lobby Congress. Obviously, the reasons for mounting a lobbying effort in the Court will vary from group to group and from case to case, but the impetus for becoming active in litigation remains the same. Interest groups get involved because they care about the outcome and how it might affect their members.

METHODS OF INFLUENCE

Interest groups might lobby the judiciary for the same reasons that they lobby other decision makers, but the methods of lobbying in the Supreme Court are quite different. Whereas a group might find myriad ways to try to shape the decision of a member of Congress—making campaign contributions, organizing constituent mailings, having personal discussions, staging rallies, and so on—there are relatively fewer avenues available in the Court. The reason is that the Supreme Court is, at least in theory, above politics. Like any court, it is obligated to dispense justice impartially, without consideration for the preferences of social or economic interests. Popularly elected decision makers, by contrast, are supposed to be responsive to political pressure. Despite this difference, however, the Supreme Court is actually quite open to the participation of organized groups. How, then, were interest groups able to participate in the *Simon & Schuster* case?

Sponsoring Litigation

There are two tactics that groups employ most often in the Court. The first is sponsorship of litigation; in other words, an organized interest will assume the costs and provide the necessary resources on behalf of a litigant in exchange for using the case as a means of advancing its goals. Obviously, furnishing lawyers, writing briefs, and paying various legal fees can be an expensive proposition. In addition, the likelihood of winning in the Supreme Court can be very difficult to gauge. Still, sponsorship of litigation is a method upon which interest groups often rely.[5] Groups recognize that cases can be

---

[5]See, e.g., Lee Epstein, "Interest Group Litigation During the Rehnquist Era," *The Journal of Law & Politics* 9:639–717 (1993).

legal vehicles for testing the law, and many have used this method with noteworthy success. Among the more well-known examples of the effectiveness of this strategy is the campaign of test cases against racial segregation, conceived by the NAACP Legal Defense and Educational Fund, as well as efforts by various groups—such as Americans United for Separation of Church and State—to limit the role of government in religious activity.[6]

Historically, political underdogs have had the benefit of group sponsorship. Disaffected litigants, without the means to shepherd cases through the lengthy and expensive appellate process, have often allowed sympathetic interests to champion their causes. Since the 1970s, though, the socially and economically advantaged parties in the Court have enjoyed the help of interest groups, as well.[7] In this case, as one of the country's largest and most successful publishers, Simon & Schuster was one such litigant, but it did not relinquish control and provide a test case for an interested organization, like the ACLU. Given that the stakes for the company were so high, it is perhaps not surprising that it retained control of the case itself, hiring a New York law firm with at least one lawyer who had handled dozens of prior cases in the Supreme Court. By contrast, New York was represented by its attorney general, a practice followed by virtually all other states.

Amicus Curiae Briefs

In *Simon & Schuster*, all of the participation from organized groups assumed the second and more common form of Supreme Court lobbying—the filing of amicus curiae briefs. Taking their name from the Latin phrase "friend of the court," these briefs are documents, submitted to the Court by interested parties, whose theoretical aim it is to provide the justices with information not furnished by the litigants in their briefs. At one time, these briefs were envisioned as sources of dispassionate advice, a way to help guarantee that the members of the Court would make fully informed decisions. Today, however, neither the justices nor interest groups harbor any illusions

---

[6]Clement E. Vose, *Caucasions Only* (Berkeley: University of California Press, 1959); Frank J. Sorauf, *The Wall of Separation: Constitutional Politics of Church and State* (Princeton, NJ: Princeton University Press, 1976).
[7]Karen O'Connor and Lee Epstein, "The Rise of Conservative Interest Group Litigation," *Journal of Politics* 45:479–89 (1983).

about the role of amicus briefs; they are designed to advanced the policy agendas of those who submit them.[8]

Paralleling the rise of interest group activity in American politics more generally, amicus briefs have been filed with greater and greater frequency over the past forty years.[9] Figure 5.1 charts this increase, showing how amici have gone from being relatively modest actors in the Court to some of its most prominent players. Amici may file their briefs only with the permission of both parties or, alternatively, the Court itself, but this has not deterred would-be lobbying efforts; despite the Court having expressed its disdain over the growing number of amicus briefs, groups of various stripes still routinely line up on both sides of an issue.[10] Like *Simon & Schuster*, most cases have not just one but several amicus briefs filed by a variety of groups. Obviously, some cases attract more attention than others, depending upon the nature of the issue. Indicative of their far-reaching policy consequences and the importance of the issues to various publics, two cases are the modern record holders for amicus participation. When the justices first considered the issue of affirmative action in *Regents of the University of California v. Bakke* (1978), fifty-eight amicus briefs were submitted to the Court. More recently, in one of its more important holdings on the issue of abortion, a total of seventy-eight briefs—signed by more than four hundred organizations—were filed in *Webster v. Reproductive Health Services* (1989).[11] Few issues, of course, draw such massive input from interest groups. Still, they are a pervasive presence; virtually every case the Supreme Court decides now has one or more amicus briefs for the justices to consider.

Typical of this pattern, there was no shortage of amici curiae in *Simon & Schuster*. It was obvious that, ever since the Supreme Court agreed to decide the case in mid-February 1991, a number of organizations had been following the case with interest and had been preparing to make their case to the Court. On April 18, 1991, the

---

[8]Samuel Krislov, "The Amicus Curiae Brief: From Friendship to Advocacy," *Yale Law Journal* 72:694–721 (1963).

[9]Epstein, "Interest Group Litigation"; Kay L. Schlozman and John T. Tierney, *Organized Interests and American Democracy* (New York: Harper and Row, 1986).

[10]Tony Mauro, "Court Gets a Tad Less Friendly to Amici," *Legal Times of Washington,* Feb. 19, 1990.

[11]Susan Behuniak-Long, "Friendly Fire: Amici Curiae and *Webster v. Reproductive Health Services,*" *Judicature* 74:261–70 (1991).

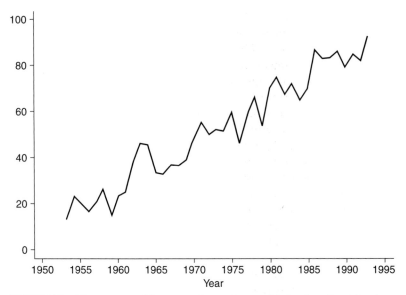

FIGURE 5.1 Percentage of Supreme Court Cases with Amicus Participation
Source: Lee Epstein, Jeffrey A. Segal, Harold J. Spaeth, and Thomas G.
Walker. 1994. *The Supreme Court Compendium: Data, Decisions, and
Developments,* 2nd ed. (Washington: Congressional Quarterly, Inc.), Table 7–24.

same day that Simon & Schuster filed its briefs with the Court, the
justices also received an amicus brief supporting the publisher's attack on the "Son of Sam" law. The following day, three more amicus
briefs arrived at the Court, two urging the Court to strike down New
York's program, one arguing in support of the law. A few weeks
later, on May 30, it was the Crime Victims Board's turn to file its papers with the justices, and five more briefs—all of them endorsing
New York's prohibition on criminals' earnings—were submitted the
very next day. A closer look at who filed these briefs reveals the considerable diversity of—and the Court's openness to—the advocacy
of organized interests.

WHO LOBBIES THE COURT?

Given that groups tend to become involved in cases that will have an
impact on their members, one might make some educated guesses

about the types of interests that would likely be drawn into a case like *Simon & Schuster*. In light of the case's implications for book publishers, for example, one might anticipate that representatives from the publishing world would draft amicus briefs. Furthermore, since the case involved a state's effort to compensate crime victims, other states having similar public policies would also have an interest in the Court's treatment of the "Son of Sam" law. Quite apart from these potential amici, the purpose of the New York law was not only to prevent criminals from exploiting their crimes but to provide financial compensation to their victims as well; thus, law-and-order groups might be keen to express their views.

Just who were the amici curiae in *Simon & Schuster*? Table 5.2 provides information about the friends of the Court in this case, classifying them under three general headings. Business associations, such as the publishers and motion picture associations who were no doubt concerned about the law's threat to their profits, constitute one group. Governments at all levels, not merely the state of New York, have an interest in reducing the incentives for crime and in compensating its victims. So governments—that is, the United States, the individuals states, and the various associations of state and local officials—comprise a second group. And advocacy groups, including the likes of the ACLU and the Maryland Coalition Against Crime, are the third. Some, like the ACLU, saw the law as a threat to free expression, while others, like the National Organization for Victim Assistance, regarded New York's policy as a legitimate means of helping those who suffer at the hands of criminals.

These three sets of actors—business associations, governments, and advocacy groups—are, in fact, the most common types of interests that file amicus briefs with the Supreme Court. Some of their briefs were filed solo; the Motion Picture Association of America, for one, submitted a brief completely on its own. Other interests, like the alliance of thirty-four state attorneys general, worked collectively upon a single brief. Whether working together or alone, it is clear that a diverse set of interests cared enough about this case to provide additional information and arguments for the justices to consider. What does this considerable variety suggest about the nature of lobbying in the Supreme Court? *Simon & Schuster* is indicative of the justices' more general openness to the input of interest groups. As two of the leading scholars of interest groups in the Court have concluded, "[T]he Supreme Court is remarkably accessible to a wide

TABLE 5.2 Amici Curiae in *Simon & Schuster v. Crime Victims Board*

In support of Simon & Schuster:
- American Civil Liberties Union, New York Civil Liberties Union, Pen American Center
- Association of American Publishers, Inc.
- Motion Picture Association of America, Inc.

In support of Crime Victims Board:
- Council of State Governments, National Association of Counties, National League of Cities, National Governors' Association, International City Management Association, National Institute of Municipal Law Officers, and U.S. Conference of Mayors
- Crime Victims Legal Clinic
- State of Florida, joined by the following states: Alabama, Alaska, California, Colorado, Connecticut, Delaware, Georgia, Idaho, Illinois, Indiana, Kansas, Maryland, Massachusetts, Michigan, Minnesota, Mississippi, Missouri, Montana, Nebraska, Nevada, New Hampshire, New Jersey, North Carolina, Ohio, Oklahoma, Pennsylvania, South Carolina, South Dakota, Tennessee, Utah, Vermont, Virginia, Wyoming
- National Organization for Victim Assistance, Security on Campus, Inc., National Organization of Crime Victim Compensation Boards, and White Collar Crime 101
- Solicitor General of the United States
- Washington Legal Foundation, Allied Educational Foundation, Citizens for Law and Order, Maryland Coalition Against Crime, National Victim Center, Parents of Murdered Children, Stephanie Roper Foundation, and forty-five Members of the New York State Legislature

array of organized interests. . . . In this sense, the Court is very much a representative institution, and in terms of the variety of organizations from which it hears, quite representative of the general mix of organizations represented in Washington."[12] With nine briefs signed by more than sixty groups, this case clearly had implications for many different social and economic concerns.

INFLUENCE ON THE SUPREME COURT

Of course, interest groups would not bother to file amicus briefs if they did not believe that their submissions had some chance of shaping the Court's decision. In case after case, policies affecting different

[12]Caldeira and Wright, "Amici Curiae before the Supreme Court."

constituencies weigh in the balance, so it seems logical that groups would file briefs in the hope of tipping the scales in their favor. Certainly the parties themselves may seek to generate outside support, as a means of demonstrating to the Court that their positions are endorsed by broad segments of society. What is less obvious is whether amicus briefs actually help determine the fate of litigants in the Supreme Court. Are the justices responsive to the lobbying efforts of interest groups? And, in particular, did organized interests have any influence in *Simon & Schuster*?

Agenda Setting

One way in which interests can affect the Supreme Court is by helping the justices locate worthwhile cases.[13] Every year, the Court is faced with thousands of petitions for review, most of which do not raise issues of sufficient importance to merit the Court's attention. For its part, the Court is especially interested in resolving cases that have nationwide significance, but finding those cases among thousands of pages of pleadings can be difficult. It is here where interest groups can help the justices.

In addition to arguing in favor of a particular outcome, amicus briefs can also be filed to persuade the Supreme Court to either accept or reject a petition for review. In other words, groups occasionally lobby the justices when they are deciding whether or not to decide a case. When filing such briefs, groups put their time, their money, and their reputations on the line, and since so many trivial cases are brought to the Court, interest groups are rather reluctant to file amicus briefs at this stage. When they do, however, these briefs act as a signal to the Court that the case has consequences for some larger constituency. This serves as reliable evidence that a case is of genuine import; consequently those cases are much more likely to be accepted.[14]

When the "Son of Sam" law was brought before the Supreme Court, two organizations—the Association of American Publishers and the Motion Picture Association of America—filed amicus briefs

---

[13]For more on the role of interest groups in case selection, see Chapter 3.
[14]Gregory A. Caldeira and John R. Wright, "Organized Interests and Agenda Setting in the U.S. Supreme Court," *American Political Science Review* 82:1109–27 (1988).

encouraging the justices to accept the case of *Simon & Schuster v. Crime Victims Board* for review. In their filing, the publishers noted that this law had the effect of blocking the publication of many books that were based upon nonfiction accounts of crime. The New York law, in their view, did not merely affect Henry Hill and Nicholas Pileggi but rather a large number of potential authors who might be interested in authoring similar books. Likewise, the motion picture group pointed to the problems the law posed for moviemaking: Film producers would either have to purge movies of their accounts of crime or simply not make their movies. In their view, films that were "based on a true story" would be watered down, if indeed they were ever made at all.

By filing these briefs, these two organizations let the Supreme Court know that the *Simon & Schuster* case mattered, not only to the publisher of a single book about the Mafia, but also to the entire publishing and motion picture industries. Later, the Court noted that it granted review in this case because "the issue is significant and likely to recur." Among hundreds and hundreds of potential cases, two major organizations helped draw the Court's attention to this one in particular; that clearly would have helped to erase any doubts the justices may have had about the larger ramifications of the controversy.

Winning and Losing

Once cases are slated on the Supreme Court's agenda, do amici make any difference in the outcomes of cases? The evidence here is not especially strong. Some scholars have studied whether the justices are affected by the sheer number of filings on one side versus another. Assuming that the Court is interested in the implications of a decision for public policy, then a party to a case should be more likely to win if it can show that its position is more widely held by different interests within society. One study developed a simple strategy for testing the influence of amicus briefs: if two cases are otherwise similar, the party with amicus support in one case should be more likely to win than the similar party without amicus support in the second case. According to this research, "The differences in the success rates of litigants who received amicus support and those who did not was trivial. . . . [T]here is no general pattern which suggests that a litigant's chances of success depend on whether or not an amicus curiae brief is filed in the litigant's behalf."[15] In short, having organized interests on one's side simply had no bearing on winning and losing in the Supreme Court.

Why would amicus briefs seem not to matter? According to one school of thought, the justices make decisions largely on the basis of their own policy preferences; if that is the case, then the participation of interest groups, or the lack thereof, should make no difference in how the members of the Court resolve cases.[16] Another view is that the Court is responsive to well-reasoned legal argument; if that were so, then a party's likelihood of success would have a lot more to do with the persuasiveness of its rationale than the number of interest groups lined up in its favor. Still another possibility is that interest groups file amicus briefs for reasons other than to persuade the Court; amicus briefs, for example, serve as a good public relations device for satisfying existing group members or recruiting new ones. Perhaps most important is the likelihood that observers of the Court have generalized about the impact of amici from a few celebrated— and atypical—successes.[17]

There is one noteworthy exception on this score. One amicus curiae in particular—the government of the United States—does indeed appear to affect the Court's decision making. The federal government is represented by the solicitor general, a lawyer in the Department of Justice whose job it is to represent the United States in the Supreme Court. Because the federal government is involved in so many cases each year, solicitors general and their staffs can accumulate considerable experience in Supreme Court litigation. Not surprisingly, with so much expertise, the solicitor general is taken quite seriously by the justices. The Court, in fact, often seeks the input of the government, by asking the solicitor general to act as a friend of the court; as a result, the United States often files briefs and even appears at oral arguments as an amicus curiae. Studies have shown, over and over again, that when the federal government files

[15]Donald R. Songer and Reginald S. Sheehan, "Interest Group Success in the Courts: Amicus Participation in the Supreme Court," *Political Research Quarterly* 46:339–54 (1993).
[16]Jeffrey A. Segal and Harold J. Spaeth, *The Supreme Court and the Attitudinal Model* (Cambridge: Cambridge University Press, 1993).
[17]Songer and Sheehan, "Interest Group Success in the Courts."

an amicus brief on behalf of a party, that party is significantly more likely to win.[18]

What relevance do these findings have for *Simon & Schuster v. Crime Victims Board*? In terms of the volume of support listed in Table 5.2, there were three amicus briefs supporting the publisher in this case, but there were twice as many briefs filed in support of New York's law. As a general rule, though, the degree of interest group support seems not to affect the outcome of a case. At the same time, the Victims Board did have the support of the solicitor general; if the justices heed the advice of the federal government, then the Victims Board would be more likely to prevail. To assess the impact of the interest groups, one needs to know how the Supreme Court resolved the dispute.

On December 10, 1991, the justices announced their decision. By a unanimous vote, the members of the Court struck down New York's "Son of Sam" law. The Court ruled that, "[w]hether the First Amendment 'speaker' is considered to be Hill [or Simon & Schuster], which can publish books about crime with the assistance of only those criminals willing to forgo remuneration, . . . the law singles out speech on a particular subject for a financial burden that it places on no other speech and no other income and, thus, is presumptively inconsistent with the Amendment." Simon & Schuster was now free to publish books like *Wiseguy*, and Henry Hill was entitled to his royalty payments.

It is true that Simon & Schuster had the backing of the book and film industries, as well as the ACLU, but New York had an impressive list of supporters of its own: a large number of law-and-order groups, several well-respected governmental associations, not to mention almost three-quarters of the states and, of course, the solicitor general. Yet none of this support seems to have mattered. The large number of proponents did not convince the justices of the acceptability of the law. New York may have been able to generate a lot of outside support, but, as is true more generally, that did not guarantee success. Even the federal government, despite its importance as an amicus, still fails to persuade the Court about 25 percent of the

---

[18]See, for example, Jeffrey A. Segal, "Amicus Curiae Briefs by the Solicitor General during the Warren and Burger Courts," *Western Political Quarterly* 41:135–44 (1988); Rebecca Mae Salokar, *The Solicitor General: The Politics of Law* (Philadelphia: Temple University Press, 1992).

time;[19] obviously, this was one of those instances. With no apparent interest group influence on the outcome, at least some of the lessons of scholarly research on the Court were borne out by the decision in *Simon & Schuster*. Does that mean that amicus briefs were unimportant in this case?

Shaping the Court's Policies

Interest groups are motivated to file amicus briefs because they recognize that the Supreme Court is crafting important policies that, in one way or another, will have an impact on them. Consequently, to most organized interests, who wins in the Court is not nearly as important as why. From their perspective, the parties may only want to see their immediate rights vindicated—a broadcaster wants a burdensome regulation removed, an employee wants a promotion that was unfairly denied, a criminal defendant wants a new trial, a religious group wants to exercise its faith freely, and so on. But the rationales that the justices employ to justify these outcomes are much more critical to groups, because these interpretations of law are binding public policies, no less than congressional legislation or administrative regulation.

For this reason, one should not dismiss the potential influence of amici too quickly. Parties may be capable of generating a wealth of amicus briefs to their cause, but if they add no new information or if they simply replicate one another, they may be of little practical use to the justices, no matter how many of them are filed. If, however, interest groups can provide new arguments, legal analysis, information, or data not otherwise available, this may affect how the members of the Court ultimately resolve the questions presented by a case. Often amici do provide the justices with unique data and analysis, and on occasion these independent arguments are incorporated into the Court's opinions.[20] According to one lawyer who has filed many amicus briefs with the Court, "A good idea is a good idea, whether it is contained in an amicus brief or in the brief of a

---

[19]See Lee Epstein, Jeffrey A. Segal, Harold J. Spaeth, and Thomas G. Walker, *The Supreme Court Compendium* (Washington: Congressional Quarterly, Inc., 1994), p. 571.
[20]James F. Spriggs and Paul J. Wahlbeck, "Amicus Curiae and the Role of Information at the Supreme Court," *Political Research Quarterly* 50:365–86 (1997).

party."[21] In this sense, amicus briefs may, from time to time, be quite important in shaping the scope, content, and impact of the Court's rulings. How might interest groups have affected the Supreme Court's consideration of *Simon & Schuster*?

In its brief, Simon & Schuster argued that the "Son of Sam" law must be reviewed by a legal test known as strict scrutiny. Ordinarily, to survive a court challenge, most laws need only bear some logical relationship to the goal that government wants to achieve. (For example, the government can impose speed limits, since they promote safety on the highway.) When, however, legislation touches upon a civil liberty, such as freedom of the press or religion, the Supreme Court usually subjects the law to a much more stringent test; it demands that the government be pursuing a very important goal—that is, a compelling state interest—by the method that least interferes with that liberty. Drawing upon that standard, the publisher argued that, since the "Son of Sam" law interfered with the First Amendment right to free expression, the law would have to be reviewed by the standard of strict scrutiny. According to Simon & Schuster, whose arguments are catalogued in Table 5.3, compensating the victims of criminals who exploit their crimes was not a vital objective of government. Moreover, since the law targeted authors whose works described their crimes, even if their books made only vague, fleeting reference to past misdeeds, the state had not chosen the least restrictive means of regulating speech. In its amicus brief, the ACLU covered much the same legal ground. Because these issues had been considered in the lower courts, such arguments would be expected to arise in the Supreme Court, as well.

Unfortunately for organized groups concerned about freedom of the press, the likes of David Berkowitz (who inspired the law) and Henry Hill are not very sympathetic figures to defend. So, in its amicus brief, the Association of American Publishers developed a strategy that permitted it to attack the law without directly defending the right to reap financial reward for such serious criminal acts. As highlighted in Table 5.3, a central argument of the publishers was that this law would inhibit the publication of a vast number of important books. Naturally, like Simon & Schuster and its other supporting amici, this group argued that the "Son of Sam" law violated the First

---

[21]Bruce J. Ennis, "Effective Amicus Briefs," *Catholic University Law Review* 33:603–9 (1984), p. 603.

TABLE 5.3 Arguments Presented on Behalf of Simon & Schuster

Argument Made by:	Requires Strict Scrutiny?	No Compelling State Interest?	Not Least Restrictive?	Impedes Production of Creative Works?
Simon & Schuster	yes	yes	yes	no
Association of American Publishers	yes	yes	yes	yes
American Civil Liberties Union	yes	yes	yes	no
Motion Picture Association	yes	yes	yes	yes

Amendment. Also as a part of their brief, though, the publishers included an additional argument: that the law had a major impact on the publishing industry, inasmuch as it created a serious obstacle to authors who might write potentially significant books. Along similar lines, the Motion Picture Association claimed that the law would have the same repercussions on the film industry. While Simon & Schuster had only alluded to these potential effects, the publishers made this the leading focus of their brief: "Crime has always been a subject of public interest and fascination, and writings about crime are a staple of our literary heritage," the amicus noted. "The reach of New York's Son of Sam law is nothing short of astonishing."

To demonstrate to the Court the law's consequences—and to remove the specter of the Mafia and serial killers from the law—the publishers included in their amicus brief a list of hundreds of existing works that would have fallen under the law. Some of these books were classics of American literature. The list included works by escaped slaves, individuals falsely accused, antiwar activists, civil rights leaders, political dissidents, prominent public officials, celebrated fiction authors, and singers and songwriters, among others. The implication was that New York's law would have theoretically deprived the reading public of the writings of such authors as Joan Baez, William Burroughs, Eugene Dennis, Merle Haggard, Patricia Hearst, O. Henry, Billie Holiday, Martin Luther King, Jr., Timothy Leary, Jack London, Malcolm X, and Henry David Thoreau. The law also would have been a barrier to the works of at least half a dozen people involved in the Watergate affair, perhaps the most important political and constitutional crisis in modern history.

By this device, this group was able to demonstrate in a clear and convincing way how the New York law, despite its understandable motives, would have major First Amendment implications. Speaking for the Court, Justice O'Connor made this aspect of the publishers' brief a highlight of her opinion. Taking her cues from the amicus brief, she extended its logic by identifying a number of prominent and respected individuals who, having committed fairly innocuous offenses, would have been subject to this law. Citing this "sobering bibliography," O'Connor wrote that the law's "provisions combine to encompass a potentially very large number of works. . . . The argument that a statute like the Son of Sam law would prevent publication of all of these works is hyperbole—some would have been written without compensation—but the Son of Sam law clearly reaches a wide range of literature that does not enable a criminal to profit from his crime while a victim remains uncompensated." As she noted, for example, even St. Augustine—hardly a criminal seeking to capitalize on his past misdeeds—would have been subject to this law for writing in his *Confessions* of past crimes, the list of which includes stealing pears from a neighbor.

In this way, the decision in *Simon & Schuster* demonstrates how interest groups sometimes have a hand in shaping the content of the Court's policies. Of course, the justices probably would have decided to strike down the New York law even without the input of these amici curiae, and while groups might often bring fresh perspectives to an issue, there is no guarantee that those views will become a part of the justices' decisions. Still, it seems clear that the publishers' long list of written works—information not contained in the parties' briefs—stimulated the justices to consider the potentially sweeping effects of the law, and this could only have solidified their skepticism of New York's program.

That the Court may, from time to time, find useful information in an amicus brief reveals the justices to be less concerned with the identity of the interest groups involved or the number of amicus briefs they file and more attentive to what those amici have to say. Stated differently, while the mere existence of an amicus brief may have little bearing on judicial doctrine, the contents of that brief may be very significant indeed.

CONCLUSION

Despite its status as a legal institution, the Supreme Court is quite open to the input of organized interests. With increased frequency, interest groups have pressed their agendas through various channels, most often as amici curiae. These interests assume many guises; they come as corporations and governments, businesses and industries, social and economic causes. Indeed, the lineup of groups before the Court is the profile of organized interests in American politics more generally. Not surprisingly, these groups lobby the justices for the same reasons that they lobby other governmental decision makers; the Supreme Court's policies have real consequences, and interest groups mobilize because they want their voices to be heard.

Simon & Schuster v. Crime Victims Board began with Henry Hill telling his story of his life as a gangster, and it ended as a major case in the U.S. Supreme Court, pitting some of the nation's most prominent interest groups against one another. Why did one man's tale of criminal intrigue spark a conflict between more than half of the states and the publishing and motion picture industries? The answer is that, while in a formal sense the case was a contest between two parties over book royalties, each of those parties represented the policy interests of much broader constituencies. Simon & Schuster wanted to be able to publish true crime stories, but the larger literary and film worlds, together with civil liberties groups, recognized a potential threat to both creativity and financial profits. New York wanted to compensate Henry Hill's victims, but governmental officials, as well as victims' rights groups, saw a challenge to a widely adopted method of providing financial help to unfortunate citizens. It is no wonder that affected organizations were anxious to express their views. Such a case is especially useful, therefore, in illuminating some of the key features of group lobbying in the Supreme Court. Ultimately, it reveals why and how interest groups take to the courts and what kind of influence they can have when they do.

QUESTIONS FOR DISCUSSION

1. As representative institutions, the elected branches of the federal government are expected to be sensitive to the interests of differ-

ent segments of society. Should the justices make similar efforts to base their decisions, at least in part, on the implications that their policies will have for various interest groups?

2. Does the participation of outside interests, either through direct sponsorship or amicus briefs, enhance or diminish the process of Supreme Court policy making? Does *Simon & Schuster* provide any answers?

3. The justices seem quite willing to have organized groups provide input into their decision-making process. What, if anything, does this suggest about the amount and quality of information provided to the Court by the parties to a case?

4. Interest group participation in the Supreme Court requires certain financial resources. To the extent that the Court listens to outside interests, is there a bias in favor of the economically advantaged? What does the interest group activity in *Simon & Schuster* suggest?

5. When filing amicus briefs, some interest groups ally themselves with one another, while others lobby alone. That is, some organizations work together on a single amicus brief, while other groups file independently. What are some of the potential benefits and costs associated with each strategy?

6. Do the justices—unelected and appointed for life—have any incentives to consider the competing voices of outside interests? What motives would the members of the Court have to appease organized groups?

7. In writing her opinion in *Simon & Schuster*, Justice O'Connor cited information provided by the Association of American Publishers in its amicus brief. Do such citations make an opinion any more compelling in either a legal or a policy sense?

SUGGESTED READING

Susan Behuniak-Long. 1991. "Friendly Fire: Amici Curiae and *Webster v. Reproductive Health Services.*" *Judicature* 74:261–70.

Gregory A. Caldeira and John R. Wright. 1990. "Amici Curiae before the Supreme Court: Who Participates, When, and How Much?" *Journal of Politics* 52:782–806.

Gregg Ivers. 1995. *To Build a Wall: American Jews and the Separation of Church and State.* Charlottesville: University Press of Virginia.

Susan E. Lawrence. 1990. *The Poor in Court: The Legal Services Program and Supreme Court Decision Making.* Princeton, NJ: Princeton University Press.

Rebecca Mae Salokar. 1992. *The Solicitor General: The Politics of Law.* Philadelphia: Temple University Press.

Kay L. Schlozman and John T. Tierney. 1986. *Organized Interests and American Democracy.* New York: Harper and Row.

Donald R. Songer and Reginald S. Sheehan. 1993. "Interest Group Success in the Courts: Amicus Participation in the Supreme Court." *Political Research Quarterly* 46:339–54.

Frank J. Sorauf. 1976. *The Wall of Separation: The Constitutional Politics of Church and State.* Princeton, NJ: Princeton University Press.

James F. Spriggs and Paul J. Wahlbeck. 1997. "Amicus Curiae and the Role of Information at the Supreme Court." *Political Research Quarterly* 50:365–86.

Stephen L. Wasby. 1995. *Race Relations Litigation in an Age of Complexity.* Charlottesville: University Press of Virginia.

CHAPTER 6

The Supreme Court's Policies and Their Impact

Buckley v. Valeo

Few issues dominate the American political landscape more than the role of money in election campaigns. Responding to concerns over corruption, excessive spending, and public accountability, policy makers have had to consider how best to reform campaign finance. One of the major forces in this debate has been the Supreme Court. In 1976, the justices decided Buckley v. Valeo, *a case questioning the legality of congressional attempts to control the way in which money could be used in federal elections. Concluding that at least some features of the law infringed upon free speech, the Court placed important and lasting limits on the ability of government to regulate the use of campaign funds. Legislators, judges, and other public officials greeted this decision with different degrees of enthusiasm. Since then, the case has had important implications— some of them unanticipated—for campaign politics. In one way or another, candidates, interest groups, and parties have been affected, as the* Buckley *decision reshaped fundraising, advertising, and spending levels in elections. What happens after the justices make a decision? This chapter considers some of the possibilities.*

The Watergate affair transformed American politics in a number of ways. One of the most important changes that it precipitated was a major overhaul in the way in which campaigns for national office were financed. During the 1972 election, the campaign organization of Republican President Richard Nixon had received untold thousands of dollars, secret campaign funds that had been used to help finance the sabotage of the Democratic Party and its candidates. These funds had apparently been used to underwrite not only a break-in at the Democratic National Committee headquarters in Washington's Watergate office building but also a wide variety of political deceptions. Revelations of these activities led to congressional investigations, criminal indictments of executive branch officials, and ultimately the resignation of the president.[1] In light of these events, Congress passed a sweeping piece of legislation known as the Federal Election Campaign Act Amendments of 1974. Designed to limit the abuse of money in national politics, this law imposed stringent regulations on the raising, spending, and accounting of funds used by presidential and congressional candidates.

Only three years before, Congress had enacted the Federal Election Campaign Act (FECA). In the hope of reducing the role of money, this law imposed several restrictions on campaign finance, but these regulations seemed to have little practical effect. Spending at the presidential level by both the Democratic and Republican parties, for example, multiplied several times over between 1968 and 1972. Given these increases, Congress again pondered reform, and the Watergate scandal sparked the efforts for change. "In 1974," notes one political scientist, "Congress thoroughly revised the federal campaign finance system in response to the pressure for comprehensive reform in the wake of Watergate and other reports of abuse in the 1972 Nixon campaign. Detailed investigations into the Nixon campaign revealed an alarming reliance on large contributions, illegal corporate contributions, and undisclosed slush funds."[2] Through a series of amendments to the FECA enacted after Nixon's resignation, Congress made comprehensive changes in when, where, and how money could be used in national elections.

Most notably, the new law limited both the contributions and expenses of candidates for federal office.[3] To reduce the role of wealthy

---

[1]For a detailed description of the events surrounding the Watergate affair written by the two principal journalists who investigated and chronicled its events, see Carl Bernstein and Bob Woodward, *All the President's Men* (New York: Warner Books, 1974).
[2]Anthony Corrado, "A History of Federal Campaign Finance Law," in *Campaign Finance Reform: A Sourcebook*, ed. Anthony Corrado, Thomas E. Mann, Daniel R. Ortiz, Trevor Potter, and Frank J. Sorauf (Washington: Brookings Institution Press, 1997), p. 32.
[3]My summary of the 1974 amendments to the FECA is drawn from Frank J. Sorauf, *Inside Campaign Finance: Myths and Realities* (New Haven, CT: Yale University Press, 1992), pp. 9–10, and Document 2.9 in Corrado et al., *Campaign Finance Reform*.

donors, the law limited individuals to giving no more than $1,000 to a candidate for any election. Contributions to political committees, such as political action committees (PACs), and political parties were also regulated, capped at annual amounts of $5,000 and $25,000, respectively. For their part, party organizations and PACs also had restrictions placed upon on how much they could contribute; neither could give a candidate more than $5,000 per election. This represented the first time that Congress had sought to place genuine constraints on the extent to which individuals and groups could channel their resources to the candidates, political organizations, and parties of their choice.[4]

No less significantly, maximum campaign spending ceilings were imposed by the 1974 law. Those with the most direct stake in the outcome of elections, political parties and their candidates, were now faced with federal controls on their spending. At the congressional level, both House and Senate candidates had maximum spending levels. In the general election campaign, for instance, House candidates could spend no more than $70,000, while individuals running for the Senate were limited to $150,000 (or $0.12 times the size of a state's voting-age population, whichever was greater).[5] Similar restrictions were established for primary elections, as well.

To curb the potential influence of personal wealth, candidates and their immediate families could not spend their own financial resources beyond the law's designated limits. Candidates for the House had a threshold of $25,000, while senatorial candidates could use no more than $35,000 of their own money. Consequently, the ability of affluent candidates simply to bankroll their own campaigns—as opposed to appealing for broad public support by soliciting contributions—was substantially diminished.

The amount of money that political parties could spend on behalf of their parties' nominees for Congress was also curtailed.

---

[4]Some earlier laws successfully curbed the contributions of corporations and labor unions to federal election campaigns. Other laws tried to limit individual contributions, but they were easily circumvented. See Anthony Corrado, "A History of Federal Campaign Finance Law," in Corrado et al., *Campaign Finance Reform*, pp. 27–35.

[5]In the case of the House of Representatives, these limitations applied to states with more than one member of Congress. A few sparsely populated states have only one member in the U.S. House; since candidates for those states' House seats, like their counterparts in Senate elections, were running statewide campaigns, their spending ceilings were made equal to those of Senate candidates.

Under the FECA, the parties' national and congressional campaign organizations, such as the Republican National Committee and the Democratic Congressional Campaign Committee, could spend no more than $10,000 in support of their candidates for the House. The maximum amount for senatorial candidates was $20,000 (or, if it were greater, $0.02 times the size of a state's voting-age population).

In mounting their national campaigns, presidential candidates were also affected by the new law; they could spend no more than $10 million in pursuit of a party's nomination. Once nominated, the Democratic and Republican candidates were limited to spending $20 million dollars each in pursuit of the presidency, but this limit was voluntary. That is, the law established a taxpayer-supported campaign fund, which would offer equal sums to the two presidential candidates. Those who declined these campaign funds for the general election could spend as much money as they wished—or at least as much as they could raise.

Of course, not all spending in an election campaign is done by candidates and their political parties. Believing that they may benefit from having certain people in national office, individuals and organized groups also use their financial resources—taking out newspaper advertisements, purchasing television time, and publishing and mailing campaign information—to advocate the election or defeat of various candidates. To minimize the impact of their money on federal elections, the 1974 amendments to the FECA stipulated that no individual or organization could spend more than $1,000 per election to support or oppose a particular congressional or presidential candidate. So, interest groups or concerned citizens who sought to undertake their own independent campaigns in a federal election were free to do so, but the amount of money they spent per candidate could not exceed the $1,000 maximum.

In order to overcome the financial abuses associated with the Watergate affair, this new law placed stringent limits on the role of money in American national elections. Candidates, organized groups, and political parties could raise money in federal campaigns, but now that money could only be raised in limited amounts. Spending would be brought under control, as well; no matter how much a candidate had—either personally or in campaign contributions—and no matter what amount of money an interest group or party might raise in an election cycle, there were strict constraints on how much they could spend. Almost any person or group that might be active in an election campaign faced new limits on its expenditures.

The goals served by the revised FECA were obvious. Among other things, the law guarded against corruption by neutralizing the so-called "fat cats" who could garner disproportionate influence in both election and subsequent policy outcomes. If donors were limited in their contributions, they would be less able to buy special consideration. Furthermore, because the law required extensive record keeping, the sources of campaign contributions would become a matter of public scrutiny. In addition, to limit money's impact on election outcomes, the contribution and spending limits reduced the financial disparities between candidates. In theory, then, decisions on election day would be based on the quality of the candidates and their policy positions, not the size of their campaign war chests. Finally, to monitor and administer federal election law, the FECA created the Federal Election Commission, a new, independent regulatory body that would oversee the financial operations of national campaigns.

Large contributions would no longer be able to dominate campaign finance. There would be an end to slush funds and undisclosed donations. Illegal money could no longer flow into campaigns unchecked. The days of excessive campaign spending corroding the electoral process were over. Or at least that is what Congress hoped. As it happened, though, Congress was never able to see how the law would actually operate. The reason was that, before the FECA went into effect, the Supreme Court declared much of it to be unconstitutional.

On October 15, 1974, President Gerald Ford signed the legislation into law. Shortly thereafter, U.S. Senator James L. Buckley of New York filed suit against Francis R. Valeo, the secretary of the Senate, in a legal challenge to the recent changes that had been made in the Federal Election Campaign Act.[6] The case quickly made its way through the federal courts, and less than a year after the law went

[6]Buckley and Valeo were the named parties, but in fact a diverse coalition of interests were involved in the case. In addition to the ideologically conservative Buckley, Democrat Eugene J. McCarthy, the former Minnesota senator and presidential candidate, was also among those contesting the law. Both liberal and conservative interest groups, such as the New York Civil Liberties Union and the American Conservative Union, were also on board. Formally, their suit was brought against a group of federal officials, including Valeo and the clerk of the U.S. House, W. Pat Jennings.

into effect, even before a new federal election had intervened, that challenge, *Buckley v. Valeo*, was in the U.S. Supreme Court.

Early in 1976, the justices announced their decision, declaring a significant portion of the law—its various limitations on campaign spending—to be unconstitutional. Specifically, the Court ruled that, because money was indispensable for political communication, any limitation on the amount of spending was, in effect, a limitation on free speech. Reflecting on the crucial connection between campaign spending and expression, the justices noted that:

> A restriction on the amount of money a person or group can spend on political communication during a campaign necessarily reduces the quantity of expression by restricting the number of issues discussed, the depth of their exploration, and the size of the audience reached. This is because virtually every means of communicating ideas in today's mass society requires the expenditure of money. The distribution of the humblest handbill or leaflet entails printing, paper, and circulation costs. Speeches and rallies generally necessitate hiring a hall and publicizing the event. The electorate's increasing dependence on television, radio, and other mass media for news and information has made these expensive modes of communication indispensable instruments of effective political speech.[7]

Limits on expenditures were, in effect, limits on speech. For that reason, they were unconstitutional. Accordingly, the Court concluded that "the provisions of the Act that impose [spending limitations] place substantial and direct restrictions on the ability of candidates, citizens, and associations to engage in protected political expression, restrictions that the First Amendment cannot tolerate."[8]

In contrast to the spending limits, the justices upheld the limits on contributions. Here, the justices agreed that the caps placed on the amounts that could be given by individuals, political groups, and parties were a legitimate means of reducing the reliance upon big donations from the wealthiest supporters. To be sure, campaign contributions were related to political expression, but, as the Supreme Court concluded, limitations on donations posed only an indirect impediment to free speech. After all, those who wanted to offer support to a candidate, PAC, or party beyond the law's specified contribution limits were always free to spend unlimited funds—and thus

---

[7]*Buckley v. Valeo* 424 U.S. 1 (1976), p. 19.
[8]*Buckley v. Valeo*, pp. 59–60.

to express themselves as freely as they wished—in support of an individual or cause.

Much of the law, then, survived; the FECA's contribution restrictions remained intact. At the same time, though, the Supreme Court determined that, however laudable the goals of equalizing financial disparities and preserving the integrity of the electoral process may have been, the spending limits violated the First Amendment. As one of the leading scholars of campaign finance neatly sums up the decision, "'Money talks' was elevated from popular saying to constitutional principle."[9] Based on that principle, a major regulatory feature of the law had been eliminated by the Supreme Court, invalidated as a violation of free speech. Congress was left with a law that was vastly different from the one it had enacted, one in which contributions were limited and expenditures were not. Candidates and political organizations could be compelled to raise money in prescribed amounts, but they were constitutionally free to engage in unlimited spending.

This decision, which reflected the Court's more general interest in developing First Amendment law, created repercussions that, in a variety of ways, were felt throughout American electoral politics. Through the lens of *Buckley v. Valeo*, this chapter tracks both the justices' policy-making priorities and the practical consequences of those decisions. To address these issues, it focuses on a number of related questions: To what extent is the decision to strike down a federal regulation of campaign speech representative of the business of the Supreme Court? What does *Buckley* reveal about the consequences of judicial policy? In short, how effective a role do the justices play in the governing process?

THE COURT'S POLICY AGENDA

Over time, the types of issues to which the justices have addressed themselves have changed dramatically. From their focus on economic regulation in the early part of the twentieth century to their concentration on individual rights beginning in the 1960s, the members of the Court have used their discretionary agenda to shift their time and resources across different social and economic questions.

[9]Sorauf, *Inside Campaign Finance*, p. 11.

Knowing the variety of policies that interest the Court from one year to the next is especially important, because it indicates, no less than it does for any other governmental institution, what problems its members consider to be most pressing and what potential course it hopes to steer. Some of the more recent shifts in the content of the Court's docket are illustrated in Figure 6.1.[10]

As these data show, the Court of the 1940s divided its time fairly equally between cases involving civil liberties, on the one hand, and government regulation of economic activity, on the other. The early 1950s saw the appointments of Earl Warren and William Brennan— justices committed to expanding the protections of civil liberties— and following their elevation to the high bench, the Court began gradually to display greater interest in issues of individual rights, while its enthusiasm for gauging government's power over economic affairs started to wane. This process of change had been in the works for some time, however; in fact, the dominant position of economic affairs on the Court's agenda had begun to decline as early as 1938, when the justices declared their intention to look more critically at questions of civil liberties. The paths represented by the two timelines in Figure 6.1 continued to diverge, and by the 1970s, most of the Court's caseload was devoted to individual rights.[11]

So, by the time the Federal Election Campaign Act was challenged in 1975, the justices had been firmly concentrating on issues such as freedom of religion, speech, and association, racial equality, and defendants' rights. Constitutional questions related to expression were a particular staple for the justices. About one of every ten cases decided by the Court concerned free speech. By asking the justices to address whether campaign finance restrictions offended First Amendment rights, *Buckley v. Valeo* represented what had become a priority for the Court, a mainstay of its policy agenda.

No less important than the substantive content of the Court's agenda is how the justices dispose of the cases on it. In *Buckley*, the decision to uphold expressive rights in political campaigns reflected the Supreme Court's ongoing liberalism, a tendency that had peaked under the leadership of Chief Justice Warren but still lingered in

---

[10]These data exclude certain policy domains, such as federalism, judicial power, and interstate relations.

[11]Richard L. Pacelle, Jr., "The Dynamics and Determinants of Agenda Change in the Rehnquist Court," in *Contemplating Courts*, ed. Lee Epstein (Washington: Congressional Quarterly, Inc., 1995).

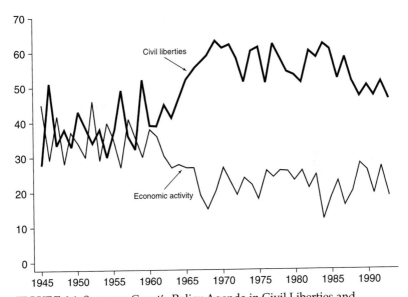

FIGURE 6.1 Supreme Court's Policy Agenda in Civil Liberties and
Economic Activity
Source: Lee Epstein, Jeffrey A. Segal, Harold J. Spaeth, and Thomas G.
Walker. 1996. *The Supreme Court Compendium: Data, Decisions, and
Developments,* 2nd ed. (Washington: Congressional Quarterly, Inc.), Table 2–9.

somewhat lesser degree on the Burger Court. Achieving this goal
meant invalidating a federal statute, something the modern Court
has not been reluctant to do, especially if a law is at odds with the
justices' policy preferences.[12] Although the justices have struck down
far more state than federal laws, rejecting questionable congressional
policy has become a fairly regular feature of the Court's policy outputs. In the first one hundred years of the Court's history, for example, the Court invalidated roughly twenty federal laws. By contrast,
the justices voided that many congressional measures during the
1970s alone.[13]

---

[12]Jeffrey A. Segal and Harold J. Spaeth, *The Supreme Court and the Attitudinal Model*
(Cambridge: Cambridge University Press, 1998), pp. 318–22.
[13]Congressional Research Service, *The Consitution of the United States of America: Analy-
sis and Interpretation* (Washington: Government Printing Office, 1987), cited in
Lawrence Baum, *The Supreme Court,* 6th ed. (Washington: Congressional Quarterly,
Inc., 1998), p. 201.

By the time *Buckley v. Valeo* was decided, issues such as freedom of expression had been dominating the court's agenda for nearly two decades. Not only that, the decision in *Buckley* reflected the general tenor of the justices' policy outputs; by 1976, the justices on the Warren and Burger Courts had laid the legal foundations for an expansive protection of individual rights from governmental interference. So a decision that sustained the speech rights of candidates, citizens, and political groups fit well within that context. Quite often, vindicating civil liberties requires overturning laws that impede the exercise of those rights. So it is scarcely surprising that, in making this legal policy, the justices declared an act of Congress to violate the First Amendment. Seen in this way, *Buckley* was indicative of what issues most interested the Supreme Court and how it resolved them.

IMPLEMENTING JUDICIAL POLICY

Providing answers to abstract legal questions is one thing, but putting those principles into practice is quite another. Declaring, as the Supreme Court did in *Buckley*, that restrictions on campaign spending violate the First Amendment certainly articulates judicial policy, but the Court cannot, on its own, guarantee that such a policy will be faithfully administered. Absent other constraints, for example, there is little to prevent a state legislature from passing laws that limit campaign spending in statewide elections. Nor is there any obstacle to lower court judges, who may be more favorably disposed to campaign finance regulation, simply ignoring the *Buckley* precedent in subsequent cases involving election law. As Alexander Hamilton explained, the Supreme Court "has neither force nor will, but merely judgment."[14] Ultimately, other governmental institutions must implement its policies.

Such implementation will often have a good deal to do with the type of policy it prescribes. Some judicial decisions are restrictive in nature, demanding conformity by imposing or prohibiting certain actions. The justices' decisions requiring the government to provide legal counsel to indigents and banning prayer in public schools are good examples of such policies. Other decisions, by contrast, are

---

[14]Alexander Hamilton, James Madison, and John Jay, *The Federalist Papers* (New York: New American Library [1787–88] 1961), p. 465.

more permissive, providing discretion to those affected by the Court's judgments. Here, the justices' opinions declaring that race could be a factor in university admissions and that the president could be sued while in office are illustrative.[15]

Buckley v. Valeo can probably best be classified as a permissive policy. Aside from sustaining a good deal of Congress's campaign law, the major thrust of the decision was its invalidation of the limitations that had been placed upon spending.[16] So, rather than require some brand of conformity, the Supreme Court gave individuals, organizations, and candidates the ability to spend as much as they wished in federal election campaigns.

To give this permissive policy its full effect, judges on other courts would have to follow precedent by adhering to the Court's interpretation of the law in subsequent cases involving campaign finance. Similarly, legislators would be bound to respect the principles of *Buckley* in drafting any new campaign finance guidelines. In addition, since the justices determined that contributions could be limited and expenditures could not, the Federal Election Commission—the regulatory body charged with administering and enforcing election law—would have to ensure that its own election guidelines clearly defined the difference between the two. Thus, implementing the *Buckley* decision required a good many government officials to follow the Supreme Court's interpretation of the law.

---

[15]For more on the distinction between restrictive and permissive policies, see Lauren Bowen, "Attorney Advertising in the Wake of *Bates v. State Bar of Arizona* (1977)," *American Politics Quarterly* 23:461–84 (1995); Jon R. Bond and Charles A. Johnson, "Implementing a Permissive Policy: Hospital Abortion Services After *Roe v. Wade*," *American Journal of Political Science* 26:1–24 (1982); Henry R. Glick, "The Impact of Permissive Judicial Policies: The U.S. Supreme Court and the Right to Die," *Political Research Quaterly* 47:207–22 (1994).

[16]In addition, it is worth noting that the *Buckley* decision also invalidated the manner in which the Congress chose to constitute the membership of the newly created Federal Election Commission. Under the original law, Congress played a role in selecting four of its six members. The Constitution invests the president with the power to appoint "officers of the United States." In *Buckley*, the justices concluded that the members of the commission were, in fact, "officers" as defined by the Constitution and that Congress, therefore, could not invest itself with the appointment power. Accordingly, Congress passed new legislation in the wake of *Buckley*, that reconstituted the commission, vesting appointment power in the president. (See Thomas E. Mann, "The Federal Election Commission: Implementing and Enforcing Federal Campaign Finance Law," in Corrado et al., *Campaign Finance Reform*.)

Ideally, of course, these officials should have conformed to the Court's mandates about campaign finance. In practice, however, there was a good deal of variation in how they responded to the decision. As with many of the Court's policies, those who were responsible for putting *Buckley* into effect reacted in several different ways.[17] One reaction was to comply, to accept the Supreme Court's interpretation of the law and try to put it into effect. Not everyone followed the Court's dictates so faithfully, though. Some implementors tried to avoid giving full force to the Court's ruling, seeking ways to bypass or circumvent the *Buckley* rules. Not only that, some government officials simply resisted the Court outright by refusing to comply with its judgment. Faced with the need to translate the Court's legal principles into practical results, then, the relevant constituencies of *Buckley v. Valeo* responded in a variety of ways. What accounts for their different degrees of enthusiasm?

Communication of the Decision

Beyond issuing its opinions, the Court has no formal mechanism for transmitting its decisions to those affected by it. Instead, the implementors of judicial policy usually are responsible for learning, on their own, what the Court has done. This has obvious consequences, since officials cannot follow a judicial decision of which they are unaware. Even those who make conscientious efforts to follow the Court's demands may often be frustrated by a lack of clarity in its opinions. For a number of reasons—not the least of which is that the Court's opinions are the product of internal debate and compromise—the opinions that emerge are sometimes ambiguous and fail to provide definitive guidance. There is no guarantee, therefore, that relevant officials will be aware of what the Court has done. Even if they are, there is no assurance that the Court's intentions will be clearly understood.[18]

---

[17]The discussion in the following section is drawn principally from Bradley C. Canon and Charles A. Johnson, *Judicial Policies: Implementation and Impact* (Washington: Congressional Quarterly, Inc., 1999), pp. 37–67, 71–89.

[18]See, for example, Robert T. Nakamura and Frank Smallwood, *The Politics of Policy Implementation* (New York: St. Martin's Press, 1980), pp. 88–92; Craig M. Bradley, *The Failure of the Criminal Justice Revolution* (Philadelphia: University of Pennsylvania Press, 1993); Stephen Wasby, Anthony D'Amato, and Rosemary Metrailer, *Desegregation from Brown to Alexander* (Carbondale: Southern Illinois University Press, 1977).

On the face of it, it seems likely that policy makers would be aware of the Court's decision in this case. After all, *Buckley* proved to be a very important and prominent piece of legal policy. Widely reported and debated, it has since framed efforts at campaign finance reform in Congress as well as in state legislatures.[19] All things being equal, one might expect to find that the Court's opinion had been effectively transmitted throughout the relevant ranks of government.

One way to estimate the extent to which *Buckley* has been communicated to public officials is to determine whether the implementors of campaign finance law have used the Court's decision as a guideline in their own decision making. Judges are a good test in this regard, because they typically must justify their decisions with written opinions that cite pertinent precedents. If lower court judges are aware of *Buckley v. Valeo*, then they should invoke that decision in resolving subsequent disputes over campaign finance.

The evidence suggests that they have done precisely that. A survey of decisions by federal courts shows that the vast majority of opinions dealing with the legal issues surrounding money in elections have relied upon *Buckley* in one way or another. Both federal trial court judges and judges on the courts of appeals are clearly aware of the high court's policy, citing the precedent in 81 percent and 86 percent of their decisions, respectively.[20] Without doubt, *Buckley* has informed the decisions of one critical set of implementors.

Simple awareness of the Supreme Court's policy, though, does not necessarily mean that it will be put into practice. Clarity in the Court's opinions is an important determinant of whether the justices' expectations will be met. This is particularly true for federal agencies, such as the Federal Election Commission, which must consider the Court's decisions as they develop and enforce their own policies.[21]

---

[19]Diana Dwyre and Victoria A. Farrar-Myers, *Legislative Labyrinth: Congress and Campaign Finance Reform* (Washington: Congressional Quarterly, Inc., 2001); Frank J. Sorauf, "What *Buckley* Wrought," in *If Buckley Fell: A First Amendment Blueprint for Regulating Money in Politics*, ed. E. Joshua Rosenkranz. (New York: The Century Foundation Press, 1999).

[20]These figures are based on data obtained from Lexis-Nexis, searching within federal court opinions from 1977 to the present for references to the general issues present in the *Buckley* decision—"Federal Election Campaign Act," "First Amendment," "contributions" (or "expenditures")—both with and without mention of "*Buckley v. Valeo*."

[21]James F. Spriggs, II, "The Supreme Court and Federal Administrative Agencies: A Resource-Based Theory and Analysis of Judicial Impact," *American Journal of Political Science* 40:1122–51 (1996).

To that end, *Buckley v. Valeo* provided considerable guidance to federal election officials by clarifying what type of election spending had to be publicly disclosed. Originally, the law specified that contributions and expenditures "relative to a clearly identified candidate" would have to be reported to the Federal Election Commission. Such a provision, as the justices noted, was inherently vague: Did that phrase mean that spending on television advertising that compared the positions of competing candidates would have to be reported? What if a newspaper ad mentioned specific candidates without endorsing them? What if a television spot discussed—and took positions on—an issue that was the focus of a particular congressional race without mentioning the candidates by name? The Supreme Court's answer was to interpret the phrase "relative to a clearly identified candidate" to mean "communications containing express words of advocacy of election or defeat [of a candidate]." The justices even went so far as to provide a precise set of illustrative statements, "such as 'vote for,' 'elect,' 'support,' 'cast your ballot for,' 'Smith for Congress,' 'vote against,' 'defeat,' [and] 'reject.'"[22]

With such a detailed roadmap for the Federal Election Commission to follow, it was a fairly straightforward matter for election officials to incorporate this language into their regulations and apply it when individuals or groups sought their guidance. In one case, a pro-life interest group asked election officials whether it was required to report the expenses associated with printing and mailing a letter discussing Senator Edward Kennedy's candidacy for president and the implications of his candidacy for abortion policy. In light of the Court's clear guidance in *Buckley*, the commission advised the group that "because the letter does not include any message which expressly advocates the election or defeat of Senator Kennedy, or any words of advocacy exhorting readers to vote for or against the identified candidate, the Commission concludes that the cost of printing and mailing the letter need not be . . . reported."[23] Such a case illustrates how the Supreme Court, crafting explicit and direct policies, can enhance the prospects of executive branch officials following its lead. By clearly delineating their interpretation of the law, the justices helped to ensure that their abstract opinion would be translated into political practice.

[22]*Buckley v. Valeo*, p. 44.
[23]Federal Election Commission, Advisory Opinion 1980-9, March 13, 1980.

Attitudes of Implementors

No matter how effectively the Supreme Court's opinions are disseminated, they must ultimately be embraced by the officials responsible for giving them force. Even the most understandable ruling will not be followed if it is not considered legitimate. For that reason, the level of compliance will have a lot to do with the attitudes of those who must follow the Court's directives. If legislators, bureaucrats, and lower court judges "are well-disposed toward a particular policy, they are more likely to carry it out. . . . But when implementors' attitudes or perspectives differ from [the justices'], the process of implementing a policy becomes infinitely more complicated."[24] If officials disagree with the Supreme Court and do not see themselves as constrained by it, they may look for ways to spurn its directives. What did the implementors of *Buckley v. Valeo* think of the decision, and how did they react as a result?

A good gauge of the attitudes of lower court judges is how vigorously they applied the *Buckley* precedent in later cases. Like many who are expected to enforce the Supreme Court's mandates, judges have discretion; they can decide for themselves how strictly they want to adhere to the Court's stated intentions. In the abstract, judges are of course bound by precedent, but as a practical matter they can skirt a precedent by determining that, even though a prior decision seemingly controls the outcome of an existing case, the two differ enough that the precedent need not apply.[25] More rebellious jurists might take a different tack by openly criticizing a precedent. To track these potential responses, Table 6.1 separates the different reactions to the *Buckley* precedent by lower courts in subsequent cases.[26] These data reveal that both federal and state court judges have demonstrated a good deal of support for the Court's decision in *Buckley*.

---

[24]George C. Edwards, *Implementing Public Policy* (Washington: Congressional Quarterly, Inc., 1980), p. 89; see also Canon and Johnson, *Judicial Policies*, pp. 33–34.

[25]Technically, this is referred to as "distinguishing" a precedent.

[26]These data were generated through the use of *Shepard's Citations*. The "complied" category are those that *Shepard's* lists as having been "followed" by the lower courts. Cases where a lower court "distinguished" or "limited" *Buckley* are treated as having "avoided" applying that precedent. The "resisted" category consists of any cases in which a lower court "criticized" *Buckley*. Note that not all of these cases necessarily involve issues of campaign finance.

TABLE 6.1 Lower Court Implementation of
Buckley v. Valeo

Response	Federal Courts	State Courts
Comply	66%	59%
Avoid	34%	41%
Resist	<1%	0%

Source: Shepard's Citations.

Far and away, the most common response to *Buckley v. Valeo* has
been to follow the Court's ruling. As many as two-thirds of the decisions from the federal courts have been substantially guided by
Buckley in their own decision making. Among recent cases, for example, a federal appeals court declared that New Hampshire's
$1,000 limit on campaign spending by political action committees
violated the First Amendment's guarantee of freedom of expression.
As the court explained, "*Buckley* controls our analysis." After noting
the similarities between the state's limitation on spending and those
originally contained in the Federal Election Campaign Act, the appeals court ruled, "Under *Buckley*, [this law] insults the First Amendment. The New Hampshire statute limits the same kind of
independent expenditures that the [Federal Election Campaign Act]
attempted to regulate, and the New Hampshire law purports to cap
those expenditures at precisely the same level ($1,000). . . . The First
Amendment does not tolerate such drastic limitations of protected
political advocacy."[27] In cases such as these, judges clearly took their
cues from the Supreme Court.

Still, the actions of some lower court judges have betrayed a desire to evade the *Buckley* precedent. In a substantial minority of cases,
a court's opinion, while reflecting an awareness of the Supreme
Court's ruling, declared that *Buckley* did not govern the outcome because the cases were too dissimilar. In one such case, Missouri imposed voluntary spending limits on its candidates for public office.
Candidates who opted against the cap were confined to raising
money solely from individual donations, while those who abided by
the limits could receive money from organized groups and political
parties, as well as individual contributors. Despite the Supreme

[27]*New Hampshire Right to Life Political Action Committee v. Gardner* 99 F3d 8 (1996),
pp. 31, 33–34.

Court's approval of voluntary spending limits in *Buckley*, the federal judges here determined that "[t]he spending limits adopted by the Missouri legislature differ substantially from the scenario described in . . . *Buckley* and are thus distinguishable. The Senate Bill 650 limits are not voluntary because they provide only penalties for noncompliance rather than an incentive for voluntary compliance. Therefore the state's reliance on . . . *Buckley* is misplaced."[28] Stated differently, because one law rewarded a candidate who accepted spending limits and the other law punished a candidate who refused them, the cases were not comparable. Even though both laws created clear incentives to limit spending, this court decided that *Buckley* did not have to be followed. This legal device—not applying a relevant precedent based on factual distinctions between cases—is quite useful for judges who wish to avoid problematic or competing precedents.[29] By this means, judges can circumvent the Court's intentions without openly challenging its authority.

For the most part, though, decision makers on federal and state courts have accepted the decision in *Buckley v. Valeo*. In fact, in virtually no instance did a maverick court reject this precedent outright. Such levels of compliance are not at all surprising; lower courts typically behave as the Supreme Court demands. After all, bucking the Court runs the risk of being reversed by the justices, an embarrassing sanction that is costly to a judge's professional reputation.[30] So, whatever their opinions about the wisdom of the *Buckley* decision, lower court judges have not been anxious to challenge the Court's interpretation of federal election law.

What did members of Congress think of *Buckley v. Valeo*? Given that much of their legislative handiwork had been invalidated by the Court, one might suspect that they would have viewed the decision unfavorably. Having just amended the Federal Election Campaign Act in 1974, Congress was dealt a blow by the Court, as *Buckley*—decided only two years later—substantially hampered its ability to achieve campaign reform. Despite this restriction on its discretion,

---

[28]*Shrink Missouri Government PAC v. Maupin* 71 F3d 1422 (1995), p. 1425.

[29]See Segal and Spaeth, *The Supreme Court and the Attitudinal Model*, pp. 49–50.

[30]Donald R. Songer, Jeffrey A. Segal, and Charles M. Cameron, "The Hierarchy of Justice: Testing a Principal-Agent Model of Supreme Court–Circuit Court Interactions," *American Journal of Political Science* 38:673–96 (1994); Frank J. Sorauf, *The Wall of Separation: The Constitutional Politics of Church and State* (Princeton, NJ: Princeton University Press, 1976).

Congress agreed to abide by it. Indeed, within just a few months after the decision was announced, legislators on Capitol Hill enacted new campaign regulations that sought to operate within the limits set out by the justices. For example, one of the legal provisions struck down by the Court was a restriction limiting presidential candidates to spending no more than $50,000 of their own personal resources in a campaign. Spending in a presidential election, the justices ruled, could only be limited voluntarily, by accepting the public funds made available to underwrite a run for the White House. Following the Court's lead, Congress reenacted the $50,000 ceiling on personal resources, this time applying it only to those candidates who accepted public money.[31] That members of Congress sought to formulate new law within the boundaries established by *Buckley* suggests that they accepted the Court's authority.

This is not always the case. Congress can (and does) try to undercut what it regards as unpalatable judicial policy, often initiating legislation aimed at limiting or overcoming a Supreme Court decision. Unpopular rulings—such as recent decisions restricting religious freedom and upholding the expressive right to burn the American flag—have been especially likely to produce congressional reaction.[32] Quite apart from legislation to limit the impact of the Court's policies, Congress has, in other instances, flagrantly ignored the justices' mandate. Unwilling to abandon the legislative veto—a device by which the legislature retains supervisory control over the federal bureaucracy—Congress continued to include it within new legislation, even after the Supreme Court had ruled it to be unconstitutional.[33]

---

[31]See Document 2.10, "Federal Election Campaign Act Amendments of 1976: A Summary," in Corrado et al., *Campaign Finance Reform*.

[32]Joseph Ignagni and James Meernik, "Explaining Congressional Attempts to Reverse Supreme Court Decisions," *Political Research Quarterly* 47:353–71 (1994); James Meernik and Joseph Ignagni, "Judicial Review and Coordinate Construction of the Constitution," *American Journal of Political Science* 41:447–67 (1997); see also Canon and Johnson, *Judicial Policies*, pp. 116–25.

[33]Jessica Korn, *The Power of Separation: American Constitutionalism and the Myth of the Legislative Veto* (Princeton, NJ: Princeton University Press, 1996). Some have suggested, however, that this result has less to do with defying the Court than it has with legislators' inability to find a viable alternative to the legislative veto. See Stephen L. Wasby, *The Supreme Court in the Federal System*, 4th ed. (Chicago: Nelson-Hall Publishers, 1993), p. 363.

To be sure, *Buckley v. Valeo* has not been without its congressional critics. Among advocates of campaign finance reform, Senator Olympia Snowe of Maine has suggested that *Buckley* "has made a mockery of the campaign laws in ways in which the system works today."[34] Another critic of the Court, Senator Byron Dorgan of North Dakota, argues that because of judicial tinkering "we have a campaign finance system in total chaos."[35] Such skepticism, though, has not produced resistance. True, some constitutionally questionable legislation has been drafted, but no such reforms have been enacted; instead, Congress has lived within the limits of *Buckley*.[36]

External Political Pressures

Translating Supreme Court rulings into public policy is also determined by broader forces in society. Different social and economic influences can conspire to distort the justices' message.[37] One of the most important of these constraints is public opinion. Without the power to implement their own rulings, the members of the Court must depend upon the acceptance and support of other political actors, many of whom are directly responsible to voters. Thus, if the public has serious misgivings about a decision by the Court, those doubts may be translated into sluggish implementation, or perhaps no implementation at all. Without public opinion on its side, the Court's will is often frustrated.[38]

Vermont legislators illustrated this tendency in 1997, when they passed the Vermont Campaign Finance Reform Act, a law that

---

[34] 144 Congressional Record S 972, February 25, 1998, p. S973.

[35] Quoted in Dwyre and Farrar-Myers, *Legislative Labyrinth*, p. 57; for a more extended discussion of congressional viewpoints on *Buckley*, see pp. 54–59.

[36] Frank J. Sorauf, "Politics, Experience, and the First Amendment: The Case of American Campaign Finance," *Columbia Law Review* 94:1348–68 (1994). For further treatment of current campaign finance legislation, see Dwyre and Farrar-Myers, *Legislative Labyrinth*.

[37] Daniel Mazmanian and Paul A. Sabatier, *Implementation and Public Policy* (Lanham, MD: University Press of America, 1989), pp. 30–35.

[38] Robert Dahl, "Decision-Making in a Democracy: The Supreme Court as a National Policy-Maker," *Journal of Public Law* 6:179–295 (1957); Gerald N. Rosenberg, *The Hollow Hope: Can Courts Bring About Social Change?* (Chicago: University of Chicago Press, 1991).

embodied the very expenditure limits that the Supreme Court had declared unconstitutional.[39] Among other things, this law put into place a variety of spending caps for candidates running for statewide office: $300,000 for governor, $4,000 for state senator, $2,000 for state representative. Clearly, such limits contradicted the principles laid down in *Buckley*. Why, then, did the legislature impose them? The answer is that there was intense public pressure on lawmakers to limit the impact of money in elections.

Like many states, Vermont actually had instituted contribution and spending restrictions before *Buckley v. Valeo*.[40] After the Court's decision, however, the legislature dutifully complied and rescinded the spending limitations. By the 1990s, though, stimulated by a blitz of media coverage of campaign finance abuses, voters were transfixed by election reform. As the federal judge who reviewed the law later explained, "Dozens of newspaper articles reflected the high level of citizen concern over the extent of money's influence over politics. [This coverage] demonstrate[s] the attention these issues received in Vermont and conveys the type of pressure that legislators must have felt to react."[41] Many of the voters in the state came to believe that politics were in the hands of the wealthy few. *Buckley* had, in effect, become quite unpopular.

Spurred by public discontent, lawmakers will often override unpopular judicial policy, rather than implement it.[42] Consequently, it makes sense that Vermont's legislature—which had previously conformed to *Buckley*—would later respond to changing public attitudes on campaign finance by enacting the very expenditure limits that its members surely knew were suspect, if not unlawful. In this sense, Vermont was not alone, as public foment prompted other state and local governments to defy the Court by establishing similar ceilings on campaign spending.[43]

---

[39]The background on this law and the litigation surrounding it is adapted from *Landell v. Sorrell* 118 F. Supp. 2d 459 (2000).

[40]For more information on the variety of state regulatory reforms, see Sorauf, "What *Buckley* Wrought," pp. 35–37.

[41]*Landell v. Sorrell*, p. 465.

[42]Meernik and Ignagni, "Judicial Review and Coordinate Construction of the Constitution."

[43]See, for example, *Kruse v. City of Cincinnati* 142 F3d 907 (1998); *New Hampshire Right to Life Political Action Committee v. Gardner* 99 F3d 8 (1996).

IMPACT OF THE COURT

By several different measures, the Supreme Court's policy in *Buckley v. Valeo* was carried out largely as the justices had intended. In the aftermath of the decision, most officials responded by implementing the principles that were set out in the opinion. That a judicial decision has been implemented, though, does not necessarily mean that it has had major consequences. *Buckley* was faithfully followed, but did the policy actually change the nature of electoral politics in any substantial way? Did it restructure the conduct of campaigns, or were its effects more modest?

Many believe the Supreme Court to be a major force in American politics; after all, its unelected, permanent membership speaks with finality to some of the most critical issues of the day. On the basis of various decisions by the Court, observers have concluded that the justices have stopped prayer in the classroom, increased abortion rates, decreased police misconduct, desegregated public schools. The evidence that the Supreme Court has actually generated such major consequences is far from conclusive.[44]

The primary ruling in *Buckley* was that governmental restrictions on campaign expenditures violated the First Amendment guarantee of free expression. Distinguishing between contributions and expenditures, the Court concluded that, while contribution limits posed only indirect burdens on expression, spending ceilings were a substantial barrier to unfettered debate. This distinction has had some notable implications for American campaigns. At the same time, though, a survey of some of these likely effects reveals that the impact of the Supreme Court has not been as dramatic as some might have expected.

Increases in Spending

One of the most noteworthy consequences of *Buckley* is perhaps the most obvious. By striking down spending limits, the Court has

[44]Keneth Dolbeare and Phillip Hammond, *The School Prayer Decisions: From Court Policy to Local Practice* (Chicago: University of Chicago Press, 1971); Donald L. Horowitz, *The Courts and Social Policy* (Washington: The Brookings Institution, 1977); Rosenberg, *The Hollow Hope.*

permitted unrestrained growth in campaign spending.[45] Using data
from elections to the House of Representatives, Figure 6.2 tracks this
growth for several different categories of candidates. There are important differences, both between candidates and across time, but
the larger lesson is that campaign spending has risen over the last
twenty years. Expenditures by incumbents and candidates for open
congressional seats have shown substantial increases. The financial
resources of challengers, while far more feeble, also show evidence
of growth. At first glance, it seems that *Buckley* uncapped a surge in
campaign spending.

It is important to remember, though, that the spending limits
thrown out by the Supreme Court were to be indexed for inflation.
Under the 1974 law, a candidate for the House could spend a combined total of $140,000 in the primary and general election cam-
paigns, and that limit was to be annually adjusted according to the
Consumer Price Index. Had those limits been allowed to remain in
place, candidates could have spent around $360,000 in 1988 and as
much $500,000 in 1998.

When those adjusted limits are compared to the actual spending
totals, the increases are not nearly as dramatic. Some ten years after
Buckley eliminated Congress's limits on expenditures, incumbents
were still spending below the law's original ceiling. In fact, it was not
until 1992 that incumbents spent significantly more than the law
would have allowed. Even in open seats, where competition tends to
drive up expenditures,[46] candidates did not seriously begin to out-
pace the 1974 law until 1986. Since then, spending for the relatively
few open House seats has escalated, but even the candidates in these
races spent at roughly the theoretical legal limit in 1992. For their
part, challengers have consistently remained well below the ceiling.

---

[45]As a practical matter, this applies only to congressional campaign spending. The
Supreme Court upheld the limits on presidential spending because they were voluntary. In exchange for public financing, presidential candidates can receive a fixed sum
to conduct their general election campaigns. Theoretically, this could have led to increases in spending by presidential candidates, but the major party nominees have
chosen to limit their spending. Since the law went into effect, no Democratic or
Republican nominee has refused the federal funds. See Sorauf, "What *Buckley*
Wrought," p. 34.

[46]See, for example, Gary C. Jacobson, "The Misallocation of Resources in House
Campaigns," in *Congress Reconsidered*, 5th ed., ed. Lawrence C. Dodd and Bruce I.
Oppenheimer (Washington: Congressional Quarterly, Inc., 1993).

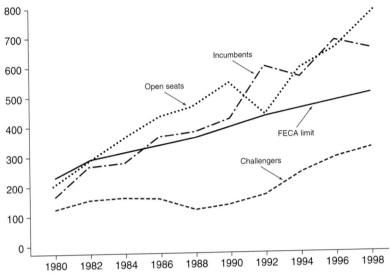

FIGURE 6.2 Average Campaign Spending in House Elections and Limits of the Federal Election Campaign Act, 1980–1998 (in Hundred Thousands of Dollars)
Source: Norman J. Ornstein, Thomas E. Mann, and Michael J. Malbin, *Vital Statistics on Congress, 1999–2000* (Washington: AEI Press, 2000), Table 3.2.

Viewed in this way, the impact of *Buckley* has not been nearly so grand as one might think. Had the limits of the Federal Election Campaign Act been upheld, they would not have seriously inconvenienced many candidates until the early 1990s.

Inequalities in Spending

A principal motive behind the Federal Election Campaign Act was to eliminate financial disparities that existed between candidates. In light of the amount of money raised by incumbents—and their staggeringly high rate of reelection—many continue to believe that money governs election outcomes. "After the alleged buying of the Congress," writes campaign expert Frank Sorauf, "it is the alleged buying of the elections to the Congress that most worries Americans. Many of them are convinced that incumbents are winning reelection at such stunning rates precisely because the incumbents have too much money and their challengers have too little."[47] Certainly, the data in Figure 6.2 document this widening gap, providing at least circumstantial evidence that the concentration of campaign resources advantages those already serving in Congress.

By eliminating the stabilizing effect of campaign spending limits, the decision in *Buckley v. Valeo* has allowed incumbents to put a good deal of distance between themselves and those who would have their seats. In 1980, for example, incumbents spent only 1.4 times more than their challengers, on average. By the early 1990s, expenditures by incumbents were nearly four times greater than the outlays of challengers. This gulf has narrowed in more recent years, but current officeholders still have a two-to-one advantage in campaign expenditures. Generated by a variety of forces—overinvestment in incumbents by political action committees, higher campaign costs, weak challengers, electoral uncertainty among House members—incumbents have been able to outspend their opposition by an increasingly wide margin.[48]

Such high levels of spending by incumbents, though, actually do little to affect their success. The evidence is quite strong that expenditures by congressional incumbents have little impact on their chances of reelection. There is no doubt that incumbents are more adept at generating campaign money, but ultimately their rates of reelection are attributable to other factors, not the least of which are name recognition, media access, and the ability to provide services to their constituents. By contrast, spending by challengers significantly increases their vote share. Consequently, the problem is not that incumbents have too much money but rather that challengers have too little.[49] If they had been upheld by the Supreme Court, spending caps might have diminished the differences between candidates. Such limits would be no guarantee, however, that those who need money the most would have enough to mount a credible challenge. The data in Figure 6.2 suggest that, even if the Court had upheld spending limits, challengers would still have difficulty raising sufficient funds.

[47]Sorauf, *Inside Campaign Finance*, p. 174.
[48]Jacobson, "The Misallocation of Resources in House Campaigns"; Sorauf, *Inside Campaign Finance*, pp. 66–77.
[49]Gary C. Jacobson, *The Electoral Origins of Divided Government: Competition in U.S. House Elections, 1946–1988* (Boulder, CO: Westview Press, 1990); Sorauf, *Inside Campaign Finance*, pp. 174–79.

In this sense, the impact of *Buckley* has been somewhat mixed. On the one hand, by eliminating the ceilings on expenditures, the justices have paved the way for greater financial inequality between candidates, and perhaps this has had the unhappy effect of contributing to public cynicism about Congress. On the other hand, perpetuating these differences has not really had genuine electoral implications. The Court may have exacerbated the inequities in campaign resources, but the *Buckley* decision has probably not altered many election results.

Wealthy Candidates

By permitting unlimited campaign spending, *Buckley v. Valeo* has also made it attractive for self-financed candidates to enter politics and conduct credible campaigns.[50] The post-*Buckley* years have been witness to a number of office-seekers financed largely through personal wealth. While other potential candidates must go cap-in-hand to individual contributors, the independently wealthy can mount viable election efforts simply by drawing from their own resources. In 1984, for example, John D. Rockefeller IV used $10 million from his personal fortune to finance his U.S. Senate race in West Virginia. More recently, Michael Huffington of California spent $28 million of his own money in a 1994 bid for the Senate. Even at the presidential level, where the sums required to run are much more staggering, wealthy candidates have been able to run respectably through self-financing. In his race for the White House in 1992, Ross Perot contributed about $64 million to his $68 million campaign. Similarly, by underwriting much of his own campaign, Steve Forbes was a reasonably strong contender for the Republican nomination in 1996.[51]

In the absence of spending caps, such candidacies have been able to flourish. Had the justices allowed the federal spending limits to remain in place, however, the benefits of personal wealth would have been seriously diminished. As it stands, candidates cannot run without substantial amounts of cash, and because of *Buckley* those who already have it can run much more easily.

[50]Bradley A. Smith, "Faulty Assumptions and Undemocratic Consequences of Campaign Finance Reform," in Corrado et al., *Campaign Finance Reform*; see also Dwyre and Farrar-Myers, *Legislative Labyrinth*, pp. 50–51.
[51]Roger J. Davidson and Walter J. Oleszek, *Congress and Its Members*, 6th ed. (Washington: Congressional Quarterly, Inc., 1998), pp. 70–74; Sorauf, *Inside Campaign Finance*, p. 258.

Fundraising

Buckley v. Valeo upheld the restrictions on contributions while striking down the spending ceilings. This distinction, say come critics, generated unfortunate consequences for how campaign money is raised. Since, after *Buckley*, donations were limited and spending was not, candidates presumably had to look for ways to raise larger sums of money as the cost of campaigning increased. Not only that, the law did not take account of the power of inflation to decrease the value of those contributions. (For a candidate who needs to purchase television time, mail campaign information, and the like, a maximum donation of $1,000 today enables a campaign to buy only about a quarter of what it did in 1974.) Effectively this means that, over time, more and more money must be raised in smaller and smaller amounts. Where do candidates turn? Because the contribution limits on political action committees are higher than those on individuals ($5,000 versus $1,000), some have feared an increased dependence upon the money of interest groups.[52]

Yet despite the increasing number of PACs, this seems not to have happened. Most contributions to congressional candidates come from individual donors, not PACs. If anything, the PACs' share of contributions has decreased in the last ten years, and what money they do give is, on average, well below the legal limit. Most of this money goes to incumbents, but this is scarcely because they are cash-poor candidates in dire need of capital. PACs invest heavily in incumbents in order to maintain long-term access to policy makers.[53]

By upholding one set of constraints imposed by federal election law while removing another, the Supreme Court injected a permissive component into an otherwise restrictive policy; candidates could engage in unlimited spending provided that they raised their funds in limited amounts. Fears that this would give a disproportionate voice to organized interests, however, have been largely unrealized. *Buckley v. Valeo* seems not to have created a system of dependence upon PACs, after all.

[52]For a review of some of the literature critical of political action committees, see Dwyre and Farrar-Myers, *Legislative Labyrinth*, p. 15.
[53]"Document 5.4, Total PAC Contributions to Congressional Candidates, 1978–96," in Corrado et al., *Campaign Finance Reform*; Norman J. Ornstein, Thomas E. Mann, and Michael J. Malbin, *Vital Statistics on Congress, 1999–2000* (Washington: The AEI Press, 2000), Table 3-8; Sorauf, *Inside Campaign Finance*, pp. 70–77.

Issue Advocacy

Campaign finance law does not apply to all political speech. In rewriting the Federal Election Campaign Act in 1974, Congress required that only expenditures "relative to a clearly identified candidate" would be affected by the law. The Supreme Court interpreted this phrase to mean only spending that actually advocated the election or defeat of a candidate would have to be reported to the Federal Election Commission. So, television and newspaper ads that urged voters to cast a ballot for or against a candidate—express advocacy—were covered by the law. Other speech that discussed the candidates, the parties, and their positions without providing instructions on how to vote—issue advocacy—was not.

This interpretation of the law reflected an effort by the Supreme Court to protect expression from excessive government control. The justices permitted the regulation of election campaign spending, while preserving the freedom of expression contained in more general political spending.[54] Stated differently, since the law regulated First Amendment rights, the members of the Court sought to protect those rights by limiting the application of the law to a narrow class of speech, express advocacy. In making this distinction, however, the justices opened the door to an immense amount of unregulated and unreported spending, much of it by interests that would otherwise be prohibited from participating in elections.[55]

Typically, issue ads praise the policy successes of officeholders, vigorously criticize candidates without calling for their defeat, or encourage voters to contact elected officials to express their views.[56]

[54]I borrow these phrases—"election campaign spending" and "general political spending"—from Richard Briffault, "Drawing the Line Between Elections and Politics," in Rosenkranz, *If Buckley Fell*, p. 123.

[55]How does one distinguish between issue advocacy and express advocacy? As mentioned earlier, the Supreme Court provided a list of typical phrases to differentiate the two. Among other things, express advocacy included statements such as "vote for," "cast your ballot," "defeat," and the like. So important were the phrases provided by the Court that some even refer to them as the "magic words." If any of the magic words are included in political speech, it is considered to be express advocacy. Other political expression, even though it may mention the candidates and their positions, is issue advocacy. See Trevor Potter, "Issue Advocacy and Express Advocacy," in Corrado et al., *Campaign Finance Reform*; Briffault, "Drawing the Line Between Elections and Politics."

[56]Briffault, "Drawing the Line Between Elections and Politics." pp. 128–29.

In 1996, for example, one such ad that was supportive of President Clinton suggested, "For millions of working families, President Clinton cut taxes. The Dole/Gingrich budget tried to raise taxes on eight million." Another ad found fault with the president, suggesting that "he gave us the largest tax increase in history. . . . Tell President Clinton: You can't afford higher taxes for more wasteful spending."[57]

Because of *Buckley*, virtually any individual or organization may raise and spend unlimited funds for this type of advocacy, and the amounts are not insubstantial. By some estimates, the amount of money spent on issue advocacy in 1996 was as high as $150 million, more than three times the combined contributions of the twenty most generous political action committees.[58] Only two years later, spending on issue advocacy more than doubled to $340 million. Of course, these are only estimates: Since issue advocacy is unrestricted by campaign finance law, it is unreported as well as unlimited. Even corporations and labor unions, which are prohibited by law from making contributions or expenditures in federal elections,[59] can sponsor issue advocacy.

By exempting issue advocacy from the Federal Election Campaign Act, the *Buckley* decision has made it possible for any number of interests to circumvent the intent of the campaign finance regulations. Congress's efforts to provide a public accounting of the spending in federal elections is easily bypassed through issue ads.[60] In fact, it is "child's play," according to one legal scholar, "for political advertisers and campaign professionals to develop ads that effectively advocate the cause of a candidate or make a powerful case against

[57]Quoted in Dwyre and Farrar-Myers, *Legislative Labyrinth*, pp. 25–26.

[58]Data on spending for issue advocacy are taken from Briffault, "Drawing the Line Between Elections and Politics." The source for spending by political action committees is Harold W. Stanley and Richard G. Niemi, *Vital Statistics on American Politics, 1997–1998* (Washington: Congressional Quarterly, Inc., 1998), Table 2-15.

[59]Of course, corporate and labor PACs can make contributions and expenditures, but their funds "are contributed voluntarily by individuals for these purposes." See Trevor Potter, "The Current State of Campaign Finance Law," in Corrado et al., *Campaign Finance Reform*, p. 10.

[60]Mark J. Rozell and Clyde Wilcox, *Interest Groups in American Campaigns: The New Face of Electioneering* (Washington: Congressional Quarterly, Inc., 1999), pp. 158–59.

the candidate's opponent but fall short of the formal express advocacy that would permit regulation."[61]

Separating express advocacy from issue advocacy is intellectually quite defensible. In practice, however, it has proven to be a distinction without a difference. One of the major effects of the policy of *Buckley v. Valeo*, then, is that it has inhibited public disclosure of financial involvement in electoral politics. The Court's conscientious attempt to protect free expression has resulted in untold dollars being used to sidestep federal law.

Reform Efforts

To the extent that there are problems with the American system of campaign finance, appropriate remedies should be within the grasp of Congress and state legislatures. Since the decision in *Buckley v. Valeo* was grounded in the First Amendment, however, this has vastly constrained what policy makers may do. Any legislative initiatives must pass constitutional muster; variations on spending limits, restrictions on issue advocacy, and even tighter reins on contributions may pose constitutional problems. When viable legislation has been proposed in Congress, many lawmakers have resisted the new regulations because of potential collisions with freedom of speech.[62] It is hardly a wonder, then, that one of the leading scholars of American electoral politics concludes that "[n]o single action had a greater impact in narrowing the reach of federal election law and in limiting the options of reformers than the Supreme Court's decision in *Buckley v. Valeo*."[63]

Efforts at the state level tell a somewhat similar tale.[64] Before *Buckley v. Valeo*, states had a wide variety of limitations on campaign expenditures in place. After the decision, these restrictions on state elections were presumably rendered invalid. Despite this setback, local lawmakers have since experimented with an array of options—limiting total receipts, offering public funds to counteract excessive spending by an opponent, and imposing controls on the flow of

---

[61]Briffault, "Drawing the Line Between Elections and Politics," p. 128.
[62]Dwyre and Farrar-Myers, *Legislative Labyrinth*, pp. 54–59.
[63]Thomas E. Mann, "Introduction," in Corrado et al., *Campaign Finance Reform*, p. 2.
[64]This paragraph is adapted from Sorauf, "What *Buckley* Wrought," pp. 35–47.

campaign money from out of state, to name a few. Often, though, state legislators have been frustrated by judicial challenges to their attempts at reform. Some have been struck down in the lower courts, but the Supreme Court's reluctance to review them makes their status uncertain.

Supreme Court Policy Making

One final implication of *Buckley v. Valeo* concerns the Court itself. *Buckley* hardly answered every question of campaign finance law. In the wake of that decision, further campaign finance litigation naturally began to make its way to the Court, asking the justices to clarify a number of campaign and election issues: Can states regulate contributions and expenditures related to ballot referenda, as opposed to candidate elections? Can one political party sue another for violation of the Federal Election Campaign Act? Does a newsletter that suggests how citizens should vote on an issue, without endorsing specific candidates, constitute express advocacy? Can political parties make unlimited expenditures in supporting or attacking a candidate?[65]

In this sense, the decision in *Buckley* generated an ongoing series of interactions between the Court and other policy makers.[66] Candidates, PACs, and political parties responded to the justices' initial decision, just as legislators and executive officials adjusted their programs. In this mix of change and uncertainty, new questions of campaign law were generated in the lower courts, whose cases found their way back to the high court.[67] An important impact of the Court's decision, then, is that it has expanded the range of legal questions in the area of campaign finance, a process that has further required the justices' time and attention.

---

[65]*First National Bank of Boston v. Bellotti* 435 U.S. 765 (1978); *FEC v. National Conservative PAC* 470 U.S. 480 (1985); *FEC v. Massachusetts Citizens for Life, Inc.* 479 U.S. 238 (1986); *FEC v. National Conservative PAC* 470 U.S. 480 (1985).

[66]See Wasby, *The Supreme Court in the Federal System,* p. 364. For a more general discussion of these issues, see Lawrence Baum, "Courts and Policy Innovation," *The American Courts: A Critical Assessment,* ed. John B. Gates and Charles A. Johnson (Washington: Congressional Quarterly, Inc., 1991).

[67]For a review of some of the leading cases, see Daniel R. Ortiz, "Constitutional Restrictions on Campaign Finance Regulation," in Corrado et al., *Campaign Finance Reform.*

CONCLUSION

The role of the Supreme Court in national policy making is evident in several different respects. Because of its discretionary agenda, the Court can change the substantive focus of its policies over time by directing and redirecting its energy to the issues that most interest its members. In this sense, *Buckley v. Valeo* typifies this feature of the Court; raising, as it did, questions about the regulation of campaign speech, it reflected the justices' more general interest in the issue of civil liberties. Since it dealt with the financing of political campaigns, this case also had the potential to have broad effects on U.S. elections. Indeed, by striking down spending limits, the Court effectively transformed the law of campaign finance.

Yet, the Supreme Court does not operate independently as a policy maker. Instead, it navigates through a larger political system, where it must cultivate the support of both government officials and the public to see its policies put into effect. After *Buckley*, the justices were dependent upon the good graces of other actors to implement the decision. With their support, the Supreme Court's intentions were largely carried out: Congress rewrote its election laws to conform to the ruling; the Federal Election Commission used the decision as a guideline in making its own regulations. Of course, there has been some degree of resistance: Federal and state judges, while not openly defying the Court, sometimes looked for ways to limit the application of the *Buckley* precedent. Similarly, the justices' interpretation of the First Amendment has not prevented legislators in some states from drafting contrary laws.

Many are quick to ascribe substantial influence to the high court. The evidence that it fundamentally altered the whole of campaign finance, though, is not overwhelming. *Buckley* certainly allowed for the possibility of unrestrained growth in campaign spending, but that growth did not really exceed Congress's original spending caps until recently. Neither has the decision led to a greater reliance upon contributions from political action committees. At the same time, *Buckley* has generated some serious reverberations. By restricting the law's application to express advocacy, for example, the Supreme Court has made it possible for an outpouring of unchecked money to flow into elections. Such issue advocacy often meets technical compliance while avoiding the spirit of federal law.

Perhaps most importantly, by equating money with speech—and thereby concluding that spending restrictions limit free expression—the Supreme Court established the terms of legislative reform. Not everyone agrees, of course, that changes are desirable, but whatever the alternatives, they must be viewed against the backdrop of *Buckley v. Valeo*. As Americans and their representatives debate changes in the system of campaign finance, their choices are necessarily framed, as they often are, by the Court's interpretation of the Constitution.

QUESTIONS FOR DISCUSSION

1. Should the members of the Supreme Court consider the practical policy implications of their decisions, or should they focus their attention strictly on reconciling competing legal principles? Should they consider, for example, the effects of unlimited campaign spending or issue advocacy?

2. When a case is before the Court, the two parties offer competing arguments over specific legal questions. How might this make it difficult for the justices to make broad and fully informed public policy?

3. Over time, the life experiences of the justices have changed a good deal. There are now more justices with judicial experience—and fewer with political experience—than there were thirty years ago. Are these changes likely to improve or lower the quality and effectiveness of the Supreme Court's policies?

4. What options are available to the Supreme Court to help ensure that its decisions are implemented? What, if anything, could the Court have done if Congress had decided to ignore *Buckley* and reenacted limits on campaign spending?

5. The justices can only decide a small number of the thousands of petitions that are brought to them every year. What effects might that have on their ability to monitor the implementation of their policies?

6. What does the mixed evidence on the impact of the Court in campaign finance suggest about the effects of its decisions more generally?

SUGGESTED READING

Lawrence Baum. 1991. "Courts and Policy Innovation." In *The American Courts: A Critical Assessment*. Ed. John B. Gates and Charles A. Johnson. Washington: Congressional Quarterly, Inc.

Bradley C. Canon and Charles A. Johnson. 1999. *Judicial Policies: Implementation and Impact*. Washington: Congressional Quarterly, Inc.

Barbara H. Craig and David M. O'Brien. 1993. *Abortion and Abortion Politics*. Chatham, NJ: Chatham House.

William N. Eskridge, Jr. 1991. "Overriding Supreme Court Statutory Interpretation Decisions." *Yale Law Journal* 101:331–455.

Louis Fisher. 1997. *Constitutional Conflicts between Congress and the President*. Lawrence: University Press of Kansas.

Donald L. Horowitz. 1977. *The Courts and Social Policy*. Washington: The Brookings Institution.

Jessica Korn. 1996. *The Power of Separation: American Constitutionalism and the Myth of the Legislative Veto*. Princeton, NJ: Princeton University Press.

James Meernik and Joseph Ignagni. 1997. "Judicial Review and Coordinate Construction of the Constitution." *American Journal of Political Science* 41:447–67.

Gerald N. Rosenberg. 1991. *The Hollow Hope: Can Courts Bring About Social Change?* Chicago: University of Chicago Press.

Donald R. Songer, Jeffrey A. Segal, and Charles M. Cameron. 1994. "The Hierarchy of Justice: Testing a Principal-Agent Model of Supreme Court-Circuit Court Interactions." *American Journal of Political Science* 38:673–696.

James F. Spriggs, II. 1996. "The Supreme Court and Federal Administrative Agencies: A Resource-Based Theory and Analysis of Judicial Impact." *American Journal of Political Science* 40:1122–51.

Index

199